Outside's
Wilderness Lodge Vacations

Outside BOOKS

Outside's

Wilderness Lodge Vacations

MORE THAN 100 PRIME DESTINATIONS IN THE U.S., CANADA, MEXICO, AND THE CARIBBEAN

Kimberly Lisagor and the editors of Outside

W. W. NORTON & COMPANY
NEW YORK ■ LONDON

Printed in the United States of America
First Edition

Manufacturing by Courier Companies
Production manager: Diane O'Connor

Library of Congress Cataloging-in-Publication Data

Lisagor, Kimberly.
Outside's wilderness lodge vacations : more than 100 prime destinations in the U.S., Canada, Mexico, and the Caribbean / Kimberly Lisagor and the editors of Outside.—1st ed.
p. cm.—(Outside books)
ISBN 0-393-32520-2 (pbk.)
1. Hotels—United States—Guidebooks. 2. Hotels—Guidebooks. 3. Vacation homes—United States—Guidebooks. 4. Vacation homes—Guidebooks. I. Outside (Chicago, Ill.) II. Title. III. Series.
TX907.2 L57 2004
917.306'2931—dc22

2003025907

W. W. Norton & Company, Inc., 500 Fifth Avenue, New York, N.Y. 10110
www.wwnorton.com

W. W. Norton & Company Ltd., Castle House, 75/76 Wells Street, London W1T 3QT

1 2 3 4 5 6 7 8 9 0

CONTENTS

ACKNOWLEDGMENTS

Many thanks to the folks at *Outside* and Norton—especially Leslie Weeden, Stephanie Pearson, and John Barstow—who trusted me with this dream assignment and offered much-needed guidance along the way. I am also indebted to the friends, travel gurus, researchers, and trip facilitators who kept the project moving: Alex Cohen, Aerin Wilson, Rich Dean, Jacq Lesko, Christie and Bob Botski, Adam Lisagor, Laura McAvoy, Chris Mott, the Murray family, Pete Norie, Luke Rice, Colin Smith, Mary Boyle, Jayne Lloyd-Jones, Nora Weber, Ron Mader, Danny Prokosch, Anne Majusiak, and the bear-repellant-toting lodge receptionist who chased me down a trail in the heart of grizzly country. Thanks most of all to my dad, who taught me to travel; to my mom, who always listens to the stories; and to my impossibly tolerant husband, Scott Bisheff, who gives me a reason to come home.

INTRODUCTION

Once, after a long, happy day of mud-slogging in a rain-drenched Northern California forest, I hung my wet hiking clothes—my *only* hiking clothes—over my cabin's porch railing to dry. It wasn't supposed to rain that night, and it didn't. But the air that had been insulated by a thick cloud cover on previous nights dropped below freezing under a clear, moonlit sky. I awoke the next morning to frost on the grass, ice on the porch, and the uncomfortable memory of a high school bra-in-the-freezer slumber party prank.

Cringing as I stepped outside, I expected to find my jeans frozen stiff. They weren't. Instead my clothes had been dried, folded, bagged, and tied to my doorknob with a note: "Thought these might serve you better thawed."

It doesn't take undue acts of heroism to make a wilderness lodge great, just a willingness to pay attention to the details. The people who run the lodges in this book take the time to get to know their guests. They understand that most folks don't mind a little comfort with their rugged outdoors. And so they've come up with ideas like setting aside a drying room for soggy climbing gear, stocking the guest rooms with trail maps and birding guides, or adding some fire starters to the kindling pile so that visiting urbanites need not feel inept.

Some of these inns, lodges, and bed-and-breakfasts have previously appeared in the pages of *Outside* magazine; others were recommended by friends and fellow outdoors fanatics. A few are surprises I stumbled onto by accident, and I can't imagine why they went unnoticed for so long. Some are included because they're so remote, while others are here because they're within weekending distance of major cities, yet bounded by wilderness. I made an attempt at geographic balance, but let's face it, you're more likely to find lodge-based bliss in Alaska than in Arkansas. Some of these places are basic and budget friendly. Others offer luxury that many of us may find too pricey. What they all share is that they are thoughtfully run base camps surrounded by wide-open playgrounds and are equipped with the means to explore them.

In this mix there's something for everyone who thinks of travel as a lifelong hut-to-hut adventure. You're sure to find a warm welcome, a cozy bed, and dreams made sweet by the promise of what lies outside.

HOW TO USE THIS BOOK

Think of this vacation guide as a menu of appetizers, not an all-you-can-eat buffet. Cataloging *every* great lodge on the continent would produce a book too heavy to lift and not nearly selective enough. However, in some cases, exclusion simply means I didn't get there yet.

Lodges in the United States are listed by geographic region, then alphabetically by state and by lodge. Canada, Mexico, and the Caribbean get their own chapters; listings are alphabetical.

At the top of each entry is a quick-access menu and a brief overview that should help you decide if a lodge warrants reading on. Distances from the "Closest Airports" are given either in distance or in time, whichever the lodge owners thought was more applicable. "Activities" are general (look under "The Sports" heading for broader descriptions) and refer to options on lodge property and in the surrounding wilderness. The "Season" heading indicates what time of year the lodge is open. When "Guides/Instruction" are available at the lodge, they are listed under this heading. Most lodges will help you find guides and instruction through nearby outfitters if they are not available on-site. Under "Services," you'll find perks like day spas, massages, and conference facilities. "Accommodations" lists the number of rooms and/or cabins and the overall lodging capacity. "Rates" were current at press time but may have changed since—the numbers you see here are guidelines, not gospel. Prices are in U.S. dollars, per night, unless otherwise indicated.

AT THE LODGE: The prototypical wilderness lodge is a hand-hewn log cabin surrounded by spruce, fir, or pines; lit by kerosene; and heated by a woodburning stove. Many of the lodges included here fit that description, but most do not. They're all situated in or at the edge of wilderness. After that, anything goes. The accommodations listed range from rustic bunkhouses with water buckets in lieu of showers, to homey bed-and-breakfasts with floral bedspreads and breakfast-table doilies. My assumption is that not everyone who loves the outdoors has the same taste, budget, or tolerance for roughing it. But every adventurer needs a base camp.

THE SPORTS: Whenever possible, I've recommended a specific hiking trail, kayak or canoe route, climbing route, or fishing water, but this section is not meant to be a self-contained activities guide. Its purpose is to whet your appetite for potential adventures, with just enough information to get you started. Without exception, the lodges are staffed by knowledgeable folks who are more than happy to fill in the details; they might even join you on the trail.

In keeping with the tradition of *Outside* magazine and the interests of most of its readers, the activities highlighted here are nonmotorized sports attuned to natural settings (e.g., no snowmobiling, hunting, paintball, or golf). But some lodges do offer all of the above and more. If you're interested in a sport that does not appear on these pages, call to ask if it's available before assuming it is not.

BACKCOUNTRY BONUS: If the lodge or a nearby outfitter offers overnight excursions that can be added onto a normal stay, this is where you'll find them. These can include great backpacking trips, horse packing trips, multiday river trips, remote fishing camps, hike-in or fly-in camps—anything that takes you even farther off the beaten path.

MEALTIME: One of nature's kindest offerings is that being surrounded by wilderness makes everything taste better. That comes in handy when all you've got for breakfast is a packet of instant oatmeal and powdered milk. But when you're staying at a lodge where made-to-order omelets, fresh baked pastries, and just-squeezed juice are standard issue, eating becomes an extraordinary experience. You may notice my bias toward places that treat every meal as a cause for celebration. In the process of researching this book, I considered moving to Big Sky so I could eat dinner at the Rainbow Ranch Lodge regularly. But gourmet fare is not a prerequisite for inclusion. Some lodges are strictly do-it-yourself establishments. Many will cook the fish you catch. Most will pack you a sack lunch to take on the trail. This section will help define your expectations.

FINE PRINT: Pet policies, age restrictions, and safety and medical information are set aside here for quick reference. This is also where you'll find the "Heads-up" section, a brief notice to be aware of certain hazards and use common sense. Some backcountry basics: If an area has biting insects, pack your bug spray or consider visiting in a bug-free season; where there are snakes, refrain from poking your hands behind rocks and into dark crevasses; to avoid scorpions, shake out your boots before inserting your feet; in bear country, hike loudly, carry bear repellant, and resist the temptation to flaunt your freshly caught salmon while shouting, "Come and get it, grizzly!" But this guide is not the place for Wilderness 101. If you are not sure how to handle potential hazards, educate yourself *before* setting out. In this section, I've also listed the nearest medical clinic (by distance or time, whichever applies).

GETTING THERE: Directions are from the nearest airport unless otherwise indicated. I've made every attempt to print accurate, up-to-date information, but roads do close and routes do change. Double-check with the lodge.

DISCLAIMER

Despite my best efforts to predict the future, unforeseen changes are bound to occur between press time and publication. Good lodges sometimes suffer under new management, raise their rates, change their pet policies, lose a great chef, or close altogether. I encourage you to post comments on the feedback forum at www.outsidelodges.com. It's more constructive than cursing my name. More important, it will help me alert other readers to any significant changes.

The United States

EAST: Maine

THE BIRCHES ON MOOSEHEAD LAKE

P.O. Box 41
Rockwood, ME 04478
Tel: 800-825-9453; 207-534-7588
Fax: 207-534-8835
www.birches.com
wwld@aol.com

Closest airport: Bangor, ME (100 miles)
Activities: hiking, mountain and road biking, rafting, kayaking, canoeing, fishing, climbing, snorkeling, diving, horseback riding, cross-country skiing, snowshoeing, wildlife watching
Season: year-round
Guides/Instruction: hiking, fishing, canoeing, kayaking guides and instruction
Services: spa, conference facilities
Accommodations: four rooms, 15 cabins, six homes; capacity 88
Rates: $70–$250 per room; weekly rates and packages available; meal plan required in July and August

In the 1930s, sportsmen came here looking to bag moose head trophies for their dens. The evolution of local recreation since then is the story of The Birches itself. Hunting gave way to cross-country skiing, canoes were joined by kayaks, and each trend spread outward from the rustic lodge that's still the epicenter of activity on this side of Moosehead Lake.

The Birches houses an expedition company that offers river rafting, kayaking, and floatplane excursions in addition to its long list of unguided activities. Spread over 11,000 acres, this place has too many possibilities to explore in a single stay, reason enough to keep coming back.

AT THE LODGE: Every building on the property maintains the flavor of The Birches' early days. The main lodge's hand-hewn logs went up in 1930. The lodge rooms have pinewood interiors and decks overlooking Moosehead Lake. The themed, one- to four-bedroom cabins have woodburning stoves, and front porches no more than 20 feet from the water. Cooking facilities range from small fridges and counter cook tops to large, full kitchens. Rambling Rose and The Honeymoon Cabin have piers just outside. Larger and more isolated than the cabins, the private, waterfront homes are located outside the resort and vary in size and style. The Adirondack-rustic Elmer Bemis cottage sits 10 feet from its own beach and dock. The A-frame Stranger in Paradise, with its beamed ceilings, hardwood floors, and unstained paneled walls, looks like a Swiss ski chalet. Most exclusive is The Grand View: four bedrooms, three bathrooms, outdoor hot tub, and a lakefront gazebo. Or, if you prefer to take your nature sans amenities, you can choose to stay in one of The Birches' tent cabins or yurts.

THE SPORTS: It's not every day you find a lodge that offers Moose Safari Kayak Eco Tours. Here you can choose from three variations: the four-hour paddle down a hidden stream to its Moosehead outlet, a three-hour trip from the main lodge to Baker Brook, or a short, moonlight kayak on the lake. Full-day, multisport itineraries combine hiking, biking, and kayaking. You can also take a floatplane over the lake and around Mount Kineo to a remote kayak/canoe spot. The all-day trip costs $125 per person, including lunch. Hikers have access to 40 miles of trails on the premises. The path up 800-foot Mount Kineo is a mile away—views are more impressive than its stature would suggest. All trails are open to mountain bikers, including 20 miles of singletrack. Cyclists can ride the rolling hills around the property for miles. You can rent kayaks on Moosehead and Brassua Lakes and take canoes down the Moose and Penobscot Rivers with very few portages. Fishing is for landlocked salmon, and brook and lake trout. Guides are available for fishing, including ice fishing. Mount Kineo offers novice climbers a little bit of belaying terrain. Whitewater junkies can brave the Class IVs and Vs of the Penobscot River or the Class IV Kennebec and Dead Rivers. Moosehead Lake, 20 by 40 miles, offers some wreck diving (though gear is not available at the lodge, so bring your own). Snorkelers are welcome, too. Horses can be found in Greenville and Jackman, both 30 minutes away. Come winter, the lodge fills with cross-country skiers. There are 40 miles of tracked trails and groomed skating lanes on the grounds.

BACKCOUNTRY BONUS: The lodge offers two overnight kayak trips. One retraces a journey chronicled by Thoreau in *The Maine Woods.* You'll set up camp after a day on the water and read essays from the book before turning in for the night. Intermediate and advanced paddlers only. The other is a yurt-based trip that explores the geology of Brassua Lake's coves. You can also create your own overnight adventure by hiking or skiing to one of the property's three backcountry yurts.

MEALTIME: The Birches' dining room is a North Woods favorite, largely because of its scenic spot at the edge of the lake. Breakfast, lunch, and dinner feature all the standards you'd expect at a sporting lodge: corned beef hash and pancakes, burgers and dogs, baby back

ribs and the weekend special prime rib roast. The meals are simple and filling. Vegetarian options and packed lunches are available.

FINE PRINT:
Pets: welcome in the cabins and wilderness yurts
Kids: bring 'em on
Credit cards: MasterCard, Visa, American Express, Discover
Heads-up: blackflies in early June; lots of snowmobiles in winter
Nearest medical: Greenville, ME (20 miles); helicopter pad for medical evacuations
Weather: A few hot days (around 100°F) in the summer and nights that drop well below zero in the winter. The lodge is at 1,050 feet and gets about 4 feet of annual snowfall.

GETTING THERE: From Bangor, take Route 15 north 99 miles to Birches Road. Airport transportation costs $120 per trip. Air taxi service is also available.

See color photo on page 129

THE LODGE AT MOOSEHEAD LAKE

Lily Bay Road
P.O. Box 1167
Greenville, ME 04441
Tel: 800-825-6977; 207-695-4400
www.lodgeatmooseheadlake.com
innkeeper@lodgeatmooseheadlake.com

Closest airport: Bangor, ME (50 miles)
Activities: fishing, hiking, mountaineering, cross-country and downhill skiing, snowboarding, snowshoeing, mountain and road biking, canoeing, rafting, kayaking, horseback riding, dogsledding, wildlife watching
Season: year-round
Guides/Instruction: fly-fishing guides and instruction, photography and canoe guides
Services: spa, conference facilities
Accommodations: five rooms, three suites; capacity 20
Rates: $205–$475 per room, double occupancy, including breakfast and hors d'oeuvres

In the heart of every resolute adventurer, there's a tiny corner devoted to priss. It's the piece that makes you giggle when you dip a tired foot into a floral-scented bubble bath, or sigh when you rub the corner of a soft blanket against your mud-streaked face. This woodsy country inn lets you revel in the comforts of a classic bed-and-breakfast without losing touch with your stalwart side. It's earthy without being gritty, simultaneously rugged and refined. Probably a lot like you.

But don't get too cozy in your fireside bed. The reason for coming to Moosehead Lake is what lies outdoors. Forty miles long by 20 miles wide, the lake itself is a nearly limitless source of water-based fun. All around it, trails run through the woods to snowy peaks. If there's an outdoor activity you want to request, the concierge desk will make sure you get to do it. Think of this place as your very own full-service, North Woods Xanadu.

AT THE LODGE: This 1917 summer home, built by survivors of the *Titanic,* is a cedar-shingled lodge with a separate carriage house that has since been converted to three guest suites. Rooms in the lodge have fireplaces, Jacuzzi tubs, and views of the mountains or lake. The original owners commissioned a local artist to hand-carve five of the beds, which feature colorful, wildlife-themed totem pole posts. Two of the beds in the carriage house suites are suspended from the ceiling, so you can rock yourself to sleep. One room has a private deck. The suites have sunken living rooms and TVs with VCRs—there's a video library in the main lodge with over 400 titles. Nature-inspired artwork and furniture fill the common areas, like the Great Room bookshelf made of twigs and the game room's 4-foot-tall beaver chew, which was pulled from a nearby stream. Picture windows highlight the lodge's bluff-top, lakeside location.

THE SPORTS: To narrow your options to a manageable number, the concierge desk has a ready list of suggested adventures that could keep you busy for nine active days. Highlights are the floatplane trip to the Penobscot River's West Branch, where a canoe and a three-hour paddle to Lobster Lake await you; a moose safari on West Branch Pond that starts with breakfast at an authentic 1800s wilderness camp; and a rafting trip on the Penobscot, Kennebec, or Dead Rivers in rapids up to Class V. Angling options include trolling for salmon and trout on Moosehead Lake, fly-fishing with an expert guide, and drift-fishing on local rivers. Come winter, this is a prime ice-fishing destination as well; gear and guides are available. Hikers can head for the Gulf Hagas Rim Trail, which skirts the edge of a 400-foot gorge that passes through a section of the Appalachian Trail. Or try a shorter hike in Lily Bay State Park, just 6 miles away. The lodge has detailed maps and trail guides with possibilities for hikers of all levels. In addition to riding on local fire roads, mountain bikers can access a nearby facility that offers 20 miles of singletrack. Overall, cyclists will find plenty of hilly terrain on lightly traveled roads. Paddlers can rent kayaks and canoes for use on lakes, ponds, and Class II and III stretches of local rivers. Guided trail rides and instruction for horseback riders are also nearby. Skiers have access to 10 kilometers of cross-country trails in nearby Monson. For downhill skiing, Squaw Mountain Ski Resort is 8 miles away. Snowshoers don't even have to leave the lodge's property to find trails. A local outfitter offers dogsled trips from November through April. Guests can arrange all of the above activities through the lodge.

BACKCOUNTRY BONUS: If you want to work up an appreciation for the lodge's cushier amenities, start your visit with an overnight at a remote cabin on a private North Woods pond. You'll take a helicopter or seaplane to the site and spend the day reeling in trout. The pantry is amply stocked with food. Cost is $400 per couple, all-inclusive. Your other backcountry options are multiday canoe or rafting trips on the Allagash and Penobscot Rivers. The lodge will make arrangements through local outfitters.

MEALTIME: The pampering doesn't stop at chow time. If anything, it rises to new levels. Breakfast transcends the ordinary with dishes like apple oatmeal crisp with Irish whiskey cream, and eggnog French toast with cranberry-apple compote. Trail lunches with gourmet sandwiches or wraps, cold salads, and drinks can be ordered in advance. Dinner is served at romantic, lakeview tables in the candlelit dining room. You might start with winter squash and apple soup before moving on to venison stew or prime rib with mushroom brandy sauce and finishing with orange-cranberry cheesecake or a slice of "Wicked Good Chocolate Cake." Vegetarian options are always available, as are midnight munchies—there's a 24-hour guest pantry stocked with juices, soft drinks, and an assortment of freshly baked snacks.

FINE PRINT:
Pets: leave 'em home
Kids: 14 and older
Credit cards: MasterCard, Visa, American Express, Discover
Heads-up: blackflies in May
Nearest medical: Greenville, ME (2 miles)
Weather: Summer highs are around 90°F, winter lows near zero. There's at least 100 inches of snowfall each year and 45 inches of rain. Lodge elevation is 1,600 feet.

GETTING THERE: Exit the airport and make a left at the first stoplight (Griffin Road). Turn right, drive to the second stoplight, and turn left onto Route 15 (Broadway). Continue to Greenville and follow the signs to the lodge. Airport transportation is available for $125 round trip.

See color photo on page 129

Massachusetts

OLD INN ON THE GREEN AND GEDNEY FARM

Route 57
New Marlborough, MA 01230
Tel: 800-286-3139; 413-229-3131
Fax: 413-229-8236
www.oldinn.com

Closest airport: Hartford, CT (40 miles)
Activities: hiking, climbing, canoeing, kayaking, rafting, fishing, horseback riding, llama treks, road and mountain biking, downhill skiing, snowshoeing, snowboarding, wildlife watching
Season: year-round
Guides/Instruction: outdoor guides
Services: spa, conference facilities
Accommodations: 39 rooms and four suites; capacity 100
Rates: $195–$365 per room, double occupancy; packages available

The 1760 Colonial Old Inn had previous lives as a stagecoach station, tavern, general store, and post office. Normandy-style Gedney Farm used to be a dairy. Careful restorations have enabled both to join New England's lodging and dining elite.

Yet there is no need to sip your afternoon tea with a raised pinky finger. The inn's proximity to fun-in-the-mud outdoor sports keeps the atmosphere comfortably low key. After a morning hike through dwarf pitch pines, you can bike dusty back roads to a bass-filled lake, then come home, splash some water on your face, and enjoy an applause-worthy dinner in the candlelit dining room. It's elegance without attitude. For East Coast urbanites this country retreat is a compulsory weekend escape.

AT THE LODGE: The character award goes to the restored cattle barns that now make up Gedney Farm. Its 16 rooms and suites have wrought-iron beds and granite fireplaces. Some also have tiled whirlpool tubs plenty big enough for two. The wood beam running through some rooms serves as a reminder that you're sleeping in a barn. Otherwise, the accommodations could be easily mistaken for an upscale bed-and-breakfast. Rooms at the Old Inn are decorated with 18th-century antiques and country furniture. Some have shared bathrooms; others have private access to the inn's front porch and its views of distant hills. All the rooms have fireplaces. Downstairs is the restaurant, with three dining rooms lit only with candlelight and furnished with Windsor chairs, mahogany tavern tables, and iron chandeliers.

THE SPORTS: The on-site Outdoor Recreation Director coordinates itineraries for hiking, biking, paddling, fishing, and climbing. Stop in or set up an appointment ahead of time. Peak seekers may be pointed to Mount Everett, where a 7.5-mile circuit leads to the 2,608-foot summit. Other nearby paths take you past fern-rimmed lakes and through scrub pine forests to waterfalls and rock outcroppings. Guided activities include a four-hour hike (anything from easy strolls to thigh-burning hill climbs; your choice), bike rides on the area's back roads, two-hour nature walks through first-growth forests and wetlands, flatwater or freestyle kayaking instruction, canoeing on nearby lakes, two- to four-hour catch-and-release sessions in the farms bass-filled ponds, and half-day climbs on the marble and granite of the Berkshire Mountains (bouldering and top roping). The lodge also offers team-building activities and a high-ropes course in a local old-growth forest. Outdoor meditation classes are held in open fields or in the forest. There's yoga and chi gong, too. Outside outfitters run Class I to III rafting and canoeing trips on the Housatonic River. A nearby farm offers one-hour horseback trail rides. Llama treks can also be arranged. Skiers and snowboarders can day trip to the Butternut Ski Area. There's plenty of snowshoeing terrain on-site.

MEALTIME: If the following doesn't make you salivate, your glands may be out of order. Appetizer: truffled lobster ravioli with mussel saffron broth and basil oil. Entrée: slowly roasted herb-crusted poussin with wild mushroom risotto and natural jus. Dessert: warm poached winter fruits with vanilla bean ice cream or molten chocolate cake with apricot sherbet and crème anglaise. These dishes were taken from former prix fixe menus at the much-lauded restaurant at the Old Inn. The menu changes monthly, but the quality and creativity are consistent enough to draw the raves of sophisticated weekenders from New York. Dietary restrictions can be accommodated with advance notice. It's only the Saturday-night menu that is fixed; dinners most other nights are served à la carte in the dining room, fireside, or (weather permitting) alfresco under a white canopy and overlooking a flower and herb garden. Breakfasts are served at the inn, and packed lunches with specialty sandwiches, salads, breads, and cheeses are available on request. If you can stand to spend a day indoors, you might consider a cooking class. Chef Peter Platt gives private lessons.

FINE PRINT:
Pets: leave 'em home
Kids: bring 'em on
Credit cards: MasterCard, Visa, American Express
Heads-up: mosquitoes
Nearest medical: Great Barrington, MA (10 miles)
Weather: Moderate summers rarely get hotter than 80°F. Winter nights can drop to 10°. The area gets less than 2 feet of snow annually and averages 29 inches of rain. Lodge elevation is 1200 feet.

GETTING THERE: From Hartford, Connecticut, take Route 44 west to Winsted, Connecticut. Take Route 183 north through Colebrook, New Hampshire, to New Marlborough and turn west onto Route 57. Gedney Farm is on the immediate right. The Old Inn on the Green is 500 yards down the road on the right. Call for directions from New York (2.5 hours), Boston (2.5 hours), Bradley International Airport in Windsor Locks, Connecticut (1 hour), or Albany (1 hour).

See color photo on page 130

New Hampshire

THE BARTLETT INN

Route 302
P.O. Box 327
Bartlett, NH 03812
Tel: 800-292-2353; 603-374-2353
Fax: 603-374-2547
www.bartlettinn.com
stay@bartlettinn.com

Closest airport: Portland, ME (75 miles)
Activities: hiking, cross-country and downhill skiing, snowshoeing, snowboarding, mountain biking, climbing, mountaineering, fishing, canoeing, kayaking
Season: year-round
Guides/Instruction: none
Services: massage
Accommodations: six rooms, 10 cottages; capacity 35
Rates: $79–$175 per room, double occupancy, including breakfast

Touristy North Conway is a better known climbers' hub than the tiny town of Bartlett. But when Conway-based guides take their charges to the famed granite of the White Mountains, Bartlett is the last place they pass along the way. Its position at the edge of the forest is part of what enticed U.K. transplants Miriam Habert and Nick Jaques to buy this much-loved inn in 2003. Aside from the notable absence of weekender traffic, the advantage of staying here is immediate, year-round access to everything you'd want to do outdoors.

AT THE LODGE: Built as a private home in 1885, the red-clapboard Victorian became a guest house in the 1920s. Many a lazy afternoon has been passed on the rocking chairs that grace its broad front porch. The cottages are separate from the original building, where most of the comfortable guest rooms have shared baths. Rooms don't have phones or TVs, but you can find one of each in the inn's living room. The cottages are self-contained units with private baths; some have fireplaces and/or kitchenettes and sun decks. All are furnished in tastefully toned-down country décor—just enough to keep the place pretty in the presence of hiker-tracked grit.

THE SPORTS: Though they're relative newbies to the area, the innkeepers have quickly acquired an encyclopedic knowledge of its outdoor offerings. One of their favorite hikes is the 4-mile trail up Mount Potash, a 2,660-foot peak with sweeping views of the Swift River Valley. A much gentler walk is the half-mile path from Bartlett Village to the rocky cascades at Dana's Baths. With over 1,000 miles of trails in the White Mountain National Forest, there's no shortage of other options. Mountain bikers are welcome on most of the singletrack and all of the roads. Four days a week there are group rides from town, ranging from 20 to 40 miles. April through November is the rock climbing season, with ice climbs the rest of the year. Mount Washington is known for its tough winter gully climbing. In the summer, peak-baggers should try the ascent on an overcast day. From the 6,288-foot summit of the Presidential Range's highest mountain, you can see the tip of second-tallest Mount Adams afloat in an ocean of clouds. The Saco River is the summertime hangout for anglers and paddlers. The river and its watershed span 100 trout-filled miles. Harbor bass, pickerel, and perch thrive in Conway Lake and nearby ponds. When the snow starts falling, skiers and snowboarders can choose from seven area ski resorts with a total of 234 trails, 36 of which are lit for night skiing. Cross-country skiers can access the 70 kilometers of groomed trails at Bear Notch Touring Center from the inn. There's limitless showshoe terrain. Though gear and guides aren't available on-site, the innkeepers will help you track down whatever you need.

BACKCOUNTRY BONUS: The Appalachian Mountain Club (603-466-2727) operates eight huts along the 170-mile stretch of the Appalachian Trail that passes through the White Mountains. Each is about a day's hike from the next. Start with a few days of rustic hut-to-hut hiking and reward yourself with a stay at the inn.

MEALTIME: Multiday visitors need not worry about breakfast becoming blasé. The always-evolving menu features new specials each day. You'll start with melon and fresh baked muffins before moving on to the main course, which could be anything from huevos rancheros to French crêpes or waffles with a fruit and cream compote. Purists have the option of ordering basics like any-style eggs served with home fries and a side of bacon, sausage, or ham (they even stock vegetarian sausage for those who are so inclined). Sack lunches can be ordered from a deli down the road. The closest restaurants are half a mile away, with many more options in nearby North Conway. For dinner, try the Barlett Village Café.

FINE PRINT:
Pets: allowed in the cottages
Kids: bring 'em on
Credit cards: MasterCard, Visa, American Express, Discover, Diners Club
Heads-up: late-spring blackflies and mosquitoes
Nearest medical: North Conway, NH (10 miles)
Weather: Summer highs in the upper 90s; winter lows below

zero. The area logs about 80 inches of annual snowfall and 50 inches of rain. Lodge elevation is 680 feet.

GETTING THERE: Take Route 302 west to the Route 16/302 junction in North Conway. Turn right at the junction and continue to the traffic light in Glen. Head west (straight) on 302 for 7 miles. The inn is at the west end of the village, a mile past the blinking light.

See color photo on page 130

NERELEDGE INN

River Road
P.O. Box 547
North Conway, NH 03860
Tel: 888-356-2831; 603-356-2831
Fax: 603-356-7085
www.nereledgeinn.com
info@nereledgeinn.com

Closest airport: Portland, ME (65 miles)
Activities: climbing, mountaineering, hiking, canoeing, fishing, cross-country and downhill skiing, showshoeing, mountain and road biking, horseback riding, rafting
Season: year-round
Guides/Instruction: none
Services: none
Specialty: catering to climbers
Accommodations: 11 rooms; capacity 28
Rates: $69–$159 per room, double occupancy, including breakfast

Okay, so anything that's within walking distance to cappuccinos and movie theaters doesn't satisfy the strictest interpretation of "wilderness lodge." But the Nereledge Inn is also within walking distance of hiking, fishing, canoeing, cross-country skiing, and some of the best rock and ice climbing in the Northeast—you can see Cathedral Ledge from half of the rooms. The inn's affable hosts are extremely tolerant of grit-loving, mud-tracking, rope-toting clientele. They've even designated a drying room for soggy gear. Proximity to North Conway aside, this place fits any definition of a top-notch base camp.

AT THE LODGE: The restored 1787 farmhouse has a wraparound porch with the rocking chairs you'd expect in such a setting. Three sitting rooms plus a game room with a dart board and a fireplace provide plenty of social space. The inn is stocked with books, magazines, and climbing videos for those who insist on wrapping their minds around the rock and ice long after their hands have let it go. The rooms are comfortable, if dizzyingly floral. All have private bathrooms, phones, and TVs.

THE SPORTS: If you think "smearing" is just a political tactic, this is a great place to enroll in Granite 101. The abundance of local climbing schools reflects the quality of the rock in these parts. Seasoned climbers will find challenges aplenty on Cathedral, White Horse, and Humphrey's Mountains, and especially on the 1,000-foot east face of Cannon Mountain. The rock season usually runs from April through November, with ice climbs the rest of the year. Beginner ice climbers can break in their crampons at Cathedral Ledge or Crawford Notch. More challenging climbs can be found at Huntington's and Tuckerman's Ravines. Consult the guidebooks in the sitting rooms for details. Hikers and mountain bikers have access to 780,000 trail-filled acres in the White Mountain National Forest, where there's on- and off-road biking terrain for all levels. Trail rides on horseback are available through nearby stables. The Saco River, a short walk away, is great for fishing, canoeing, or just splashing around on a hot summer day. There's also river rafting, up to Class V, in the spring. And come winter, five major ski areas are less than a half-hour drive away. Marked and maintained cross-country trails are 8 miles from the lodge at Jackson Ski Touring Center. Gear and instruction for all of the above activities are available in town.

BACKCOUNTRY BONUS: Local outfitters offer summer and winter traverses of the Presidential Range. You can also sign up for a guided climb up Mount Washington, the region's tallest peak at 6,288 feet. Contact Bartlett Backcountry Guides Service (603-374-0866; www.bartlettadventures.com) for information.

MEALTIME: Warm apple pie à la mode first thing in the morning? Sure, why not? The inn's huge country breakfasts suffer no shortage of sweet-tooth appeal. You could easily induce a diabetic coma with the chocolate chip pancakes, which are always a big hit among the hyperactive. Tamer options include classic French toast, design-your-own omelets, blueberry pancakes, and good ol' ham and eggs. The menu may vary, but you can count on starting the day with a full belly. No other meals are served at the inn, but the innkeepers will pack a trail lunch on request. They'll also make reservations for dinner in town. Two favorites are Schooner Fare, a seafood restaurant in North Conway, and Jackson Bistro, 9 miles away.

FINE PRINT:

Pets: leave 'em home
Kids: bring 'em on
Credit cards: MasterCard, Visa, American Express, Discover
Heads-up: bears, mosquitoes, blackflies, poison ivy
Nearest medical: North Conway (1 mile)
Weather: Extreme. Summer highs to 90°F; winter lows far below zero. The lodge gets as much as 300 inches of annual snowfall and 40 inches of rain. Lodge elevation is 484 feet.

GETTING THERE: From Portland, take Route 302 west to North Conway, where it joins Route 16 north at a T junction (turn right). Stay on Route 16/302. At the sixth set of traffic lights, there is a Citizen's Bank on the right. Turn left onto River Road. The lodge is 500 yards farther down on the right.

See color photo on page 131

New York

ADIRONDAK LOJ

Adirondak Loj Road
P.O. Box 867
Lake Placid, NY 12946
Tel: 518-523-3441
Fax: 518-523-3518
www.adk.org
adkinfo@northnet.org

Closest airport: Lake Clear, NY (30 miles)
Activities: hiking, climbing, mountaineering, fishing, canoeing, road biking, birding, cross-country and downhill skiing, snowshoeing, snowboarding, rafting
Season: year-round
Guides/Instruction: education programs, on-site naturalist, children's programs
Services: conference facilities (limited)
Accommodations: five bunk rooms and four private rooms; capacity 46
Rates: $30–$55 per person (10 percent discount for Adirondack Mountain Club members)

In the beginning, it was just a lodge. Henry Van Hoevenberg opened it in 1890, carved trails into the surrounding mountains, and spread the word to any hiker who would listen. Plenty did. The High Peaks area has since become the epicenter of New York mountaineering activity, with paths leading to 46 summits that exceed 4,000 feet. Adirondak Loj, rebuilt in 1927, remains a favorite place to congregate before a climb.

Now operated by the nonprofit Adirondack Mountain Club, the Loj serves double-duty as a schoolhouse. The club's Education Department holds outdoors skills seminars here in everything from pine needle basket making to survival orienteering. But there's no need to wait for formal instruction. Just outside is the biggest natural classroom in the East.

AT THE LODGE: Don't come here to escape humanity. Even in the private rooms, you're likely to hear the bustle in the bunk rooms, including the occasional high-decibel snorer. Of course, there's plenty of opportunity to flee the crowds once you venture outside; but indoors, you're part of a boisterous Loj family that sometimes includes Cub Scouts in a sugar-cereal frenzy. This rustic, Adirondack-style bed-and-breakfast is more like a hostel than a hotel. It does have the basics, like flush toilets and hot showers, but the shared bathroom facilities are not luxurious. Four of the five bunk rooms are designated for families. The fifth, and largest, is coed. By far the best feature is the common room, where a moose head oversees haggard hikers gathered around the large stone fireplace. The lodge stocks a modest library of nature-themed books for your perusal. There's also a small nature museum on-site, staffed by a natural history expert in the summer.

THE SPORTS: Hundreds of miles of marked trails branch outward from the lodge. Your first outing should be the short walk to the High Peaks Information Center, where you can check weather conditions; pick up maps, snacks, and other supplies; and schmooze with the locals before choosing your peak. The most ambitious destination is Mount Marcy, the state's tallest point at 5,344 feet. The 15-mile out-and-back trail is heavily traveled on clear days. Next on the altitude roster is Algonquin Peak, an 8-miler that tops out at 5,114 feet. It's a steep, tricky walk through Norway pines, spruce, and firs, and ends with some grin-stretching views. If you prefer to stay closer to home, you can paddle Heart Lake, which is just outside the lodge. Proficient canoeists can seek out challenging waterways, some with up to Class IV rapids, nearby. Anglers can troll, fly-fish, or ice-fish on local lakes and streams. The best-known spots are on the Ausable River, which holds mostly trout and pike. Climbers who'd rather conquer walls than peaks can find bolted routes up to 5.11. Cyclists with thighs of steel can retrace a portion of the hilly Iron-man route. Skiers and snowboarders can head for Whiteface Mountain, 20 minutes from the lodge. Cross-country and snowshoe trails (ungroomed) start outside the lodge. Outfitters for all of the above activities are located nearby. Be sure to check with the Adirondack Mountain Club (see Outdoor Resources appendix) for programs that will coincide with your stay.

BACKCOUNTRY BONUS: The Adirondack Mountain Club also operates a backcountry lodge, 3.5 miles from the nearest road. **Johns Brook Lodge** has two family rooms and two coed bunk rooms that can accommodate up to 28 guests. There's no electricity and no indoor plumbing, just a warm place to sleep after a day on the trails. The lodge is open from mid-May through mid-October. The cost is $27 to $30 per person from June 28 through September 1, with basic meals available for $5–$14. All other times, beds cost $15.50 to $17.50. Bring your own food and bedding.

MEALTIME: The summer camp–style breakfast buffet features three hot items (usually pancakes along with an eggs-and-meat combination dish), fresh fruit, juices, cereals, and coffee for $5. Trail lunches can be ordered during breakfast; for $5.50 you get a sandwich, trail mix, fruit, and the ever-famous homemade "Marcy bar." Dinner must be booked 24 hours in advance and is served family style around the wood-paneled dining room's indoor picnic tables. You'll feast on soup, salad, a simple but tasty entrée like baked fish or pasta, and a hefty slice of apple pie, all for $14. The kitchen can accommodate most dietary restrictions with advance notice.

FINE PRINT:

Pets: allowed (leashed) on the grounds but not in the lodge

Kids: bring 'em on

Credit cards: MasterCard, Visa, American Express, Discover

Heads-up: bears, blackflies, mosquitoes, and gnats from mid-May through June

Nearest medical: Lake Placid, NY (8 miles)

Weather: Expect extreme winter conditions from January through March, which can mean freezing rain or heavy snow or subzero temperatures. Summertime highs are in the mid-80s, with nights in the upper 40s. Annual snowfall is 120 inches, with 38 inches of rain. Lodge elevation is 2,179 feet.

GETTING THERE: Take Route 86 east through Saranac Lake and Raybrook, then turn left onto Old Military Road. Turn at the junction onto Route 73 and follow it about a mile to Adirondak Loj Road. Turn left and follow the road about 5 miles until it dead-ends at the lodge.

ADIRONDACK ROCK AND RIVER LODGE

P.O. Box 219
Keene, NY 12942
Tel: 518-576-2041
Fax: 518-576-9827
www.rockandriver.com
ed@rockandriver.com

Closest airport: Albany, NY (2 hours)
Activities: climbing, mountaineering, cross-country and downhill skiing, snowshoeing, snowboarding, hiking, mountain and road biking, rafting, kayaking, canoeing, fishing, horseback riding
Season: year-round
Guides/Instruction: climbing and mountaineering guides and instruction, hiking and kayaking guides, wilderness medicine First Responder courses
Services: none
Specialties: climbing and mountaineering
Accommodations: 10 standard rooms, 1 bunk room; capacity 25
Rates: $65–$85 per room, double occupancy, including breakfast; $15–$30 per person for lean-to or bunks

If you simply must have access to an indoor climbing wall first thing in the morning, then this is the lodge for you. In fact, it just may be the only lodge on the continent where rope-toting rock jocks far outnumber every other type of clientele. The reason is its proximity to Adirondack Park's best rock and ice, and dozens of peaks over 4,000 feet. Not to mention the staff of American Mountain Guides Association (AMGA)–certified guides who lead climbers of all levels into the backcountry just about every day of the year.

The focus is definitely on vertical ascents, but nonclimbers have reasons to come here, too. The 30-mile Jackrabbit Ski Trail starts outside the lodge's front door; the closest neighbor is a horseback outfitter; lodge activities include guided flatwater kayak trips; and the hiking opportunities are too numerous to describe here. Even if you never touch a harness, you'll have no trouble keeping pace with the rock-and-ice storytellers at the end of the day.

AT THE LODGE: This 1800s homestead was rebuilt in 1990 with aged wood exteriors and simple, Emersonian décor that help maintain the flavor of its past. The two riverside lodges, Climbers Lodge and Guides House, have private rooms, kitchens, and stone fireplaces. The indoor climbing wall (made of real rock) is inside Climbers Lodge, a renovated barn. Guides House has a slide show area, climbing classroom, and gear storage room. Half the rooms have views of the Adirondacks.

THE SPORTS: The accommodations, while plenty nice, are not this lodge's reason to be. It's the legendary Rock and River guiding service that draws the bulk of the clientele. Whether you've never strapped on crampons or have bagged too many peaks to number, Adirondack Park has challenges to suit your skills. Beginners can take a two-day starter course ($185 for rock, $205 for ice) with the guiding service to get acquainted with the basics. Most of the advanced courses have a two-to-one guide-to-client ratio and cover everything from lead climbing ($240 for the first two-day section) to big-wall skills ($100 for two days). Some of the multiday excursions combine climbs with kayaking, canoeing, and camping. Or you can opt for a water-only guided flatwater kayaking trip on local lakes. Instructors teach the basics of boat design and stroke technique, and may even show you an Eskimo roll. Guided hikes cover all of the area's peaks and slides. The High Peaks region has 46 peaks that exceed 4,000 feet, but guides will also accommodate requests for mellower strolls. A popular day trip is the 11-mile point-to-point hike to Rocky Peak Ridge. The trail starts with a thigh-burning ascent that climbs 3,000 vertical feet in the first 3 miles. You can bike or drive to the trailhead and have someone from the lodge pick you up at the end. Horseback riding, fishing, skiing, snowshoeing, and Class IV rafting can be arranged through nearby outfitters. Ask at the lodge for details.

BACKCOUNTRY BONUS: Rock and River has a long list of multiday backcountry adventures. Among the most requested is the easy overnight Noonmark summit. The 90-foot cliff at the top of this west-facing peak has crack and face climbs ranging from 5.3 to 5.9. The campsite is a half mile down the trail at Round Pond. For a combination kayaking and climbing adventure, head for The Palisades, a scenic, 80-foot, 5.7+ climb approached by a 5-mile paddle on Lake Champlain.

MEALTIME: The culinary goal here is sustenance, not chichi cuisine. Old-school, homestyle breakfasts are served in the large, sunny dining room. You can count on the homebaked goodies to fuel you through the day. Trail lunches contain sandwiches, granola, fruit, cheese, and whatever else the kitchen happens to deem sack-worthy. For dinner, you'll have to drive to town, five minutes away. Ask for recommendations at the lodge.

FINE PRINT:
Pets: leave 'em home
Kids: bring 'em on
Credit cards: MasterCard and Visa
Heads-up: blackflies in June
Nearest medical: Lake Placid, NY (15 minutes)
Weather: Summer highs can reach 90°F, winter lows can drop to 10 below. Prepare for every weather option; blue skies in the morning don't necessarily mean blue skies all day. Lodge elevation is 1,800 feet.

GETTING THERE: From Albany, take Interstate 87 north to exit 30. Follow Route 73 through Keene to Alstead Hill Road, 1 mile outside of town. Rock and River is at the end of the road.

See color photo on page 131

ELK LAKE LODGE

P.O. Box 59
North Hudson, NY 12855
Tel: 518-532-7616 (summer); 518-942-0028 (winter)
Fax: 518-532-9262
no email or web address

Closest airport: Albany, NY (two hours)
Activities: hiking, fishing, canoeing, mountain and road biking, wildlife watching
Season: May through October
Guides/Instruction: none
Services: none
Accommodations: six lodge rooms and eight cottages; capacity 54
Rates: $95–$150 per person, including all meals; two-night minimum

The faithful fans of Elk Lake Lodge love it for what it *doesn't* offer: phones, televisions, dinner ingredients you can't identify. Heck, at Elk Lake Lodge they won't even take your credit cards. What the lodge does offer is exclusive access to a 600-acre private lake on a 12,000-acre private forest reserve, where motors are strictly shunned and the trout and salmon run in dizzying numbers. This is a genuine, turn-of-the-19th-century Adirondack mountain experience. If you're looking for a modern-amenities buffet, look elsewhere.

At the heart of it all is 3-mile-long Elk Lake, flanked by 4,000-foot peaks on three sides and dotted with more than 30 islands. A naturalist could talk your ear off about the resident hawks and warblers, exotic gentian blooms, and mycological wonders. But most guests prefer to sit alone in a canoe and absorb it all in silence.

AT THE LODGE: Much of the original 1904 structure remains intact, including the fieldstone fireplace—the focal point of the living room and the gathering place after a day on the trail. Lodge rooms are basic but comfy, with twin beds and private bathrooms. The newer cottages vary in size, holding two to eight guests. Some have kitchens and fireplaces. All have living rooms, full bathrooms, and lake, forest, or mountain views that could make it mighty tempting to hunker down in an Adirondack chair and spend your days loon-watching from the porch.

THE SPORTS: Adirondack Park is just a few hours' drive from major East Coast cities—great news for anyone who likes to share trail space with the multitudes. For those who prefer solitude, Elk Lake Lodge offers 40-plus miles of maintained hiking trails that are open only to lodge guests. Paths run through the thick hardwood forest to open overlooks; in the distance, clumps of aspen are conspicuous among the white pine. Sugar maple leaves float in the creeks and collect at beaver dams. The trails are lined with columbine and anemone in spring, blueberries and blackberries in summer. Guests are issued trail maps on arrival. The arduous 6.9-mile hike to the Mount Dix summit takes the better part of a day. Park at the lot at the top of the hill on Elk Lake Road and start climbing. When you've passed the Slide Brook and Lillian Brook lean-tos, you'll know you're halfway there. Pause to congratulate yourself, then keep climbing to the 4,850-foot peak, which offers views that stretch clear across the reserve to the Colvin Range. It's a good idea to pack a flashlight for a potential in-the-dark descent. Access to 600-acre Elk Lake and 200-acre glacial Clear Pond is also restricted to lodge guests. Paddle out in one of the lodge's rowboats or canoes and spend a full day exploring inlets, bays, and islands. Bring your fishing gear (the lodge does not offer gear or guides) and you stand a better-than-decent chance of reeling in lake trout, brook trout, and landlocked salmon. Lake and stream fishing are best through mid-June. For cyclists, there's mile after mile of lightly trafficked pavement that dips and climbs through the mountains. Point your bike eastward and set out on the Blue Ridge Road (bicycle rentals are not available).

MEALTIME: The menu is frills-free home style: steak and potatoes, turkey and gravy, spaghetti and meatballs. Think summer camp with fancier plates. If you clean your fresh catch, the kitchen staff will grill it for you. Trail lunches are just like mom used to make: sandwich, carrot or celery sticks, fruit, cookies, juice. Vegetarians can be accommodated with advance notice. Last but not least, if you like a glass of wine with your dinner, bring your own; the lodge doesn't have a beverage license. Whatever Elk Lake Lodge lacks in culinary panache, it more than makes up for in ambience. Meals are served fireside in a dining room overlooking the lake.

FINE PRINT:
Pets: leave 'em home
Kids: bring 'em on
Credit cards: none
Heads-up: blackflies, especially in June (head nets available)
Nearest medical: Schroon Lake, NY (18 miles)
Weather: highs in the 80s, lows in the 30s (the lodge is closed in winter). Lodge elevation is 2,000 feet.

GETTING THERE: From Interstate 87 or U.S. Route 9, turn west at North Hudson and drive toward Newcomb on the Blue Ridge Road. After 4 miles, turn north at the Elk Lake Lodge sign and follow the private road for 5 miles to the lodge. Transportation from the airport is not provided.

See color photo on page 132

THE POINT

P.O. Box 1327
Saranac Lake, NY 12983
Tel: 800-255-3530; 518-891-5674
Fax: 518-891-1152
www.thepointresort.com
info@thepointresort.com

Closest airport: Saranac Lake, NY (20 minutes)
Activities: hiking, mountain biking, canoeing, fishing, horseback riding, mountaineering, cross-country and downhill skiing, snowboarding, snowshoeing, ice skating
Season: year-round
Guides/Instruction: hiking, fishing and canoeing guides and instruction
Services: massage
Accommodations: 11 rooms; capacity 22
Rates: $1,250–$2,400 per room, double occupancy ($14,500 for entire property), all-inclusive (meals, all activities, open bars)

It's summer 1933. William Avery Rockefeller, nephew of the esteemed John D., has just invited you to weekend at his newly completed Adirondack retreat on Upper Saranac Lake. Suddenly you're the envy of New York society, because everyone who's anyone knows that an invitation to one of the exclusive Great Camps, built between 1880 and the Depression, is the ultimate status symbol among Manhattan's elite.

Back then, the retreat was known as Camp Wonundra. In 1980, new owners David and Christie Garrett redubbed it The Point and transformed it into a luxury wilderness resort fit to host any modern-day Rockefeller. Name a hospitality distinction and this place has earned it: Mobil's five stars, Zagat's best small resort, *Wine Spectator*'s "Best Resort for Wine Lovers." The list goes on and on. By staying here, you run the risk of forgetting that a normal life awaits you at home. Then again, that's exactly The Point.

AT THE LODGE: The last of three prominent Adirondack camps designed by architect William Distin, the 1929–1933 buildings embody the design themes of the era, with the use of natural materials like native-cut stone and halved Canadian pine logs. The lodge and guest houses were built around boulders and rock ledges. Rooms are detailed with large bay windows, wrought-iron hardware, and massive fieldstone chimneys. Animal skins and Native American rugs cover the wide-board pine walls and floors. The couches and beds are all oversized. In addition to the lodge and guest house accommodations, there's a large room above the boathouse. A new, rustic one-room cabin for daytime use—"Camp David"—has no bathroom but does have a full, stocked bar. Rooms do not have phones or televisions (communication with the outside world is entirely unnecessary), but they do have broad views of Saranac Lake.

THE SPORTS: The Point likes to think of Adirondack State Park as its own 6-million-acre fitness center. Whether you're paddling a canoe on a glassy lake or pedaling one of the house Cannondale mountain bikes up a narrow trail, every workout puts its indoor, urban gym counterpart to shame. Hiking paths on and around the property are covered with wildflowers, fall foliage, or winter snow. More than 2,500 area lakes, streams, and ponds contain landlocked salmon, bass, and pike. Fishing gear and boats are provided for use on Upper Saranac; guides can be hired for other locations. The boathouse stocks canoes, small outboards, sailboards, and Adirondack guide boats. Racks of cross-country skis and snowshoes are available to guests. Downhill skiing and snowboarding are accessible at Whiteface Mountain. There's skating and ice fishing on Saranac Lake. Nearby Lake Placid has the nation's only public bobsled and luge runs. Eight miles from the lodge, Cold River Ranch and XTC Ranch offer horseback riding. The cost of all on-site activities is included in the room rates.

MEALTIME: "What comes in the bottle is more than wine," says co-owner David Garrett, who shops at auctions to find rare vintages and fill special requests for frequent guests. His sleuthing ensures that each bottle contains a story, and uncorking the bottle is akin to sharing a gift with friends. In fact, the entire dining experience at The Point has the feel of an exclusive, gourmet house party. After cocktails, meals are served family style in the Great Hall, where fireplaces bookend the antiques-filled room, and hunting trophies adorn the walls. The menu changes daily, each dish a unique expression of the chef's best creative efforts. One of his past favorites is an appetizer of farm-raised goat cheese served three ways, side by side: pistachio-crusted with cider reduction, fondant with toasted brioche and white truffle oil, and ravioli with a century-old balsamic vinegar. Dressing up for dinner is a must—on Wednesday and Saturday black tie is required. Depending on the weather, meals are preceded by a champagne cruise or followed by a bonfire overlooking the frozen lake. In accordance with the house party theme, stocked, serve-yourself bars are abundant. Worry not, the employees who knock on doors to deliver the morning coffee and breakfast are instructed to do so very quietly.

FINE PRINT:
Pets: bring 'em on
Kids: 18 and older
Credit cards: MasterCard, Visa, American Express
Heads-up: blackflies in June
Nearest medical: Saranac Lake, NY (25 minutes)
Weather: Highs in the upper 80s; winter lows below zero. Lodge elevation is 1,100 feet.

GETTING THERE: Directions to this exclusive lodge are sent only on receipt of your reservation deposit. The Point is less than three hours by car from Burlington, Vermont, and Albany, New York. Transportation from the Saranac Lake airport is included in the cost of a stay.

See color photo on page 132

TRAIL'S END INN

62 Trail's End Way
Keene Valley, NY 12943
Tel: 800-281-9860; 518-576-9860
Fax: 518-576-9235
www.trailsendinn.com
innkeeper@trailsendinn.com

Closest airports: Albany, NY, and Montreal, Québec, Canada (two hours)
Activities: hiking, cross-country and downhill skiing, snowshoeing, snowboarding, fishing, climbing, mountaineering, horseback riding, llama trekking, mountain and road biking, rafting, canoeing, kayaking, orienteering, birding, wildlife watching
Season: year-round
Guides/Instruction: none
Services: massage, conference facilities
Accommodations: 12 rooms and three cottages; capacity 40
Rates: $85–$195 per room, double occupancy, including breakfast

This aptly named bed-and-breakfast sits at the end of the Rooster Comb Trail, which leads to the first summit of the Great Range and continues for as many miles as your boots will take you. The inn's location makes it a perfectly situated base camp for hikers, climbers, snowshoers, and anyone else hoping to experience Adirondack State Park on more than a sip-hot-cocoa-by-the-fire basis.

Which isn't to say that you can't opt for the latter. Rooms with sleeping porches and fireplaces do lend themselves to lounging. And the mountain-sized breakfasts are as likely to launch you into a post-binge nap as they are to energize you for a day outdoors. Whatever your choice, the hospitable innkeepers will help you nail down a daily itinerary and find gear and guides. They'll also remind you to wind down with a warm bath at the end of the day.

AT THE LODGE: Each of the large bedrooms in this sprawling, 1902 summer home has a distinct look, from the red-walled Terry Room with its stark white accents and Palladian, lawn-view window to the classic Bigelow Room's antique oak bed and sleeping porch overlooking the trees. Rooms come standard with fireplaces or woodstoves, phones, and claw-foot tubs or two-person whirlpool tubs. Some have skylights, screened porches with beds, wood floors, and private bathrooms. From the inn's front porch, you can look out past the lawn to the woods at the edge of the 2.5-acre property. The three separate cottages, which sleep up to six, are self-contained homes with full kitchens and TVs. Algonquin is the only cottage that's on the property; the others are 5 miles from Keene Valley (breakfast is not included at the off-site cottages).

THE SPORTS: Though the inn doesn't stock gear or hire in-house guides, the keepers have long-standing relationships with many local outfitters and are happy to help you plan any type of adventure. In addition to the Rooster Comb Trail, hundreds of miles of other hiking trails traverse the park, many of which are just a few miles from the inn. The woods are heavily forested, but the trails are well marked—this has been a popular hiking destination for more than a century. In the winter, snowshoers have access to all the hiking trails. Cross-country ski trails can be found at the Mount Van Hoevenberg ski center; downhillers and snowboarders can head for Whiteface Mountain, which has the longest vertical drop in the East (3,340 feet). Both ski areas are open to mountain bikers in the off-season. Cyclists can ride the bike portion of the North American Ironman, which runs on wide-shouldered mountain roads near the inn. Climbers will find more than 1,000 routes in the High Peaks, many within a few miles of Trail's End, and there's ice climbing in the winter. The Adirondack Mountain Club (see Outdoor Resources appendix) runs workshops on orienteering. You can also drop in on birding trips led by the local Audubon chapter. There's world-class fly-fishing on the Ausable River, which winds through the valley a third of a mile from the inn. Class V rafting is on the Hudson River, an hour away. Guide service is available locally for just about all of the above activities.

BACKCOUNTRY BONUS: The innkeepers work with local outfitters to help you add overnight backpacking, rafting, canoeing, or kayaking trips to your stay. There are plenty of canoe/camping options on the Fulton Chain or in the St. Regis Canoe Area, both nearby. Mountaineers frequently stay at the inn before and after conquering any or all of the area's famed 46 High Peaks (all are over 4,000 feet; Mount Marcy is the highest at 5,344 feet).

MEALTIME: Ask for the Hiker Quick-Start breakfast if you plan to get an early start on the trail. Coffee, tea, hot cocoa, fruit juice, cereal, and fresh baked goods should fuel you through the morning. If you can wait for the full breakfast, expect dishes like cranberry multigrain pancakes, granola waffles, fruit-filled French toast, omelets, and vegetable quiches. The main dish is always vegetarian, with meat served on the side. Special diets are accommodated on request (the innkeepers are especially proud of their vegan French toast and pancakes). The breakfast room is a glass-enclosed porch with views of birds at the feeders, the farm's original stone wall, and the woods in the distance. Request a trail lunch the night before ($7) or first thing in the morning ($8) and you'll get a PBJ, ham, turkey, or cheese sandwich, along with fresh fruit, a granola bar, a cookie, and juice or water. An outdoor sink and hose are available for cleaning any trout you catch. You can grill them on the outdoor barbecue grills. The inn's cooking facilities are open to guests, including a fridge, microwave, cook top, toaster oven, and propane grills.

FINE PRINT:

Pets: dogs are allowed in some rooms and in all cottages
Kids: bring 'em on
Credit cards: MasterCard, Visa, American Express, Discover
Heads-up: late-spring blackflies, some mosquitoes, poison ivy at lower elevations, bears
Nearest medical: Keene Valley, NY (five minutes)
Weather: With 100-plus inches of annual snowfall in the Keene Valley area, you can count on a white winter. Nighttime temperatures can drop below zero. Summer weather is cool, rarely topping the mid-70s. Yearly rainfall averages 39 inches. Lodge elevation is 1,000 feet.

GETTING THERE: From Albany, take Interstate 87 north to exit 30. Get on Route 73 and follow it 11 miles to the inn. From Montreal, Canada, follow the signs into the United States and take Interstate 87 south to exit 30. Drive along Route 73 for 11 miles to the inn.

See color photo on page 133

Vermont

BLUEBERRY HILL INN

Forest Road 32
Brandon, VT 05733
Tel: 800-448-0707; 802-247-6735
Fax: 802-247-3983
www.blueberryhillinn.com
info@blueberryhillinn.com

Closest airports: Rutland, VT (35 minutes), and Burlington, VT (75 minutes)
Activities: cross-country skiing, snowshoeing, hiking, mountain biking, canoeing, fishing, horseback riding, birding, wildlife watching
Season: closed midweek November and April, closed first three weeks of December
Guides/Instruction: cross-country skiing guides and instruction, children's programs
Services: conference facilities
Specialty: cross-country skiing
Accommodations: 11 rooms, one cottage; capacity 32
Rates: $125–$160 per person, double occupancy, including breakfast, dinner, winter trail pass

The bumpy dirt road to Blueberry Hill acts as a buffer between the real world and the inn. It slows you to a meditative rumble, so that by the time you've finished the drive, any stress you were feeling has been pounded to a gelatinous goo. Whatever remains can be melted away in the sauna, which sits next to a spring-fed pond. You'll recharge with a candlelit dinner and a solid night's sleep, waking to conquer the trails with the vigor of a born-again hedonist.

The innkeepers do their best to perpetuate a relaxed mood, so whatever your normal-life priorities, you're bound to realize at some point during your stay that what really matters is skiing home in time for soup and cookies. Such relaxation-induced epiphanies are the house specialty.

AT THE LODGE: This historic 1813 farmhouse sits in the Moosalamoo Region of the Green Mountain National Forest, surrounded by more than 22,000 acres of berry-filled woods and orchid-rimmed lakes and streams. The inn's sunny common space centers around the open kitchen, where copper pots hang above an antique stove. Flowers and herbs grow in the greenhouse, where you can sip your morning coffee in the shadow of dripping ferns. The cozy guest rooms and separate cottage are furnished with antiques and handmade quilts. There are no televisions, of course, but you can gaze at the pond from four of the rooms. All rooms and the cottage have private baths. Some have skylights and family-friendly lofts. Outside, the Adirondack chairs are perfect for lazing on the lawn. Everything about Blueberry Hill Inn is peaceful.

THE SPORTS: Seventy-five kilometers of groomed and wilderness trails spiderweb the 120-acre property. The ski center carries backcountry and skating skis and snowshoes (a separate trail for snowshoers keeps the ski tracks from getting crunched). At 2,800 feet, the Halfdan Khlune Trail is the state's highest maintained trail. For less altitude, opt for the much flatter Moosalamoo Trail, which runs to a great picnic spot in the Forest Service campground. In the summer, 60 miles of maintained hiking trails are accessible from the inn. About 20 of them are open to mountain bikers; rentals are available on-site. For an early-morning wake-up walk, climb the short trail to Rattlesnake Point, where you can look down onto Lake Dunmore and Silver Lake. There's canoeing on those lakes and nearby Sugar Hill Reservoir. Anglers must pick up a permit before fly-fishing for rainbow, brown, and brook trout. With advance notice, arrangements can be made for horseback rides. Birders should head for the Moosalamoo Birding Trail, where the resident bluebirds, osprey, warblers, and peregrine falcons are visited by the occasional white-tailed deer or moose.

BACKCOUNTRY BONUS: Make Blueberry Hill your starting point for an inn-to-inn ski weekend on the Catamount Trail. Covering the entire 300-mile route across Vermont could take weeks, but you can make a challenging two-nighter of the 25-mile section between Goshen and Killington, Vermont. Contact the Catamount Trail Association (802-864-5794; www.catamounttrail.org) for route and lodging information.

MEALTIME: The breakfast and dinner menus change daily, but you can count on waking up to homemade granola and fresh baked goodies like almond croissants, in addition to a hot main dish like shiitake omelets. For lunch, request a sack lunch with a sandwich, fruit, juice, and the house chocolate chip cookies (which, by the way, you can order online later as a tasty reminder of your stay). Bring any fish you catch to the kitchen to be cleaned and grilled to your preference. The dinner menu is an eclectic mix of dishes using garden-fresh herbs and veggies whenever possible. You'll start with an assortment of cheeses before sampling appetizers like garlic fish soup or a mousseline of scallops in a saffron sauce and partaking of a main

course such as pan-fried duck breast with apple-onion sauce or roasted rack of lamb with rosemary. You can take many of the recipes home with you—the inn's cookbook is for sale here.

FINE PRINT:
Pets: allowed only in the cottage
Kids: bring 'em on
Credit cards: MasterCard, Visa, American Express
Heads-up: blackflies and mosquitoes in May and June
Nearest medical: Middlebury, VT (14 miles)
Weather: Summer highs to 80°F, winter lows to 20 below. The area gets about 32 inches of annual rainfall and 9 feet of snow. Lodge elevation is 1,800 feet.

GETTING THERE: From Burlington, take Route 116 south to Route 125 east. Drive 4 miles through Ripton. One mile later, turn right onto Forest Road 32 (unpaved) and continue 5.5 miles to the inn. Airport transportation costs $20 each way from Rutland, $40 from Burlington.

See color photos on pages 133 and 134

ON THE LOOSE EXPEDITIONS YURTS

1035 Carse Road
Huntington, VT 05462
Tel: 800-688-1481; 802-434-7257
Fax: 802-434-4837
www.otloose.com
info@otloose.com

Closest airport: Burlington, VT (35 minutes)
Activities: snowshoeing, cross-country and backcountry skiing, hiking, mountain and road biking, kayaking, canoeing, fishing, birding, climbing
Season: closed during mud season, April through early May
Guides/Instruction: skiing and snowshoeing guides and instruction, hiking and wilderness skills guides, children's programs
Services: conference facilities (limited)
Accommodations: two yurts; capacity 20
Rates: $135 per yurt, up to 10 people

Nomads wandering the frozen mountains of Mongolia created the yurt as a practical, portable home; it was sturdy enough to withstand subzero climes, but its lightweight walls could be easily disassembled for travel. Centuries later, it remains the Mongol dwelling of choice, even in big cities. But the rest of the world has been slow to catch on.

Beth Whiting and Bruce Hennessey brought yurts to their 150-acre hilltop farm in 1998 as a funky and affordable home base for hiking, skiing, and snowshoeing adventures. Vermont's winters may not pack quite the frigid punch of wintertime in the far-east, but anyone who has hunkered down in a Vermont storm will forever sing the praises of the wood-and-canvas dome.

AT THE LODGE: Something of a compromise between a tent and a cabin, each 24-foot-diameter, circular yurt has a wood frame, a pine floor, canvas walls with windows, and a central skylight. It may be chilly when you first step inside, but body heat and a woodstove can quickly generate a tropical interior climate. Bunk beds line the perimeter, and a table and chairs define the cooking/eating/living area. The open floor plan means you'd better like your yurt mates—the only place to hide out is behind the changing-room curtain. The interior is lit by candles and propane lights that turn the structure into a glowing lantern at night. A composting toilet is just outside. Yurt rentals include firewood and water; bring your own sleeping bag.

THE SPORTS: The Long Trail, which runs for 270 miles across Vermont, passes through the woods near the farm. Hikers and snowshoers can also head east on the Beane Trail, which runs to nearby mountains that top out at nearly 3,000 feet. Snowshoes are the only equipment available for rent, but the area's snowmobiling trails make great backcountry ski touring paths if you've got your own gear and don't mind the occasional roar of a snowmobile engine. There's also easy access to the 300-mile-long Catamount Trail. Cyclists will find lots of rolling valley roads nearby. Mountain bikers must stick to the fire roads, which provide perfect terrain for beginners. There's kayaking on Lake Champlain (40 minutes away) and slow-water canoeing on the Winooski River. Beth and Bruce can refer you to fly-fishing guides. Birders should check in at the Green Mountain Audubon Nature Center, just 6 miles from the farm. Climbers will find a wide range of rock and ice within an hour's drive. In addition to its year-round outdoor programs for adults, On the Loose runs a summer day camp for kids ages 7 to 12.

BACKCOUNTRY BONUS: On the Loose offers all-season backpacking trips in the Green Mountains. You choose the distance, and the guides will set the itinerary accordingly. Food, tents, and other gear can be provided. Bring your own backpack, preferably prestuffed with the items on the outfitter's recommended equipment list. Trips start at $150 per day for two people.

MEALTIME: You're pretty much on your own for chow. The yurts have propane stoves, cookware, utensils, and dishes, but no food. Five miles away, there's a country store that stocks enough basics to keep you from starving, but you'd be wise to do a grocery run before leaving town. In the worst-case scenario (e.g., you overcook your macaroni), good restaurants are just 15 minutes away. Or you can play it safe by hiring a camp chef.

FINE PRINT:
Pets: welcome
Kids: bring 'em on
Credit cards: MasterCard, Visa
Heads-up: mosquitoes and blackflies in spring; snowmobiles use the trails
Nearest medical: Burlington, VT (25 miles)
Weather: Highs in the mid-80s, lows to 20°F. Average yearly snowfall is 5 to 6 feet. The yurts are at 1,500 feet.

GETTING THERE: Take Interstate 89 south to exit 11 (Richmond). Turn right onto Route 2 and right again at the stoplight onto Main Road. Drive about 11 miles, through Huntington, and turn left on Moody Road. After 1 mile, cross the bridge and take the first left onto Carse Road. Continue to the farm at the end of the road and hike or snowshoe the half-mile trail to the yurts.

See color photo on page 134

MIDWEST: Michigan

BIG BAY POINT LIGHTHOUSE

#3 Lighthouse Road
Big Bay, MI 49808
Tel: 906-345-9957
www.bigbaylighthouse.com
keepers@bigbaylighthouse.com

Closest airport: Marquette, MI (45 minutes)
Activities: hiking, kayaking, canoeing, cross-country and downhill skiing, snowboarding, snowshoeing, mountain and road biking, fishing, dogsledding, birding, scuba diving
Season: December 27 through November 14
Guides/Instruction: none
Services: spa
Accommodations: seven rooms; capacity 14
Rates: $104–$185 per room, double occupancy, including breakfast

There aren't many historic lighthouses left in North America that allow overnight guests. Of them all, Big Bay Point may be the only one where the ghost of the former keeper has been known to make noisy, early-morning recruiting calls for fishing buddies (not that you'll need any spectral nudging to get out and explore Lake Superior and the Huron Mountains). More notably, the lighthouse lays sole claim to this unusual perk: a private trail that runs from the tower to a massage hut at the wooded lakefront, where guests can indulge in a mud slather or skilled rubdown of the sort you'd expect from a big-city day spa.

AT THE LODGE: Though it still functions as a lighthouse, Big Bay Point was converted to a bed-and-breakfast in 1986. The 60-foot tower adjoins a cliff-top, two-story home, where some of the spacious guest rooms have exposed brick walls, cathedral ceilings, fireplaces, and incredible views of the Upper Peninsula. All rooms have private bathrooms; none have televisions or phones. Guests congregate around the fireplace in the living room, where there's an expansive book, music, and video library, along with a TV and VCR. The lighthouse houses a sauna. Climb to the top of the tower, 120 feet above the lake, for 360-degree views of electrical storms over the water, the aurora borealis, or pine and hardwood forests climbing up the Huron Range. The 12-by-12 massage hut has screened front walls to let in the sounds and smells of the lake without inviting in any biting insects. The spa treatments range from Swedish massage to an exotic assortment of facial masks and body wraps. The hut is open from Memorial Day weekend through October 15. Spa packages are available.

THE SPORTS: Hiking trails run through the inn's 47 wooded acres, far into the Huron Mountains. You can walk from the base of the lighthouse to nearby waterfalls and pine-topped peaks. Twenty-five miles of logging roads are open to mountain bikers. An outfitter in Big Bay (4 miles away) will rent you bikes and/or take you on guided rides. Twelve miles from the inn, you can fly-fish for trout in the Yellow Dog River; or, even closer, cast from shore into Lake Superior at Black Rock Point. Local outfitters rent kayaks for use in the lake, with or without a guide. There's portage-free canoeing a couple of miles away. In nearby Marquette, you can find road biking, scuba outfits, and ski slopes. Marquette Mountain has 22 downhill runs. The only gear the lighthouse stocks is snowshoes, which come in handy when the walk to the massage hut would otherwise put you knee-deep in powder. Birders should ask about the May birding package; these expert-guided walks are included in a two-night stay.

BACKCOUNTRY BONUS: Great Northern Adventures (906-225-TOUR; www.greatnorthernadventures.com) offers overnight dogsled tours. You can spend a weekend learning to mush a team of Alaskan huskies in the Hiawatha National Forest. Trips include gear, meals, instruction, and lodging in rustic cabins or full-service lodges (including Big Bay Point Lighthouse). Multiday cross-country skiing, snowshoeing, kayaking, and mountain biking itineraries are available, as are multisport itineraries.

MEALTIME: The smells of fresh coffee and homemade blueberry muffins start creeping into the guest rooms long before food hits the table. Breakfast is served family style in the lighthouse dining room, where hot entrées like raspberry pancakes with berry butter or hot apple pie French toast are served with fresh fruits, breakfast meats, cereals, and an assortment of fresh baked goods. Coffee, tea, and hot chocolate are available all day, with cookies in the evening, but you're on your own for lunch and dinner. The town of Big Bay, 4 miles away, is home to

the famous Thunder Bay Inn, where the good food is overshadowed by its history as the inspiration for the best-selling book and 1959 Jimmy Stewart movie *Anatomy of a Murder.* (A copy of the video is in the lighthouse library.)

FINE PRINT:
Pets: leave 'em home
Kids: 16 and older
Credit cards: none
Heads-up: lake flies (on humid days when there's a south wind)
Nearest medical: Marquette, MI (27 miles)
Weather: Summer highs to 85°F; winter lows to 10°F. The area doesn't get much rain but logs 165 inches of annual snowfall. Lodge elevation is 800 feet.

GETTING THERE: From Marquette, take Highway 550 north into the town of Big Bay, then follow the lighthouse signs for 3.5 miles to the point and inn.

See color photo on page 135

JOLLI-LODGE

29 North Manitou Trail
Lake Leelanau, MI 49653
Tel: 888-256-9291
www.leelanau.com/jolli
jolli@chartermi.net

Closest airport: Traverse City, MI (25 miles)
Activities: kayaking, canoeing, sailing, fishing, hiking, mountain and road biking, horseback riding, diving, snorkeling, surfing, cross-country and downhill skiing, snowboarding, snowshoeing, windsurfing, kiteboarding, hang gliding, birding
Season: May 15 through November 1
Guides/Instruction: children's programs
Services: none
Accommodations: 16 cottages, six lodge rooms; capacity 96
Rates: $70–$85 per room, $900–$1,600 weekly per cottage

On the backyard clothesline, bedsheets billow in the Lake Michigan wind. Children push shuffleboard discs as their parents watch from white Adirondack chairs on a closely cropped lawn. If this sounds like a scene stolen from a summer day in 1955, there's a reason. Very little about Jolli-Lodge has changed since it opened back then.

This classic Midwest family retreat has been run by the Joliffe clan from the very beginning—the third generation of Joliffes are the current owners. Its décor has survived the journey from contemporary to passé to retro with admirable grace. Families who've been coming here for years swear summers wouldn't be the same without their annual weeklong stay. Jolli-Lodge elicits the kind of loyalty that's as hard to come by these days as a vintage electric card-shuffling table (in case you're wondering, there's one in the corner of the dining room).

AT THE LODGE: Built by a wealthy sportsman in the 1920s, the big white lodge had separate servants' quarters that have since been converted to cottages. The screened front porch opens onto a sprawling lawn with a sandy Lake Michigan beach at its edge. All lodge rooms and cottages have television (in color!), but the only phone is a shared outdoor pay phone. Some of the rooms have fireplaces; most have decks with broad lake views. The cottages have full kitchens. The eclectic furnishings were collected at garage sales over the years, hence the prevalence of kitsch. Ask the Joliffes, and you'll find out that many of the knickknacks have a history. Case in point: the OPEN sign, crafted by an Acme sign maker the owners hired after seeing him on the 1950s game show *What's My Line?*

THE SPORTS: Three sit-on-top kayaks are available for guests to drag into the lake, as are the house sailboats. You can also paddle on nearby Lake Leelanau and Glen Lake. Lake Michigan fishing yields mostly salmon. The smaller, warmer lakes often turn up bass, pike, and walleye. There's fly-fishing not far away. Hikers can head for Sleeping Bear Dunes National Lakeshore, where 50-plus miles of trails run through hardwood forests and over Sahara-like dunes. Birders can keep an eye out for eagles, vultures, and owls. The area's lightly trafficked roads make for great cycling terrain. The Vasa Trail, which starts 28 miles away in Traverse City, is 20 miles of single- and double-track that's open to mountain bikers. Horseback instruction and guided rides are available through nearby outfitters. Divers can rent gear in Traverse City and explore shipwrecks in the lake—this area is part of the Manitou Bottomland Preserve. There isn't much for snorkelers to look at, but you're welcome to give it a shot. Surfing here is only for the brave. If there's snow before the lodge closes for the winter, snowshoers can head for the woods. The closest skiing is just 5 miles away (but don't get your hopes up; the Midwest isn't known for its slopes).

MEALTIME: In the early years, the lodge served three meals a day. But after a family squabble in the kitchen that drove the mother and daughter-in-law cooking team to quit, the Joliffes decided to focus on lodging instead. Now guests staying in the lodge rooms can get a continental breakfast (coffee, juice, rolls) from July 1 through Labor Day. Otherwise, you're on your own. Across the street, there's a small market/bakery/winery that can take care of your basic picnic needs. Three miles away in Leland, you'll find four restaurants and a grocery store. Once a week, the lodge has a potluck picnic and a marshmallow roast.

FINE PRINT:

Pets: allowed in the off-season (spring and fall)
Kids: bring 'em on
Credit cards: MasterCard, Visa
Heads-up: some years dead alewives wash up on the beach
Nearest medical: Northport, MI (16 miles)
Weather: Summer days can hit 90°F; nighttime temperatures from spring through fall can drop to 45°F. Lodge elevation is 450 feet.

GETTING THERE: Take M-37 south 4 miles, then M-22 north for 15 minutes. Turn onto M-204 west and take it 8 miles to M-22 south. Drive ¾ mile to the lodge.

PINEWOOD LODGE

P.O. Box 176
Autrain, MI 49806-0176
Tel: 906-892-8300
Fax: 906-892-8510
www.pinewoodlodgebnb.com
pinewood@tds.net

Closest airport: Marquette, MI (40 miles)
Activities: cross-country skiing, snowshoeing, hiking, mountain and road biking, kayaking, canoeing, fishing, snorkeling, diving, surfing, birding
Season: closed April and November
Guides/Instruction: none
Services: none
Accommodations: three rooms, three suites; capacity 12
Rates: $115–$145 per room, double occupancy, including breakfast

From the gazebo in the Pinewood Lodge's backyard, you get a bite-sized view of Lake Superior, framed by tall red pines. That's just about perfect, since the lake is too darn big to be digested whole. As you venture off the grounds, you'd do well to take a snack mentality with you: The lodge's central location on Michigan's North Coast gives you access to an overwhelming number of adventure possibilities.

For starters, there's Hiawatha National Forest, just across the highway. Down the road you'll find Grand Island National Recreation Area, where you can hike or bike the entire rim; and Pictured Rocks National Lakeshore, where coastal trails are groomed for skiers in the winter. Then again, you could easily confine yourself to the lodge's sandy beach, where you can hike a little, splash around, and then head home to warm up by the fire.

AT THE LODGE: Three of the six rooms and suites in this 8,400-square-foot log cabin overlook Lake Superior. All have private bathrooms, TVs (just three channels), and VCRs (a video library is on-site). The three suites have separate sitting rooms. Décor ranges from rustic/woodsy to refined/antique. The lodge was designed to feel homey, so quiet nooks for napping or taking in the views abound. Common areas include the library, sauna, gazebo, atrium, front porch, and back deck. In the great room, big windows light up the natural wood.

THE SPORTS: The North Country National Scenic Trail passes by the area on its way from New York to Washington, D.C. You can access a portion of it 3 miles from the lodge, or drive to Pictured Rocks to walk the Lakeshore section that hugs the Lake Superior shoreline. Many trails in the area are multi-use, like the 9-mile Bruno's Run loop, where hikers, mountain bikers, and snowshoers share a forested path to a number of small lakes. The 25-mile Valley Spur Route has been set aside for mountain bikers. It runs through hardwood forest, meadows, and red pine groves, with four separate loops that range from flat and gentle to technical and hilly. Ideal for road bikers, Highway 28 has a comfortable, 10-foot-wide shoulder. A network of river-connected lakes makes Hiawatha National Forest an ideal canoeing spot. Try the Indian River Canoe Trail, which starts at nearby Fish Lake and runs for about 36 miles. Get a license and you can fish for brown trout. If angling is your main ambition, though, you'd do better to head for Lake Superior to cast for lake trout and steelhead. Charter companies run sportfishing trips from May through October. For the most part, the lake is too rough for small craft—pontoon boats are the preferred mode of transport here—but kayakers can paddle the calm bays along the Picture Rocks and Grand Island coastlines. Other in-the-water endeavors include snorkeling (shipwrecks, rock formations, sand reefs), diving (more of the same, but colder), and surfing (short, fast waves best suited to short boards). When the snow starts falling, it's cross-country time. The Valley Spur Trail has 11 groomed loop trails of varying difficulty, for a total of 38 miles of terrain. If you prefer less manicured snow, try the McKeever Hills Ski Trail—an intermediate 5-mile loop that skirts McKeever Lake. The lodge will help track down gear and guides for all of the above.

MEALTIME: A full breakfast is served near the great room fireplace or in the dining room. The menu varies, but you can expect to see omelets, Finnish pancakes, or waffles on the table. Vegetarians should warn the kitchen in advance, as meat is a breakfast standard. Though you can't see any signs of civilization from the lodge, there are quite a few restaurants within a few miles. Ask at the lodge for lunch and dinner recommendations.

FINE PRINT:
Pets: leave 'em home
Kids: 13 and older
Credit cards: MasterCard, Visa, Discover (deposits by check only)
Heads-up: biting flies from late June through August
Nearest medical: Munising, MI (16 miles)
Weather: On summer days, temperatures range from 70° to 85°F. Winter temperatures are usually 10° to 25° but have been known to drop far below zero. Average yearly snowfall is 220 inches. Lodge elevation is 623 feet above sea level, 22 feet above lake level.

GETTING THERE: Drive through Marquette and take Highway 28 east 27 miles. The lodge is on your left.

See color photo on page 135

Minnesota

BEARSKIN LODGE

124 East Bearskin Road
Grand Marais, MN 55604
Tel: 800-338-4170; 218-388-2292
Fax: 218-388-4410
www.bearskin.com
stay@bearskin.com

Closest airport: Duluth, MN (136 miles)
Activities: cross-country skiing, showshoeing, fishing, canoeing, kayaking, hiking, mountain and road biking, diving, wildlife watching
Season: year-round
Guides/Instruction: fishing and cross-country skiing guides and instruction, snowshoeing guides, on-site naturalists, children's programs, naturalist programs
Services: massage
Accommodations: 11 cabins, four lodge suites; capacity 85
Rates: $100–$375 per room, double occupancy; $650–$2,300 per week

They call it the Lake Effect. It's what happens when absurdly cold air (the northeastern Minnesota kind) is pushed over a relatively warm body of water (say, Lake Superior) to produce great quantities of chalky snow that can then be groomed to silky perfection. The 126-mile Gunflint system is famous for this snow, and there's no better place to access it than the Bearskin Lodge, where 70 kilometers of marked and maintained trails start just outside the lodge door.

When the snow melts, hikers take over the trails, and paddlers make a dash for the water. Bearskin is the only lodge on East Bearskin Lake, which feeds into the Boundary Waters Canoe Area Wilderness and Quetico National Park. Together they offer thousands of miles of paddling possibilities. As all-season lodges go, this one ranks highest in adventure potential.

AT THE LODGE: The homey cabins are spread around the lakeshore, each with a path leading to a private dock. Most were built of spruce or cedar logs or planks, with screened porches overlooking the lake. Some of the older cabins date back to the 1920s. Norway Pine #11, the most recent addition, has panoramic views and an outdoor hot tub. All cabins have full kitchens, freestanding fireplaces, separate dining areas, and private bathrooms. The welcome absence of TVs and phones keeps you focused on the outdoors. Each of the two-story suites, next to the main lodge, hold up to eight guests. They have all the amenities of the cabins, plus open-air decks with lake views. There's a laundry facility at the edge of the property, and a gift shop with fishing tackle and outdoor duds. At the Hot Tub Hus, the sauna and eight-person Jacuzzi can be reserved for private use.

THE SPORTS: For starters, there are gorgeously groomed skiing and skating trails, with rentals available on-site. This is the gateway to the Central Gunflint system, which could keep all-level skiers busy for a good long while. Itty-bitty holiday lights that line the lake and some of the trails ensure that the fun doesn't have to end with the daylight. This is especially key for late-night ice skating and broomball games. If the activities ended with skiing and snowshoeing, that would be enough; but things really start happening once the 440-acre, 4-mile-long lake has thawed. Fishing guides will help you find the walleye, small-mouth bass, and northern pike, by canoe. Or you can drop a line from your private dock—all necessary gear is available at the lodge. Paddlers can cross East Bearskin Lake and portage to other lakes in the Boundary Waters Canoe Area Wilderness. Canoe and kayak rentals are available at the lodge and in Grand Marais (for use on Lake Superior). If you've got a very thick wetsuit and your own scuba gear, you can dive in East Bearskin or Lake Superior. Those who prefer land have immediate hiking access to all of the lodge's ski trails, plus a few million acres of terrain in the surrounding Superior National Forest. Many of the trails and logging roads are open to mountain bikers; bikes can be rented at the lodge. The road biking is on steep, gravelly hills. Keep an eye out for moose, bears, wolves, foxes, beavers, lynx, and pine martins. Naturalist-led hikes in the summertime include programs for kids over age 3.

BACKCOUNTRY BONUS: Use this lodge as a jumping-off point for Boundary Waters canoeing/camping trips up to several weeks long. In addition to renting you a canoe, many area outfitters will prepare your gear and food, chart a course, and reserve your campsites. Call 877-550-6777 for permits and reservations. For logistical information, check out www.canoecountry.com.

MEALTIME: Each cabin and town house has its own fully applianced kitchen, but the nearest full-service grocery store is 30 minutes away. The gift shop sells basics like milk and trail mix. Breakfast baskets are available on request, as are trail lunches (sandwich, fruit, chips, cookies, drink). If you fish with a guide, cleaning your catch is part of the service, but you'll have to do the grilling yourself. There's a hot lunch every winter day. A sit-down dinner is served two or three nights a week, advance reservations required. In addition to warm bread, salad, veggies, homemade soup, and pie, you'll choose from three home-style entrées: New York strip steak, a vegetarian dish, and a nightly special (i.e., walleye in parchment, orange-glazed roast duck, or beef tenderloin kabobs). The cost for adults is $25. Kids can order from their own menu (grilled cheese sandwich, spaghetti, PB&J, etc.) for $3 to $15 each. The candlelit dinners are served beside the massive granite fireplace in the lodge's lakeview dining room.

FINE PRINT:

Pets: leave 'em home
Kids: bring 'em on
Credit cards: MasterCard, Visa, American Express, Discover
Heads-up: bears, moose, mosquitoes, blackflies
Nearest medical: Grand Marais, MN (26 miles)
Weather: Summer highs to 100°F, winter lows to an unfathomable 60 below. Yes, that's 60° below zero. The good news is that there's more than 100 inches of annual snowfall.

GETTING THERE: Take Highway 61 north to Grand Marais. Turn left onto County Road 12 (the Gunflint Trail) and stay on it for 26 miles. The lodge is on the right.

BIG LAKE WILDERNESS LODGE AND OUTFITTERS

3012 Echo Trail
P.O. Box 359
Ely, MN 55731
Tel: 800-446-9080
www.biglakelodge.com
info@biglakelodge.com

Closest airport: Ely, MN (26 miles)
Activities: canoeing, fishing, kayaking, hiking, mountain and road biking, birding, wildlife watching
Season: May through mid-October
Guides/Instruction: fishing and canoeing guides, basket weaving instruction, children's programs, on-site naturalist
Services: none
Specialties: fishing and canoeing
Accommodations: 13 cabins, two tents; capacity 84
Rates: $105–$340 per room or tent, including some activities; weekly rate $640–$1,360

Simplicity is an underrated amenity, both in lodges and in life. Big Lake Wilderness Lodge stands as a reminder that you don't need much more than a canoe and a fishing rod to attain summertime bliss. With a full-service outfitter on-site, it's easy to get on the water, and 1,920-acre Big Lake—which connects to 1,200 miles of canoe routes—is just steps from your cabin or tent.

Affable owners Eric and Sharon Schneider have made a point of creating a family-friendly environment. Guided kids' activities from kite making to movie nights leave moms and dads free to enjoy the area's simplest pleasure—silence.

AT THE LODGE: Fishing and hunting trophies line the log walls of the 1947 main lodge, along with a generous smattering of other paraphernalia collected over the years. Each of the half-log-sided cabins has its own deck, a full kitchen, and a full private bath. Set amid pines near the edge of the water, all cabins have splendid lake views. Three of the cabins have fireplaces. None have phones or TV (though there's one of each in the main lodge). The base camps on Spirit and Loon Islands have two-bedroom tents big enough to wrap around a Manhattan studio apartment. They're stocked with cots, sleeping pads, and warm sleeping bags. Each campsite has its own wood dock and a screened gazebo with a picnic table. All cooking gear (pots, pans, utensils, propane stove, fuel, fresh water) is provided, along with ice, a cooler, and firewood for the stone fire pit. There's a portable toilet at both campsites, but you're welcome to paddle to the main lodge for the hot showers, sauna, and indoor plumbing.

THE SPORTS: Guests get free use of the house canoes, paddle boats, and kayaks. From the lodge's dock, you can take an easy canoe trail on 5 miles of river and lake. With thousands of miles of canoe trails in the surrounding Boundary Waters Canoe Area Wilderness, there's no shortage of daytrip options. Guides are on-site to answer questions, map courses, or take you as far into the wilderness as you want to go. Kayakers can paddle around the lake and nearby islands. An extensive selection of fishing boats is available for rent, and tackle is for sale at the lodge store. Guide service is offered on three local lakes, where the catch includes walleye, northern pike, smallmouth bass, and yellow perch. Landlubbers can hike the two on-site trails in a single day. They run through boreal forest along the lakeshore for 5 miles. Logging trails and paved roads are open to bikers; mountain bikes and helmets can be rented at the lodge. The resident naturalist gives weekly talks on the local flora and fauna. Guided children's nature walks are offered several times a week. More than 100 species of birds have been seen in the area—binoculars are available. Wildlife seekers can also day-trip to the International

Wolf Center in Ely (23 miles) and the Vince Shute Bear Sanctuary in Orr (50 miles).

BACKCOUNTRY BONUS: The lodge's outfitter service offers a dozen or so overnight paddling and hiking itineraries with as much or as little gear and guidance as you want. Since there's a daily quota for each entry point, be sure to make reservations early.

MEALTIME: There's no restaurant, just your cabin or camp kitchen. Basic edibles are for sale in the lodge store, but you'll be better off getting groceries in Ely. The nearest restaurants are also in Ely, 23 miles from the lodge. If you catch any fish while you're here, the staff will clean and pack them for the trip home. This service is included in the cost of a stay.

FINE PRINT:
Pets: on a leash; $18 per day, $90 per week
Kids: bring 'em on
Credit cards: MasterCard, Visa, American Express, Discover
Heads-Up: mosquitoes and blackflies
Nearest medical: Ely, MN (24 miles)
Weather: Average highs range from the mid-50s (October) to the upper 70s (July).

GETTING THERE: Take St. Louis County Road #1 3 miles to Ely. Turn right on MN 169 (Sheridan Street) and drive 0.5 mile. Just past the International Wolf Center, turn left onto St. Louis County Road #88 and drive 2 miles. Turn right onto St. Louis County Road #116 (Echo Trail) and drive 20 miles. The lodge is on your left. Airport transportation is available for $25.

BLUEFIN BAY ON LAKE SUPERIOR

Highway 61 and Sawbill Trail
Tofte, MN 55615
Tel: 800-BLUEFIN (258-3346); 218-663-7296
www.bluefinbay.com
bluefin@bluefinbay.com

Closest airport: Duluth, MN (79 miles)
Activities: kayaking, canoeing, skiing, snowshoeing, hiking, mountain and road biking, diving, surfing, fishing, climbing, mountaineering, horseback riding, wildlife watching, dogsledding, skijoring, skating
Season: year-round
Guides/Instruction: guides and instruction for most activities
Services: massage, conference facilities
Accommodations: 73 rooms and town houses, 2 to 12 guests each; capacity 375
Rates: $55–$479 per room, including some activities

It's the rare resort that tries to be all things to all guests, and succeeds. Though no one would ever call this place quaint, plenty have called it romantic and family friendly, remote and convenient, upscale and laid back—all in the same breath. That's quite an accomplishment for a massive complex that can hold hundreds of guests and claims to cater to just about everyone.

Admittedly, the die-hard adventurer may occasionally feel compelled to flee the busy grounds, but that's easy to do when you're surrounded by Lake Superior, the Boundary Waters Canoe Area Wilderness, and the Sawtooth Mountains. Besides, rugged outdoor playtime is just that much sweeter when you know there's a bubble bath waiting at home.

AT THE LODGE: The site's lodging history dates back more than a century, but the resort didn't exist in its present incarnation until the mid-1980s. Since then, expansion has been an ongoing process. Designed to look like the historic coastal village of Tofte, which was almost

completely gutted by a forest fire in the early 1900s, the pale blue buildings are bright and breezy and filled with nautically themed art (a wooden steering wheel here, a model clipper ship there). Accommodations range from basic hotel rooms to three-bedroom town houses with fireplaces, Jacuzzis, and kitchens. The Grand Superior Master Bedroom has high, wood-paneled ceilings and a great big bathtub next to a picture window overlooking the lake. All rooms have views of Lake Superior or the Sawtooth Mountains. Floor plans are posted online (www.bluefinbay.com/floorplans.html). Whatever it lacks in rustic funkiness (from the water, it could be mistaken for a sprawling condo complex), Bluefin makes up for in amenities: Internet access, a fitness center, pools, saunas, and spas.

THE SPORTS: Entire books have been written about this region's outdoor sports; the list of options is almost paralyzing. Start with a trip to the Activities Desk for information on the guided kayak trips on Lake Superior that are included in your stay. Also gratis are the house mountain bikes and canoes, guided hikes and showshoeing, cross-country ski equipment and access to 55 kilometers of groomed trails. A statistic for the geographically inclined: Lake Superior is 370 miles long by 160 miles wide, which makes it the world's largest body of fresh water. That translates to a whole lot of paddling, but you can find 120 more miles of water in the Boundary Waters Canoe Area Wilderness. The water sports here aren't limited to the above-the-surface variety—the clear water makes for unbeatable wreck diving, and extreme surfers like to tackle the southwest shore at Park Point. Prepare for very, very cold water. Hikers and mountain bikers can get trail maps at the front desk. Eight nearby state parks have trails that parallel creeks and lead to rocky gorges, cauldrons, and waterfalls; many of them are fat-tire friendly. Tofte Charters takes Bluefin guests fishing for king and coho salmon in warm weather, and ice fishing for brook trout in the winter. They'll clean and cook your catch. Climbers can head for Tettegouche State Park, where routes range from beginner to expert. Summiting 2,301-foot Eagle Mountain may not seem like a great mountaineering feat, but try it in snowshoes and you may reconsider. For kids, there's a play area and an activities program. There's also an ice skating rink on-site.

BACKCOUNTRY BONUS: Though it's not officially offered through the lodge, you can combine a stay with a multi-day canoe trip in the Boundary Waters Canoe Area Wilderness or some backpacking on the existing sections of the Superior Hiking Trail, which will run 250 miles from Duluth to the Canadian border when it is complete.

MEALTIME: It takes three restaurants to feed the masses here. Most upscale (though still pretty casual) is The Bluefin Restaurant, with a gourmet menu and lake views that bring a steady stream of out-of-towners to the resort just for dinner. The more low-key Breakers Bar and Grill serves burgers, sandwiches, and bar food. Coho Café is the Italian bistro and bakery. Locals claim it has the best pizza in the state. Coho is also the place to order your trail lunches, which include the standard sandwich/chips/cookie combination or you can order customized specials.

FINE PRINT:

Pets: allowed in some rooms

Kids: bring 'em on (14 and older for kayaking)

Credit cards: MasterCard, Visa, Discover

Heads-up: poison oak, seasonal blackflies and mosquitoes

Nearest medical: Grand Marais, MN (25 miles)

Weather: Minnesotans may pass off their winters as "chilly," but the rest of us consider 20 below utterly intolerable. Fortunately, Lake Superior creates a buffer that makes winter here slightly less miserable than elsewhere in the state (unless there are onshore winds). Still, pack the warmest layers you can find. Temperatures during the rest of the year are pleasant, with highs in the 80s and lows in the 40s, and rain- and snowfall are moderate. Lodge elevation is 620 feet.

GETTING THERE: Take Highway 61 north from Duluth and drive approximately 79 miles to the town of Tofte. The lodge entrance is on your right.

See color photo on page 136

NORTHERN ROCKIES: Idaho

IDAHO ROCKY MOUNTAIN RANCH

HC64 Box 9934
Stanley, ID 83278
Tel: 208-774-3544
Fax: 208-774-3477
www.idahorocky.com
idrocky@ruralnetwork.net

Closest airport: Sun Valley, ID (70 miles)
Activities: hiking, mountain and road biking, fishing, rafting, kayaking, canoeing, horseback riding, climbing, mountaineering, cross-country skiing, snowshoeing
Season: mid-June through mid-September; December through March; only two cabins are open in winter
Guides/Instruction: none
Services: massage
Accommodations: four rooms, 17 cabins; capacity 50
Rates: $109–$127 per person, including breakfast, dinner, and some activities

It's a shame that lightning and water don't mix, because watching an electrical storm light up the Sawtooth Mountains while you're soaking in a hot-spring-fed swimming pool would rank among the most mind-blowing experiences at the Idaho Rocky Mountain Ranch. Unfortunately, a single stray bolt could lead to some mind blowing of the most unpleasant kind—best to head for dry land when the electrons start flying.

The wicker rocking chairs on the lodge's front porch are an acceptable alternate venue. They're among the many comfy touches that belie this lodge's "ranch" moniker—it's more a high-end retreat than a rough-and-tumble wrangler's place. Built in 1930 as a private hunting lodge by wealthy Frigidaire distributor Winston Paul, it was available by invitation only in the early years. The current owners, who opened it to guests in 1977, have preserved the ranch's tradition of mountain luxury.

AT THE LODGE: The 8,000-square-foot, hand-hewn log lodge is on the National Register of Historic Places. Its historic integrity has been carefully maintained, as evidenced by the monogrammed china. The rooms and cabins have electricity and private bathrooms, but no televisions, phones, or clocks. Not that you'll miss them. Handmade quilts cover the hand-crafted log beds. Walk-in dressing rooms and fireplaces are standard amenities, and every lodgepole pine cabin has views of the Sawtooth and White Cloud Mountains and/or the Sawtooth Valley. The hot-spring swimming pool is the lodge's best stargazing spot. In the winter, only two housekeeping cabins (with kitchens) are open to guests.

THE SPORTS: The 1,000-acre property has its own valley-to-ridgetop trails and a stocked, catch-and-release fishing pond with a paddle-boat. There's also access to the Salmon River, where local outfitters run family-friendly rafting and kayaking trips on Class II to IV rapids. The whitewater season runs from June through late August. Some of the mellower stretches are open to canoes, as are many local lakes. Guides and gear can be procured for anglers, though they're not available on-site. You'll be casting into the area's dozens of rivers and lakes for cutthroat, bull, rainbow, and brook trout, as well as steelhead and whitefish. Nearby stables offer guided trail rides in the White Cloud range. Mountain bikers will want to explore the area's miles and miles of buffed-out singletrack. Cyclists can ride the long stretches of mountain roads—everything from slow, easy grades to challenging mountain passes. Climbers can find bolted routes up to 5.12, including many multipitch routes. Peak baggers have plenty to choose from in the 10,000- to 12,700-foot range. Climbing guides can be hired in town. If you and your family are looking for a place to splash around or paddle, Redfish Lake is a popular spot; expect to have plenty of company. Guided nature walks are also available. In the snowy season, there's backcountry skiing through forestland to open meadows, plus 25 miles of groomed cross-country snowshoeing trails.

BACKCOUNTRY BONUS: Outfitters in nearby Stanley offer multiday river trips and llama, horse, and mule treks that can be tacked on to a lodge stay. You can also plan a backpacking trip in the Sawtooth National Forest or Frank Church/River of No Return Wilderness (not quite as daunting as the name would imply, this 2.4-million-acre preserve is the largest wilderness area in the lower 48). In winter, there's hut-to-hut skiing.

MEALTIME: You'll be picked up by wagon for the short ride to the weekly Monday-night barbecue and Dutch oven cookout. Expect a cowboy serenade as you nibble on barbecued ribs at the edge of the forest. Other meals are served fireside in the dining room, where you can choose between two-person corners and more social, family-style tables. Breakfasts are hearty, with fresh baked pastries and fruit preceding hot entrées. Packed lunches (sand-

wich, trail mix, fruit, juice, homemade cookie) can be ordered for $4.95 to $8.50. Dinners feature four or five entrées that vary according to the chef's mood. Choices usually include fresh trout, lamb, steak, pasta, and a vegetarian option. Appetizers, soup, salad, and dessert are included in the entrée price. Wine and beer are available; there's a corkage fee if you bring your own bottle.

FINE PRINT:

Pets: leave 'em home
Kids: bring 'em on
Credit cards: MasterCard, Visa (June through October only)
Nearest medical: Stanley, ID (9 miles)
Weather: Summer highs are usually in the upper 70s, with lows often dropping to freezing (there are only 30 or so frost-free nights each year). In winter, expect days in the 20s and nights that get bone-chillingly close to zero. Yearly snowfall averages 150 inches. Lodge elevation is 6,600 feet.

GETTING THERE: From Sun Valley, drive north on Highway 75 and look for the ranch entrance between mile markers 180 and 181. The lodge and cabins are a half mile from the east side of the highway.

See color photo on page 136

Montana

BIG EZ LODGE

7000 Beaver Creek Road
P.O. Box 160070
Big Sky, MT 59716
Tel: 877-244-3299; 406-995-7000
Fax: 406-995-7007
www.bigezlodge.com

Closest airport: Bozeman, MT (43 miles)
Activities: fishing, hiking, paddling, cross-country, back-country, and downhill skiing, snowboarding, snowshoeing, horseback riding, mountain and road biking, rafting, wildlife watching
Season: mid-May through mid-October; mid-November through mid-April
Guides/Instruction: fishing guides and instruction, horseback riding and hiking guides
Services: spa, conference facilities
Accommodations: 12 lodge rooms and one suite; capacity 26
Rates: $299–$1,400 per room, double occupancy, includes breakfast and some activities (all-inclusive package also available)

Genuine cowboys may scoff at the absence of rough edges here, but a few minutes spent in the massive outdoor hot tub that overlooks Big Sky's snow-tipped peaks should melt away any cynicism. Big EZ Lodge was designed to let you enjoy Montana's unparalleled outdoors without the slightest twinge of discomfort. Any adventure you can dream up is yours for the asking, and you can count on coming home to pure indoor luxury.

The owners, communications magnates from Austin, Texas, fashioned the entryway after their state's capitol building and imported much of the Western-style furniture and original artwork from home. Since they spend part of each year living on-site, every detail of the operation must live up to their discriminating standards. Staffer Julie Pfingst describes the lodge as aptly as anyone: "It's like a cruise ship in the mountains."

AT THE LODGE: The Internet-obsessed will be thrilled with the in-room laptop, which has high-speed Internet access and a personalized screen saver message welcoming them to the Big EZ Lodge. It's a standard amenity in every spacious room, along with satellite television and a direct-dial phone number. If that's not enough to tempt you to relocate your office, there's the stocked mini-fridge (complimentary) and, in six of the rooms, an over-the-desk window view of Gallatin National Forest. The décor is high-end but homey, with handmade quilts, unique tile accents, and artwork that matches the state-themed rooms (e.g., an antique needlepoint Confederate flag in the Tennessee room). Guest rooms are separate from the main lodge, where meals are served in a small, open dining area overlooking an airy common room. The 1,850-square-foot Lone Start Suite, where the owners stay when they're in town, features a kitchen that would earn the envy of any chef, a workout room, a full office, and a private outdoor hot tub. The staff's favorite touch: the heated toilet seat in the master bathroom.

THE SPORTS: Hundreds of miles of fire roads and trails make the world outside the front door a hiker's and biker's paradise. The mountain biking tends to be steep and technical, but the scenery makes the effort worthwhile. There's paddling on nearby lakes, and technical climbing in the canyons. The skiing and snowboarding at the Big Sky Resort (transportation available) rank among the nation's finest, though you wouldn't know it from the absence of lift lines. Snowcat and cross-country skiing aren't far away. The trout fishing in stocked ponds on the property and in local rivers is legendary. Class II to IV rapids make rafting an option in summer. And there's an 18-hole putting course in the front yard. Virtually any guest request for exploring the surrounding wilderness can be arranged by the lodge. Any gear that's not available on-site can be rented from nearby outfitters. Two 6-mile, round-trip day hikes—one to Beehive Basin and one to Lava Lake—will take you far from civilization. Both have elevation gains that will make the Jacuzzi all the more welcome when you return. The first starts in subalpine surroundings and takes you up above tree line. The lake hike climbs 1,500 feet to a serene mountain lake.

BACKCOUNTRY BONUS: Overnight horse packing trips in the Spanish Peaks Wilderness Area, in Yellowstone National Park, and in Gallatin National Forest can be arranged with advance notice.

MEALTIME: Unless you've opted for the all-inclusive package, breakfast is the only meal that doesn't come with a bill. Then again, with the Texas-sized servings, you could feasibly accomplish a whole day's eating before 11 A.M. Fresh fruits and juice smoothies accompany your eggs, Baileys-espresso blueberry pancakes, or sweet potato cake. For lunch, the dining room is open; sack lunches with a sandwich, salad, chips, drink, and pastry are available on request. And if you don't feel like seeking dinner down the hill in Big Sky, you'd do quite well to settle into one of the private dining rooms or open dining area at the lodge. Game features prominently, but the menu includes gourmet options for fish-eaters and vegetarians as well. The wine list is more than adequate, and the desserts plenty dangerous. Dining options in Big Sky include the world-class restaurant at Rainbow Ranch Lodge (see lodge listing on page 65) and the casual but tasty Corral restaurant, just across the highway from Rainbow Ranch.

FINE PRINT:
Pets: leave 'em home
Kids: bring 'em on
Credit cards: MasterCard, Visa, American Express
Heads-up: bears
Nearest medical: Big Sky, MT (8 miles)
Weather: Few summer days top 90°F, though summer nights can get as low as 40°; winter temperatures usually hover in the 20s but can get colder with little warning. The yearly snowfall averages 400 inches. Lodge elevation is 7,500 feet.

GETTING THERE: From Bozeman, head south on Highway 191 and drive past the Big Sky Resort turnoff. Two miles after that, you'll pass the Ophir School on the right. Turn right at the SCHOOL ACCESS sign (just past the school) onto Main Beaver Creek Road (unmarked at this intersection). About a mile down the road is a gate, where you can dial the Big EZ Lodge for access. Continue 4.8 miles to the lodge. Transportation from the airport is available for a fee.

See color photo on page 137

THE BUNGALOW BED AND BREAKFAST

P.O. Box 168
Wolf Creek, MT 59648
Tel: 406-235-4276
bungalow@montana.com

Closest airport: Helena, MT (38 miles)
Activities: hiking, fishing, canoeing, mountain and road biking, horseback riding, wildlife watching
Season: April through December
Guides/Instruction: none
Services: conference facilities (limited)
Accommodations: four rooms; capacity 10
Rates: \$110–\$150 per room, double occupancy, including breakfast

Think of this place as a miniature replica of Yellowstone National Park's ever-heralded Old Faithful Inn—same architect (Robert Reamer), same era (early 1900s), but with a notable absence of national park traffic and solace-snatching snowmobiles. Like the park lodge, the Bungalow's asymmetrical shape was designed to reflect the disorder of nature. Unlike the park lodge, its limited capacity and off-the-path location allow you to experience that disorderly nature with a minimum of human interference.

Three miles from the small town of Wolf Creek, Montana, The Bungalow fits snugly against a hillside. Its stone fireplace columns blend seamlessly with a tall granite face in the background. The local trout fishing's every bit as good as what you'd find on better-known rivers to the south, and the surrounding wilderness looks much like it did when Lewis and Clark explored it 200 years ago. Sure, there's something to be said for the classic Old Faithful Inn vacation; but this place offers something a park lodge never could: the feeling that it's yours to enjoy alone.

AT THE LODGE: The lodgepole pine log lodge was built between 1911 and 1913. It's been in the O'Connell family since 1946; current owner Pat O'Connell Anderson turned it into a bed-and-breakfast in 1993. Her focus on preservation helped earn it a listing on the National Register of Historic Places two years later. For a small lodge, it has a very open feel, mainly because of the high ceilings and massive stone fireplace in the Great Room. This is where guests gather to read by the fire or watch the tastefully hidden TV. You can look onto the ground level from the open, second story, where Native America rugs and animal pelts are draped over the railings. The rooms are bright and simple, with views of the mountains or a pasture. Those with their own bathrooms have a shower and a claw-foot tub.

THE SPORTS: A 7-mile drive takes you to a stretch of the Missouri River that would be legendary in fly-fishing circles if anyone decided to spread the word. There's stream and lake fishing, too, particularly on beautiful Holter Lake, where you can yank trout into a rented boat. Guides and gear can be found all over the place. The Gates of the Mountains Wilderness Area, 12 miles from the lodge, is a 28,500-acre wildlife reserve on the east side of the Missouri. Bighorn sheep, mountain goats, ospreys, and eagles live in the area's limestone canyons, where trails parallel creeks to remote waterfalls. Local outfitters offer canoe trips on the Missouri and Dearborn Rivers. Bikers can pedal logging roads or ride the lightly traveled canyon roads. Local guest ranches sometimes offer horseback rides to nonguests, if they make prior arrangements. Insurance restrictions prevent the lodge from affiliating itself with any outfitters, but brochures with contact information for all of the above activities are available.

BACKCOUNTRY BONUS: Wolf Creek Outfitters (406-235-9000; www.wolfcreekoutfitters.com) offers overnight float trips that retrace the path of Lewis and Clark on a quiet stretch of the Missouri River. You'll paddle a replica fur trader canoe between towering cliffs, then camp out by the river. The cost is $250 per adult, $225 per child (12 and younger), including meals, tents, and guides.

MEALTIME: A gigantic breakfast graces the 12-person table in the log dining room each morning. Your choices might include ginger pancakes with lemon sauce, eggs Benedict, peach melba French toast, or a fresh herb frittata, all accompanied by breakfast meats, fresh fruit, and fresh baked goods like berry muffins, scones, cinnamon rolls, sticky buns, and homemade honey whole wheat bread for toast. Cereal is available for anyone who'd rather go light. Sack lunches with a sandwich, fruit, chips, and dessert are available with advance notice. You're on your own for dinner, unless you've rented the entire lodge and have made prior arrangements. In that case, the menu features mountain standards like grilled steak, garlic lime chicken, or poached fresh salmon with dill sauce, along with salad, potatoes or rice, bread, and a choice of two or three desserts.

FINE PRINT:
Pets: leave 'em home
Kids: bring 'em on
Credit cards: none
Heads-up: bears, occasional mosquitoes
Nearest medical: Helena, MT (38 miles)
Weather: Summer highs to 90°F; winter lows to zero. Expect cool nights year-round. There's very little precipitation, about a foot of rain and 10 inches of snow each year. Lodge elevation is 4,300 feet.

GETTING THERE: Take Interstate 15 to exit 228. Drive 1.2 miles on Highway 287 and turn left at the BUNGALOW sign. Drive 1 mile up the gravel road to the inn.

See color photo on page 137

CHICO HOT SPRINGS RESORT

#1 Chico Road
Pray, MT 59065
Tel: 800-HOT-WADA; 406-333-4933
www.chicohotsprings.com
chico@chicohotsprings.com

Closest airport: Bozeman, MT (50 miles)
Activities: horseback riding, hiking, rafting, canoeing, fishing, climbing, windsurfing, cross-country skiing, snowshoeing, dogsledding
Season: year-round
Guides/Instruction: horseback riding guides and instruction
Services: spa, conference facilities
Specialties: hot springs and horses
Accommodations: 103 rooms
Rates: $39–$325 per room, double occupancy

The story goes something like this: Some nineteenth-century prospectors strike hot water instead of gold; start selling soaks, along with hot food and a clean bed, to weary miners; throw in plenty of booze, women, and dancing at a saloon that's done its best to keep this part of the West wild—and the rest is more than a century's worth of history.

"Most people come here because there's still rustic funk," says general manager Colin Davis. To understand that as a compliment, you have to toss back some drinks in the dusty, antiques-filled bar, where a long list of celebrity guests has hidden out over the years, then step into the dimly lit dining room for a fat steak served with gourmet accoutrements. The addition of high-end rooms and a conference center opened this Paradise Valley classic to a new set of patrons, but the reasons to love it have stayed the same: It's old-school, it's campy, and it's undeniably cool.

AT THE LODGE: If there's anything that can be said generally about the rooms at Chico, it's that you can't generalize about the rooms. At the simple end, they've got an antique bed, a sink, squeaky floorboards, and a shared bathroom down the hall. The other extreme is a fully equipped log-cabin-style home with a kitchen, woodburning stove, Jacuzzi, and capacity to hold 20 guests. Neither the rooms nor the cabin have phones or televisions, but a separate business lounge can handle your communication needs. Room rates include access to the hot springs pools, open 6 A.M. to midnight. The three-story main lodge is the original structure, built in 1900. It is on the National Register of Historic Places and is decorated accordingly. The 152-acre grounds also include a horse barn, activity center, greenhouse, gardens, conference center, saloon, and day spa.

THE SPORTS: Diamond K Outfitters (406-580-0928; KLKendall@aol.com) runs one-hour to full-day guided horseback rides from the Chico barn ($25 to $150, ages 6 and older; Western Horsemanship lessons cost $75). The gentle horses are the main attraction here, but just about any diversion can be arranged through the on-site Activity Center. You're 3 miles from fly-fishing and Class II to III rafting on the Yellowstone River, 30 miles north of Yellowstone National Park, and surrounded by the Absaroka Beartooth Wilderness, where hundreds of miles of trails lead to high peaks, lakes, and waterfalls. Low-key hikers can take a half-mile path through the woods and up the mountainside to the resort's private catch-and-release trout pond. Climbers can tackle rocky, 10,919-foot Emigrant Peak. Windsurfers head for nearby Daley Lake. And cross-country skiers have access to groomed trails a few miles from the resort. Some recommended outfitters include Big Sky Flies and Guides (888-315-3789; www.bigskyflies.com) and Absaroka Dogsled Treks (406-222-4645; www.extrememontana.com), who will set you up with a team of Siberian huskies to drive through the Montana backcountry. All arrangements can be made through the Activity Center.

BACKCOUNTRY BONUS: Combine your Chico stay with a multiday horse packing trip in the Yellowstone backcountry. All-inclusive, five-day tent camping trips costs $1,950. Three-day trips cost $1,200. Obtain information and make reservations through Diamond K Outfitters (406-580-0928; KLKendall@aol.com).

MEALTIME: If the resort served basic meat and potatoes, nobody would complain. Instead, it has transcended its down-home roots with menu items like Gorgonzola filet mignon rubbed with toasted fennel and coriander and a *Wine Spectator* award-winning wine list. Dishes in the upscale but cozy Chico Dining Room emphasize local meats and fish, as well as herbs and veggies grown in the year-round greenhouse and gardens. A small, private wine cellar dining room accommodates up to 16 guests. At the more family-friendly Percie's Poolside Grill you'll find reasonably priced items like burgers and fries. Sack lunches (sandwich, chips, fruit, cookie, drink) can be packed on request. Just about everyone spends time in the saloon, where a bar menu specializing in baby back ribs complements the eight on-tap microbrews. On weekend nights, live music draws a steady stream of locals from Livingston and beyond.

FINE PRINT:
Pets: $5 per animal, per stay
Kids: bring 'em on
Credit cards: MasterCard, Visa, American Express, Discover
Heads-up: bears
Nearest medical: Livingston, MT (25 miles)
Weather: Summer high of 95°F; winter lows to zero. Lots of wind. Up to 4 feet of annual snowfall. Storm clouds can fill a clear blue sky in minutes. Prepare for all weather conditions. Lodge elevation is 5,280 feet.

GETTING THERE: Take Interstate 90 east from Bozeman to Livingston. Turn south onto

Highway 89. After 22 miles, look for the CHICO HOT SPRINGS sign on the left. Follow the signs to the resort.

See color photo on page 138

MOUNTAIN MEADOWS GUEST RANCH

P.O. Box 160334
Big Sky, MT 59716
Tel: 888-644-6647; 406-995-4997
www.mountainmeadowsranch.com
mmgr@mcn.net

Closest airport: Bozeman, MT (43 miles)
Activities: hiking, horseback riding, fly-fishing, mountain biking, rafting, climbing, cross-country and downhill skiing, snowboarding, snowshoeing, wildlife watching
Season: November 15 through April 15; June 1 through October 1
Guides/Instruction: cross-country skiing guides, fly-fishing clinics, on-site naturalists
Services: spa, conference facilities
Specialties: families, cross-country skiing
Accommodations: seven lodge rooms, two log cabins; capacity 30
Rates: $150–$330 per adult, $99–$165 per child; all-inclusive (meals, most activities, airport transportation)

If your favorite uncle had a private mountain hideaway, staying there would feel a lot like a stay at Mountain Meadows. Want a midnight snack from the kitchen? Sure, help yourself. Feel like flipping through the family photo album? Go right ahead ("family" snapshots include not only the owners' children and grandchildren, but just about every guest who has ever slept within the lodge's walls). For two generations, the hospitable Severns have owned and operated Mountain Meadows, making sure that a night spent here is more like a friendly sleepover than an impersonal lodge stay. If not for professional touches like the morning coffee at your doorstep and the plush robe in your closet, you might forget there's a bill to pay.

AT THE LODGE: Giant picture windows in the log-cabin-style dining room and bedrooms frame Lone Mountain and the Spanish Peaks. The lodge rooms and cedar log cabins are homey, with pine-post beds, overstuffed comforters, and Western décor. Rooms have private decks; cabins have gas fireplaces. All have satellite television, if stargazing from the outdoor hot tub isn't entertainment enough. The lodge's living room centers around a massive river rock fireplace, conveniently situated next to the Ping-Pong table. Co-owner Chuck Severn, a retired neonatologist, sometimes breaks from his duties as breakfast chef and bartender to play a few games with his guests.

THE SPORTS: Yellowstone National Park's northern border is just 18 miles from the lodge, but many guests don't venture that far. There's no reason to when you're surrounded by enough terrain to keep you hiking, biking, fishing, or cross-country skiing for weeks (and especially when most activities are included in the cost of a stay). Winter sports are a specialty here: 25 kilometers of groomed cross-country trails start from the lodge's front door (gear available on-site); downhill skiing and snowboarding at the Big Sky ski resort are a short shuttle drive away; sleighs, sleds, and snowshoes cut daily tracks through the powder. In the warm season, local rivers have Class II to IV rafting. The house stocks mountain bikes for the fire roads and nearby trails. Hikers can hire a naturalist guide or venture out on their own. A favorite route is the half-day trip to Lava Lake, a slow 3.5-mile ascent through the woods to a pristine mountain lake. Keep your eyes peeled for deer, moose, elk, and the very occasional bear. The trailhead is 15 miles from the lodge.

Just outside the front door, you can follow a short path to the not-so-wild animals at the Mountain Meadows petting barn, which is stocked with goodies for them. Insider's tip: Charlie the goat is a cookie hog; keep him at bay long enough and you might coerce the shy alpaca into taking a snack.

MEALTIME: Grandpa Chuck fires up the kitchen before sunrise so his guests can wake to the smell of fresh coffee, blueberry muffins, and eggs. The kitchen staff will pack a basic sack lunch if you're spending your day off-site. Cocktail-hour appetizers like Asian chicken wings are served around the Thirsty Moose Bar while the kitchen staff puts the finishing touches on dinner. Dishes are a touch more creative than your standard home-style fare, but the menu generally features a salad, bread, and meat and potatoes—served family style in the glass-walled dining room. Vegetarians are accommodated on request. No one leaves the table hungry.

FINE PRINT:
Pets: leave 'em home
Kids: bring 'em on
Credit cards: MasterCard, Visa, American Express, Discover
Heads-up: bears
Nearest medical: Big Sky, MT (15 minutes)
Weather: Summer highs in the 90s, lows in the 60s. Winter highs around 50°F, lows can hit zero. Roughly 400 inches of annual snowfall. Lodge elevation is 7,000 feet.

GETTING THERE: From Bozeman, head south on Highway 191 and drive past the Big Sky Resort turnoff. Two miles after that, you'll pass the Ophir School on the right. Turn at the SCHOOL ACCESS sign, just past the school, onto Main Beaver Creek Road (unmarked at this intersection). About a mile down the road is a gate and phone, where you can dial Mountain Meadows for access. Then continue 7 miles to the lodge. Transportation from the airport is available.

See color photo on page 138

PAPOOSE CREEK LODGE

1520 Highway 287 North
Cameron, MT 59720
Tel: 888-674-3030; 406-682-3030
www.papoosecreek.com
papoose@papoosecreek.com

Closest airport: Bozeman, MT (75 miles)
Activities: hiking, canoeing, fishing, horseback riding, mountain and road biking, wildlife watching
Season: early May through mid-October
Guides/Instruction: canoeing, fishing, hiking, horseback riding guides and instruction, cooking classes
Services: massage, conference facilities
Accommodations: five lodge rooms and three cabins; capacity 16
Rates: $400–$675 per person, all-inclusive (meals, guided hiking and canoeing); multisport package, weekly rates, and lodge buyout also available

The front porch of Papoose Creek Lodge is a better place than most to witness one of Montana's greatest natural phenomena: chronically high-strung out-of-towners unwinding at record speeds. Maybe it's because of the creek trickling through the property or the quaking aspens fluttering over the decks, or maybe it's just that there's no cell phone signal to distract their attention from the scenery. This is a lodge designed with relaxation and luxury in mind, and it succeeds on both fronts.

Which isn't to say that visitors are limited to low-key pursuits. On-site guides with grizzly-sized personalities will direct your days on the trail or on the water. Between the Madison River and the surrounding Lee Metcalf Wilderness Area, there's no shortage of terrain. You'd be wise to make it back in time for cocktail hour, when you can sip wine with the very few other guests before retreating to the dining room for a gourmet repast. It's no wonder that this new lodge, which opened in 2002, already boasts a long list of repeat clientele. It's the kind of place you want to think of as your own.

AT THE LODGE: Every detail at Papoose Creek Lodge is high-end, from the heated bathroom floors to the in-room sound system and CD collection. The upstairs rooms in the log-cabin-style lodge have private decks. All rooms have cushy comforters, armchairs, and writing desks next to forest-view windows. The extremely eco-minded owners built the cabins out of reclaimed lumber; this makes them look weathered, although they're the property's newest structures. Original artwork, mainly the work of locals, decorates the walls. Paths from the cabins and main lodge lead to an outdoor hot tub by the creek, the perfect place to recover from an activity-packed day.

THE SPORTS: If you don't mind the thunder of an occasional semi blasting down the small, two-lane highway, you can practice your casting on the lodge's reed-rimmed pond. Four-foot-tall sandhill cranes like to share the space, but you'll otherwise have it to yourself. The guides at Papoose Creek will take you fishing on the peaceful Madison River, on nearby lakes, or inside Yellowstone National Park, which is less

than an hour away. Guided fly-fishing costs $350 to $500 per day for one or two anglers. Hikers can head for the trail that climbs the hill directly behind the property and passes through adjacent Sun Ranch. The Papoose Creek Trail starts just behind the stables and runs 8 miles through steep rock canyons and wildflower-filled meadows to the alpine Crater Lakes, where a flip of your fly-rod could land you a cutthroat or two. An all-day hiking option is the 15-mile trip to Lobo Mesa on the Little Elk River Trail. From a vantage point of over 9,000 feet, you can spot peaks in Wyoming and Idaho on a clear day. Moose and elk make occasional appearances on this stretch of the Gravely Range. There is plenty of trout, too. Quarter horse rides and instruction can be tailored to any skill level, and there are hundreds of miles of trails to choose from. Guided horseback rides costs $115 per person for half a day, $175 for a full day. Canoeists can navigate Quake Lake, where trees poke through the 174-foot-deep body of water that was formed by a 1959 earthquake. For cyclists, there's plenty of scenic highway available. All activities and gear rentals can be arranged through the lodge, as can the post-sport, in-room massage ($100 per hour).

MEALTIME: Fresh fruit and baked snacks are yours for the grabbing all day long on the counter at the edge of the open kitchen. It's worth nabbing an apple just to get a close look at the chef in action. Food is an integral part of the experience at Papoose Creek, with five-course dinners starting around sunset and often stretching into the wee hours. From your seat beside the tall dining-room window overlooking the pond, you might sip spinach leek soup as the sun dips behind the Gravely Range. By the time the ginger flan is set before you, you'll be begging for a second stomach. Breakfast can be anything from simple fresh fruit and granola to an egg-heavy feast—your choice. Simple sack lunches (sandwiches, fruit, cookies) come in an insulated lunch box to keep your goodies from getting crushed on the trail.

FINE PRINT:
Pets: leave 'em home
Kids: 12 and older (except family week)
Credit cards: MasterCard, VISA, American Express, Discover
Heads-up: bears
Nearest medical: Ennis, MT (32 miles)
Weather: Summer highs can hit 100°F, with much cooler nights. Spring and fall vary widely—even snow is possible. Lodge elevation is 6,000 feet.

GETTING THERE: From Bozeman, head west on Highway 84 to Norris. Turn south onto Highway 287. Look for the PAPOOSE CREEK LODGE sign on the left, 32 miles past Ennis. Transportation to and from the airport costs $300 for up to 10 guests.

See color photos on page 139

PINE BUTTE GUEST RANCH

HC58-Box 34C
Choteau, MT 59422
Tel: 406-466-2158
www.nature.org

Closest airport: Great Falls, MT (80 miles)
Activities: horseback riding, hiking, wildlife watching, fishing
Season: early May through early October
Guides/Instruction: hiking and horseback riding guides, on-site naturalists and wranglers
Specialty: natural history
Accommodations: 10 cabins; capacity 25
Rates: $1,300 per person, per week (Sunday to Sunday), all-inclusive (meals, activities, airport transportation); $1,000 children ages 1–12

A typical grizzly track measures 14 inches in length. That's not counting the claw, which can easily add another 5 inches. The first time you stumble onto (or into) one as you're hiking around Pine Butte, your hair may stand on end. Worry not, you'll get used to these tracks after a while. The East Front is the last place in the United States where grizzlies still wander the plains. And wander they do. Naturalist-guided hikers who seek them out in the spring or fall have a pretty good chance at a sighting.

But grizzlies pale in comparison to the area's better-known giants. The Pine Butte Swamp Preserve contains one of the richest dinosaur beds on the planet. It was here in 1978 that a paleontologist found the first dinosaur eggs known to North America. It's also home to the world's first dinosaur embryo discovery. Guests at the ranch, which is owned and operated by The Nature Conservancy, can join experts on a dig. Not many lodges can offer such an intimate interaction with the natural world.

AT THE LODGE: From 1930 to 1978, these grounds were home to Circle 8 Ranch. The original cabin now serves as the Natural History Center and Bookstore, home base to the ranch's naturalist programs. The new handcrafted log lodge was built in 1962. Like the guest cabins, it was constructed entirely of native wood and stone, and decorated in homage to its dude ranch past. Each cabin has a fireplace, a private full bath, and handmade hardwood furniture. The only phone on-site is in the main lodge. Don't bother looking for a television. Cabin windows look

out onto the mountains, a stream, or into the mouth of a canyon.

THE SPORTS: The resident wrangler leads two daily trail rides into the high country. Though rides are suitable for all skill levels, kids must be eight years old to join the group. The Nature Conservancy's 18,000-acre Pine Butte Swamp Preserve is surrounded by millions of acres of protected land, including Lewis and Clark National Forest and the million-acre Bob Marshall Wilderness. Hikers can take the 3.5-mile A. B. Guthrie Memorial Trail from the preserve's information kiosk to the top of a ridge overlooking the swamp and the Rocky Mountain Front. Naturalists lead guests on mammal tracking expeditions, wildflower walks, and photography tours throughout the preserve. Other workshops are offered seasonally. There's a minimal amount of fishing gear on-site for use on a high mountain lake or in the property's small stream. There's also a small river nearby, where tubing is popular in the summer. At Egg Mountain, the site of the dinosaur dig, you can find eggshell fossils scattered amid the rocks, and massive bones protruding from the ground. Tours of the swamp and the working cattle ranch are also given regularly.

MEALTIME: When the weather allows, the ranch offers breakfast and dinner cookouts; otherwise, meals are served in the main lodge, where four large, eight-person tables are surrounded by picture windows. Hummingbird feeders just outside provide the chow-time entertainment. Meals are simple and healthy, but tasty, with an emphasis on garden fresh produce and homemade breads, soups, and pastries. Any dietary needs can be accommodated, and the lodge will gladly clean and cook any fish you catch. Guests fill out sack-lunch order forms for meals on the trail. Sandwiches are on bagels or homemade bread, and include anything from ham and Swiss to veggies and hummus. Consistent with The Nature

Conservancy's preservation ethic, lunch bags are reused for the duration of your stay, and food and drink containers are recycled.

FINE PRINT:
Pets: leave 'em home
Kids: bring 'em on
Credit cards: MasterCard, Visa, American Express
Heads-up: bears
Nearest medical: Choteau, MT (27 miles)
Weather: Summer highs in the 90s; in-season lows around 30°F. The area gets a foot and a half of annual rainfall. Lodge elevation is 5,100 feet.

GETTING THERE: From Choteau, head north on U.S. 89. Turn left onto (paved) Teton River Road, which is halfway between mileposts 46 and 47. Follow the road toward the mountains for about 17 miles to a junction marked by two rural mailboxes and a sign that says PINE BUTTE GUEST RANCH. After about 0.3 mile on a dirt road, you'll pass a cluster of rural mailboxes. Twenty yards past them, turn right and continue 3 miles. Turn left just before the bridge that crosses the creek. The ranch is a quarter mile ahead. The lodge provides transportation from the airport.

See color photo on page 140

POTOSI HOT SPRINGS RESORT

P.O. Box 269
Pony, MT 59747
Tel: 888-685-1695; 406-685-3330
www.potosiresort.com
potosi@potosiresort.com

Closest airport: Bozeman, MT (one hour)
Activities: fishing, hiking, horseback riding, backcountry and cross-country skiing, mountain and road biking, rafting, canoeing, climbing, mountaineering
Season: year-round
Guides/Instruction: fly-fishing guides and instruction; climbing, hiking, rafting, and horseback riding guides
Services: spa, conference facilities
Specialty: hot springs
Accommodations: four cabins; capacity 24
Rates: $200–$330 per room, double occupancy; meal and activity packages available

So many of Montana's best lodges were built as tax breaks for out-of-state multimillionaires that it's beyond refreshing to find a notable exception. Nick Kern and Christine Stark were tending bar and waiting tables in Bozeman when one day they drove past the idyllic Potosi property while on a camping trip. Shortly thereafter, Christine overheard a customer saying it was for sale. It took months to find a bank that would approve the loan, and when they finally made the purchase, it took another month of cleaning to undo years of neglect. But by the time they opened in April 2000, they had created a retreat that's easily on par with its best-financed neighbors.

The lodge is run almost entirely by the owners—Nick doubles as a fishing guide, and Christine dons chef garb when she delivers your evening meal. Although this is a huge plus, the true selling point is the lodge's remote location amid 6,000 square miles of national forest. The property is bordered by fishing creeks, climbable peaks, and natural hot springs that give the valley its own mini-ecosystem, replete with rare lichen and ferns. The millionaires can have their made-to-order hideaways. A stay here is unlike any wilderness lodge in the state.

AT THE LODGE: The comfortable, creekside cabins are made of rough-hewn timber and furnished with woodburning stoves and cookware-stocked kitchens. Front porches open up to South Willow Creek, where you can practice your casting, then walk up the hill to the hot springs. The first of them flows into a pool that's long enough for swimming laps, and almost cool enough, at 90° to 94°F. It's set in a deck at the base of a moss-dripping granite cliff, with a Finnish sauna at the edge. Just up the path and over a footbridge is the smaller, hotter pool, enclosed in a fairytale wood cabin with a stained-glass window. At 102° to 104°F, it's just right for a long soak on a cool night. The two-story main lodge serves as the dining room, gathering spot, and the owners' home, unless they're camping out in one of the two on-site tepees.

THE SPORTS: "If you see water in Montana, there's fish in it," says Nick. The lodge's two creeks are no exception; you can expect to catch and release plenty of rainbows, cutthroats, and browns without leaving the property. If you feel like branching out, the Madison, Gallatin, and Yellowstone Rivers flow nearby. The Beaverhead–Deerlodge National Forest has unlimited hiking, starting with the short trail that runs past the hot springs to a granite crag that houses a century-old eagle's nest. Obviously, there's no climbing there, but you're welcome to boulder on some of the property's less inhabited rocks. The Tobacco Root Mountains offer granite climbs, too, some on peaks over 10,000 feet. Horseback rides on mountain trails are available only with guides. Local rafting on Class II to V rivers

runs from May through September. There's backcountry and cross-country skiing on ungroomed trails and treed slopes nearby. And Yellowstone National Park is just 90 minutes away. Be sure to end at least one day in the massage tepee, where you'll get a rubdown next to a woodburning stove and set to the natural soundtrack of the creek.

BACKCOUNTRY BONUS: You can also add a backcountry camping trip to your stay. A guide will take you 3 to 5 miles on foot, bike, or horseback to an alpine lake. From there, you can hike to a peak, fish the lake, or find a flat spot in a quiet meadow and sprawl out for an open-air nap. Food and gear are provided.

MEALTIME: Wherever the hot springs bubble above the surface, watercress grows year-round. Christine also harvests wild strawberries, raspberries, and huckleberries on the grounds. She might even pick berries from the chokecherry bushes to boil into syrup or jam. Suffice it to say, keeping meals organic is no great feat. Most of the produce is local, as are the dairy and eggs. For breakfast you might have almond poppyseed pancakes with applewood-smoked bacon and fresh fruit, or an omelet with grilled Atlantic salmon, sautéed asparagus, scallions, and Gruyère cheese. More likely, Christine will offer both, and then some. Lunches are always packed for the trail and could contain turkey, veggies, and Brie, wrapped in a spinach tortilla; a grilled ahi tuna salad sandwich with fresh dill on sourdough; or any number of choices that will redefine your concept of brown-bagging it. Come dinnertime, there's an emphasis on game. Whether it's grilled elk tenderloin or oven-roasted rosemary pheasant that starts your three-course meal, you'll be amazed that you can eat this well in the middle of nowhere. Christine may not be academy trained, but she could easily claim to be. The three-meal plan costs $75 per person, per day. If you're doing your own cooking, pick up your groceries in Bozeman. The closest town is Pony, 7 miles down a dirt road, but short of bar snacks, it has nothing to offer an empty stomach.

FINE PRINT:
Pets: bring 'em on
Kids: 13 and older (except with full lodge buyout)
Credit cards: MasterCard, Visa, American Express
Heads-up: bears
Nearest medical: Ennis, MT (45 minutes)
Weather: Summer highs in the 80s; winter lows near zero. Weather can change dramatically with little notice—prepare for all possible conditions. Lodge elevation is 6,200 feet.

GETTING THERE: From Bozeman, take Interstate 90 west through Three Forks to Highway 287 south. At Harrison, head west on Highway 283 and drive 6 miles to Pony. Turn left at the red caboose onto South Willow Creek Road and drive 3 miles. Turn right at the fork and continue 3.5 miles to the lodge. Transportation from the airport can be arranged on request.

See color photo on page 140

RAINBOW RANCH LODGE

P.O. Box 160336
Big Sky, MT 59716
Tel: 800-937-4132; 406-995-4132
www.rainbowranch.com
info@rainbowranch.com

Closest airport: Bozeman, MT (43 miles)
Activities: fishing, horseback riding, cross-country and downhill skiing, snowboarding, snowshoeing, hiking, mountain and road biking, rock climbing, dogsledding, whitewater rafting, kayaking, canoeing, wildlife watching
Season: year-round (restaurant closed mid-October through mid-December)

Guides/Instruction: guided horseback rides and instruction
Services: spa, conference facilities
Accommodations: 16 rooms; capacity 44
Rates: $145–$295 per room; packages available in winter

Patrick Hurd talks about his wine cellar in the way most parents talk about their children—if he carried a snapshot of his favorite Italian red in his wallet, no one who knows him would be at all surprised. It has been his goal since becoming proprietor of the historic Rainbow Ranch Lodge in 1995 that the wining-and-dining experience be on par with New York's finest, and you'd be hard-pressed to find a former patron who'd say their chimichurri-rubbed buffalo ribeye was anything less than sublime.

If that isn't reason enough to travel to Big Sky, there's the lodge itself, where guest-room decks are a fly-rod's toss from the trout-heavy Gallatin River. Though the property abuts the highway, you'd never know it as you lie in your cushy lodgepole bed with a fire blazing and the window cracked just enough to let in the sound of rushing water. Bottom line: Patrick has every reason to be a proud papa.

AT THE LODGE: Lodge history dates back to 1919, when the Lemon family bought the land in a failed attempt to start a cattle ranch. Their next venture, the Halfway Inn (so named because it's halfway between Bozeman and West Yellowstone), proved much more successful. The lodge changed hands, and names, a few times before getting a major overhaul from the current owners in 1995. But old lodge photographs, a faded ranch sign from the 1930s, and original Western artwork carry the spirit of the lodge's early days. Rooms have river rock fireplaces and chopped wood on their riverfront decks. Anachronistic amenities like satellite TV and VCR are thoughtfully hidden inside antique reproduction furniture. Outside, there's a gazebo grill and covered deck, the site of barbecues and weddings during summer. A 12-person outdoor hot tub in front of a tall river rock fireplace has allowed many a guest to soak comfortably with a glass of wine during a nighttime dusting of snow.

THE SPORTS: On-site Full Moon Outfitters (406-580-3257) offers two-hour to all-day guided horseback trips for $60 to $138. Riders leave directly from the lodge, which happens to sit at the edge of a million acres of national forest. ("It's basically a backyard that, luckily, we don't have to pick up the mortgage on," says Patrick.) But equestrians don't have all the fun. Hiking and biking trails in the Gallatin Mountains and Lee Metcalf Wilderness run deep into the heavily wooded backcountry, where wild geraniums, columbine, and berries color the meadows in spring and summer. The trout fishing on the nearby Madison, Yellowstone, and Missouri Rivers would be worth a day trip, except that there's no reason to venture that far—the Gallatin River (of *A River Runs Through It* fame) is a few steps from the lodge's back door. Come ski season, Rainbow Ranch shuttles guests the 15 miles to Big Sky Resort and its 3,600 acres of crowd-free skiable terrain. Cross-country skiers and snowshoers can hit the trails without getting in a car. All the above activities can be organized through the lodge. Last, and probably least, there's the quirky addition of a sand volleyball court between the lodge and the river, for anyone who's so inclined.

MEALTIME: To call it the best food in Montana would be an insult to the chef; this menu was created with international peers in mind. Top nod goes to the pan-seared sea scallops with oxtail marmalade, salsify, parsley puree, and horseradish cream. But every dish on the menu has wowed food critics with palates accustomed to big-city venues. If you're impressed by the award-winning wine list, be

sure to ask for a tour of the cellar, where 7,000-plus bottles rest behind heavy iron gates, and water trickles down ancient-looking river rock walls to cold slate floors. Occasional wine-tasting dinners are served around the cellar's long harvest table, which was made from an old ranch sign rescued from a woodpile in the barn. The main dining room (upscale ranch house décor; no dress code) is open for dinner only. Though there's morning coffee service in the common room, your best bet for a substantial breakfast is Corral, the restaurant/bar across the street. Sack lunches can be ordered from a local bakery.

FINE PRINT:
Pets: yes, with a $40 per day housekeeping fee
Kids: bring 'em on
Credit cards: MasterCard, Visa, American Express, Discover
Heads-up: bears
Nearest medical: Big Sky, MT (9 miles)
Weather: Summers are very mild; nights can be chilly. Winter temperatures plunge far below zero. Blue skies can fill with thunderclouds in less time than it takes to unpack your Gore-Tex.

GETTING THERE: From Bozeman, drive south on Highway 191. The lodge is 5 miles south of Big Sky, on the left at mile marker 43. Transportation to ski resorts is available in the winter. Transportation to and from the airport is not available.

See color photo on page 141

TRIPLE CREEK RANCH

5551 West Fork Road
Darby, MT 59829
Tel: 406-821-4600
Fax: 406-821-4666
www.triplecreekranch.com
tcr@bitterroot.net

Closest airport: Missoula, MT (75 minutes)
Activities: horseback riding, fishing, hiking, cross-country, backcountry, and downhill skiing, snowboarding, snowshoeing, whitewater rafting, road and mountain biking, wildlife watching
Season: year-round
Guides/Instruction: fly-fishing and horseback guides and instruction
Services: spa, conference facilities
Accommodations: 19 cabins; capacity 46
Rates: $510–$995 per room, double occupancy, all-inclusive (meals, drinks, most activities)

Calling Triple Creek a ranch is a bit like calling Godzilla a house pet. This 400-acre deluxe hideaway in the Bitterroot Mountains—the fantasy-come-true enterprise of Intel CEO Craig Barrett and his wife, Barbara—is the ultimate example of backcountry decadence. The quarter horses featured prominently on the activities roster are merely a pleasant aside.

Your first clue that this isn't an ordinary cowpoke hangout: Prada purses outnumber saddlebags. But the resident fishing and horseback riding guides pride themselves on transforming anyone who's willing into a reeling and riding machine. With a staff that outnumbers the guests, a steady supply of gourmet meals, and on-site managers bent on personalizing every stay, there's little chance that any guest will go home disappointed.

AT THE LODGE: None of the 19 log cabins is lacking in amenities, but those deemed "luxury" earn the designation with private hot tubs (indoors or on a deck) and double steam showers. Standard in all the cabins: woodburning fireplaces, satellite television and VCR, phones with data ports, and a fully stocked wet bar. Shared hot tubs nestled in the forest are a short walk from your front door. With the exception of Stage Stop, which is 1.9 miles away, all cabins are scattered around a pine-log main lodge. Meals are served in the lodge's high-beamed dining room. Diners are surrounded by three-story-high picture windows that look out onto lodgepole pines during the day and reflect the dining room's candlelight at night.

THE SPORTS: You may come here in stilettos, but chances are you'll go home in a Stetson. The very fishing guide who choreographed Brad Pitt's casting technique for his role in *A River Runs Through It* is available to help you land browns on the Bitterroot River, just a few miles from the lodge. The 40 resident quarter horses are flawlessly trained, and the horseback riding guides have been known to break into cowboy songs on the trail. Marked hiking paths run deep into the national forest that abuts the property on three sides. One option: a 6½-mile ramble through elk, moose, and mountain goat country that skirts the perimeter of swimmable, peak-rimmed Lake Como. For a full-day adventure, hike up Trapper Peak. It's 5 miles from the trailhead through thick pine and cedar to the 10,157-foot summit, the highest point in Montana's jagged Bitterroot Mountains. The views give a whole new meaning to the name Big Sky Country. Winter sports include downhill, backcountry, and cross-country skiing, snowboarding, and snowshoeing into the mountainous high country. If you want gear and guides for other activities, just ask at the lodge. All on-ranch activities (horseback riding, hiking, swimming, tennis, pond fishing, cross-country skiing, and snowshoeing) are included in the cost of your stay, along with a lift ticket for Lost Trail Powder Mountain. Off-site sports cost extra.

BACKCOUNTRY BONUS: Most folks don't come here to sleep in a tent, but if you're bent on

adding a backpacking leg to your visit, 19 million acres of options await you in the surrounding national forest. A popular two-nighter is the 9-mile hike up the Easthouse National Recreation Trail to Palisade Mountain. Maps and information are at the Stevensville Ranger District (406-777-5461).

MEALTIME: If you wake up feeling daring, TCR's breakfast lasagna could be the way to start the day. The less adventurous may opt for apple French toast or good old-fashioned oats. Every menu features options that appeal to carnivores and vegetarians, health nuts and grease hounds. Creativity and quality are the constants. In addition to the sit-down lunch menu, pack lunches are available. Don't expect your mama's bologna on white bread, however; the choices are all gourmet. Dinners can be packed as well, though you'd be missing out on menu items like squab confit ravioli and wasabi-crusted filet mignon. You can start your evening with a glass of wine by the fireplace on the riverview rooftop lounge, then retreat to the downstairs dining room. Not feeling social? Any meal can be delivered to your cabin on request.

FINE PRINT:
Pets: 20 pounds and under
Kids: 16 and older
Credit cards: MasterCard, Visa, American Express, Discover
Heads-up: bears; snowmobilers use the trails
Nearest medical: Darby, MT (12 miles)
Weather: Summer highs in the 80s; winter lows in the 20s. Darby gets around 15 inches of annual snowfall. Lodge elevation is 4,600 ft.

GETTING THERE: From Missoula, head south on Highway 93 toward Hamilton. Four miles past the town of Darby, turn right onto West Fork Road (Highway 473) and continue west 7.5 miles. The TRIPLE CREEK RANCH sign and driveway are on the right. Airport transportation costs $200 round trip per carload. Transportation by helicopter is also available.

See color photos on pages 141 and 142

Wyoming

BITTERROOT RANCH

1480 East Fork Road
Dubois, WY 82513
Tel: 800-545-0019; 307-455-2778
Fax: 307-455-2354
www.bitterrootranch.com
bitterrootranch@wyoming.com

Closest airport: Riverton, WY (85 miles)
Activities: horseback riding, fishing, hiking, canoeing
Season: late May through September
Guides/Instruction: horseback riding and fly-fishing guides and instruction
Services: conference facilities (limited)
Specialties: trail riding, cattle drives, and roundups
Accommodations: 12 rooms; capacity 30
Rates: $1,500 per week, per person, double occupancy, all-inclusive (meals and activities)

At Bitterroot, it's all about the horses. Mostly Arabians, bred right here, with a few quarter horses, Appaloosas, and mustangs thrown in for kicks. There are so many horses that each guest is assigned three on arrival: one horse is for rides through sagebrush-scented canyons into the Absaroka Mountains; the other two graze in wide-open meadows until it's their turn to play.

Aspiring wranglers can join cattle drives and roundups in the summer. The saddle-sore can take a day off to fly-fish or hike. The ranch is bordered by Shoshone National Forest, which runs all the way to Yellowstone National Park, so there's no shortage of terrain. With internationally acclaimed instructors, applause-worthy cuisine, and accommodations fit for a softer-than-cowboy crowd, this ranks among the best dude ranches in North America.

AT THE LODGE: The simple log cabins are set along both sides of a trout-filled stream, with the tree canopy and the sound of rushing water blocking out most evidence of your neighbors. Cabins have their own bathrooms, woodburning stoves, private decks, and electric heat. No phones or TVs, of course (though there's a phone in the lodge if you really need it). The main lodge is the only original building, constructing in the 1930s. Those added during expansions in the 1950s and 1990s are consistent with the original style. Most cabins are a long walk from the lodge, where you'll find the hot tub, pool table, dining room, and video- and book-stocked library. The distance is great for privacy, but not so great if you're wiped out after a long day.

THE SPORTS: Since the quality of the horses is the major draw, most guests know a stirrup from a saddle before they arrive. But riders of all levels are welcome—there are even ponies for kids. The owners, who have lived here since the early 1970s, lead many of the trail rides themselves. Mel grew up riding on a farm at the base of Mount Kilimanjaro. Bayard has lived all over the world. Both know Shoshone and the high plains of the Wind River Indian Reservation as if they had spent every day of their lives studying the terrain. In addition to the two daily, two- to three-hour rides, more experienced riders can join cattle drives and roundups in early July and late September.

The cows graze on a 50-square-mile area of untamed parkland. You'll be pushing them up the Elkhorn Trail to a mountain known locally as Shangri-la, or gathering them in from forests at elevations as high as 10,000 feet. This is the only U.S. ranch of its kind that is certified by the British Horse Society. Videotaped instruction is available. Though the emphasis is definitely on four-legged recreation, there's a lot to be said for the fly-fishing. A mile-long stretch of the East Fork of the Wind River runs through the property, and guests can access sections nearly inaccessible from outside the ranch. These stretches of water hold a virtually untapped supply of cutthroats, rainbows, and browns. The ranch also has stocked trout ponds. Guides and gear are available, including canoes for use on local lakes. Guests who come here only to fish stay at a reduced rate.

BACKCOUNTRY BONUS: The lodge will arrange two- to three-day guided horse packing trips into remote parts of Shoshone National Forest. The cost is $50 extra per person, per day, including gear and food.

MEALTIME: Meals are served at 10-person tables in the bright, airy dining room. The theme here is hearty home style, with no ingredients that require the use of a dictionary. Breakfast usually includes pancakes with eggs, toast, and sausage. In-house lunches can be anything from a ham and turkey quiche to beef tacos. Packed lunches are made to order, with sandwiches, fruit, homemade cookies, and candy bars. If you land any trout, the staff will clean it and cook it. For dinner, you might see a leg of lamb with roasted potatoes and Yorkshire pudding, or salmon with Hollandaise, broccoli, and rice. Veggies come fresh from the garden, meats are ranch raised, and breads are baked on-site. Wine and cocktails are available with dinner.

FINE PRINT:
Pets: leave 'em home
Kids: bring 'em on
Credit cards: MasterCard, Visa, Discover, American Express
Heads-up: bears
Nearest medical: Dubois, WY (26 miles)
Weather: Summer days top out at 85°F; in-season lows can drop to 30°. There's not much precipitation, just over a foot of snow- and rainfall combined. The lodge is at 7,500 feet.

GETTING THERE: Take U.S. 287 from Riverton and turn onto East Fork Road, 10 miles east of Dubois. The lodge is 16 miles up the unpaved road. Airport transportation costs $185 per carload.

See color photo on page 142

BOULDER LAKE LODGE

P.O. Box 1100
Pinedale, WY 82941
Tel: 800-788-5401; 307-537-5400
www.boulderlake.com
blodge@coffey.com

Closest airport: Jackson Hole, WY (100 miles)
Activities: horseback riding, fishing, hiking, canoeing, biking, climbing, wildlife watching
Season: June through October
Guides/Instruction: horseback riding guides, fishing guides and instruction
Services: conference facilities (off-season only)
Specialty: horse packing trips
Accommodations: nine rooms; capacity 34
Rates: $180 per room, double occupancy

Boulder Lake Lodge should have a sign at the end of its property saying THIS WAY IN. The point of staying here isn't so much the lodge itself (though it's a pleasant place) as its location amid 2 million acres of Bridger-Teton National Forest and Wilderness Areas. Every morning, wranglers take guests far into the high country, where water lilies float on trout-filled ponds, and horse trails climb through thick stands of spruce and pine to the western edge of the Continental Divide. Think of the ranch and lodge as a comfortable, convenient, family-friendly refueling station—the wilderness is your destination.

AT THE LODGE: Set at the edge of 6-mile-long Boulder Lake, the ranch was part of an early-1900s homestead. The old barns and corrals sit next to the log-style lodge, which was built in 1957. In the Great Room, a massive moose head stares down from the top of the large stone fireplace, where a guitar-strumming cowboy sings ballads after dinner. Game mounts line the walls of the living and dining rooms. A hallway leads to the guest wing, where each room has a private bath and a wagon wheel bed. There's a house phone for guest use, but there are no phones or TVs in the rooms.

THE SPORTS: Riders who've spent plenty of time in the saddle can take the lodge's more spirited horses on all-day treks on forest trails. There are gentler horses for beginners to ride along Boulder Creek and around the lodge. Guided rides cost $15 (one to three hours) to $100 (all day) per person; riders of all levels are welcome. Full-day fishing trips start with a hot breakfast at the lodge before you saddle up for the ride to a local lake or stream, where you'll fly-fish, spin-cast, or troll for rainbows, brookies, cutthroats, graylings, and goldens. All the dirty work is done by the guides, including the trailside lunch preparations. The cost is $150 to $175 per person.

Lake fishing and river float trips on the Green and New Fork Rivers cost $285. Off-the-saddle options include hiking the hundreds of miles of national forest trails that parallel creeks and run through wildflower meadows to waterfalls; mountain biking the sagebrush-lined doubletrack forest roads (no singletrack riding allowed in the national forest; bring your own bike); or paddling a canoe on Boulder Lake ($15 per day, including paddles and vests). The lodge also offers a pack-in service for climbers, but it provides only access, not gear or guides.

BACKCOUNTRY BONUS: Boulder Lake specializes in 4- to 10-day horse packing trips in Bridger-Teton National Forest and beyond. Itineraries range from a one-way spot pack, where backpackers are taken by horseback into the high country and dropped off for the walk home ($160 per person), to the weeklong Summer Package, which combines a lodge stay with a pack trip to a high-mountain fishing camp for horseback riding, trout fishing, and river floats ($1,385 per person). All backcountry trips include guides, meals, and gear. Bring your own sleeping bag. Customized itineraries are available.

MEALTIME: Guests and staff share table space in the Great Room, the dining room that overlooks grazing horses and the foothills of the Rockies. Ranch-style, meat-and-potatoes fare is the standard, with a menu that changes daily. Past breakfasts have included fresh-from-the-fryer homemade donuts, French toast and hash browns, and a breakfast burrito bar. The in-house lunch menu could be burgers and dogs, pizza and orzo salad, or turkey chili with cornmeal rolls. Trail lunches with sandwiches, chips, fruit, juice, pudding, and a candy bar are also available (if you're on a guided excursion, expect something along the lines of a fat steak grilled trailside). There are appetizers before dinner, then main dishes like country ham with maple gravy and barbecued brisket with ranch-roasted red potatoes. The breads, and desserts like rhubarb-buttermilk cake and blueberry cheese pie, are all homemade. If you deliver your catch of the day to the kitchen, the staff will clean and cook it for dinner.

FINE PRINT:
Pets: leave 'em home
Kids: bring 'em on
Credit cards: none
Heads-up: mosquitoes
Nearest medical: Pinedale, WY (24 miles)
Weather: Expect daytime temperatures as high as 80°F, with nights dropping as low as 35°. Rain is possible throughout the season. Lodge elevation is 7,300 feet.

GETTING THERE: Take Highway 191 south through Pinedale and turn left on Route 353 at Boulder. Drive 2 miles, then turn left onto the gravel road. Continue 10 miles to the ranch and lodge. Airport transportation costs $130 for two passengers, $10 for each additional passenger.

See color photo on page 143

BROOKS LAKE LODGE

458 Brooks Lake Road
Dubois, WY 82513
Tel: 307-455-2121
www.brookslake.com

Closest airport: Jackson Hole, WY (70 miles)
Activities: fishing, canoeing, horseback riding, hiking, cross-country skiing, snowshoeing, dogsledding
Season: late June through mid-September; late December through mid-March
Guides/Instruction: fishing and horseback riding guides and instruction
Services: spa, conference facilities
Accommodations: six lodge rooms, one suite, six cabins; capacity 36
Rates: $140–$325 per person, all-inclusive (meals, activities, guides, equipment); two-night minimum in winter

City dwellers from out-of-state have long fled to Wyoming to get away from it all; Wyoming natives head for the Wind River Mountains. Nestled in these off-the-path peaks, a half-hour drive from the nearest little town, Brooks Lake Lodge has served as a wilderness hideaway since 1922. Its listing in the National Register of Historic Places is evidence of its authenticity, but careful renovations have kept the comfort level up-to-date. Staying here is far from roughing it.

On-site guides make it easy to venture into Shoshone National Forest, Grand Teton National Park, or Yellowstone National Park for adventures on horseback, dogsled, foot, or canoe. The surrounding mountains offer 5,000 square miles of wilderness to explore. Coming home to High Tea and city-caliber cuisine will halt your Wild West fantasies just long enough to keep you civilized for the return home.

AT THE LODGE: Lodgepole walls, lodgepole beds, lamps carved to look like trophy animals: there's no forgetting you're in a wilderness lodge, no matter how groggy you are when you emerge from the thick pile of down comforters in the morning. In the cabins, woodburning stoves complete the rugged-chic décor. The deluxe Sheep Suite tops them all, with a large living room, kitchen, two-person Jacuzzi, and broad views of the Pinnacle

Mountains. The new (2003) 4,000-square-foot spa has a Jacuzzi, steam room, and fitness room, though it's hard to fathom why anyone would choose to sweat indoors when there's so much to do outside.

THE SPORTS: The area's alpine lakes, creeks, and rivers are littered with brook, rainbow, and cutthroat trout—in some spots you could scoop them up with your bare hands. Or, take advantage of the resident guides and work on your casting technique from a canoe. You can also access little-known fish hangouts by hiking in or by guided horseback ride. Licenses and fishing gear are available at the lodge. Horses trained here are accustomed to the steep terrain and thin air, so you can push yourself on all-day rides. Favorite hiking destinations are Austin's Peak, Brooks Mountain, or the Jade Lakes, all of which may leave you breathless—those can be arduous climbs. In the snowy season, groomed cross-country trails start at the lodge's front door. You can follow the powder deep into the forest on skinny skis, snowshoes, or a dogsled. Best of all, the fishing doesn't end when the lakes freeze over. Ice-fishing guides will auger a hole, serve you hot chocolate, and transport your fresh catch to the dining staff. Gear and guides for all ofthe above activities are available through the lodge.

BACKCOUNTRY BONUS: From mid-July through early September, you can take a guided, one- or two-night horse packing trip to the lodge's Cub Creek wilderness camp. A two-hour ride in the Teton Wilderness takes you to a riverside tent site, where your fly-fishing catch may determine what's for dinner. You'll have your very own wrangler to lead the way and set up camp (as comfy as roughing it gets, straight down to the goose down pillow), and a cook to make sure coffee is the first smell you register in the morning. The cost is $200 per person, per night.

MEALTIME: No fish is tastier than the one you catch yourself, especially when the dirty work of cleaning and cooking it is left to trained professionals. The kitchen staff is happy to receive your catch but will also tempt you with dinner options such as duck, bison, and caribou (the latter prepared with a roasted escallot herb demiglaze). Breakfasts are equally gourmet; choose among simple fruit and fresh pastries to design-your-own omelets and malted waffles with berries on top. Eat your lunch in-house or have it packed up for the trail. Either way, be sure to end your activities in time for High Tea and entertainment by local musicians, artists, and guest speakers in the tearoom.

FINE PRINT:

Pets: leave 'em home
Kids: bring 'em on (6 and older for horseback rides)
Credit cards: MasterCard, Visa, American Express
Heads-up: bears—lots
Nearest medical: Dubois, WY (35 miles)
Weather: highs in the 70s; lows can dip to 20 below. Lodge elevation is 9,200 feet.

GETTING THERE: From Jackson Hole, head north on Highway 191/26/89 to Moran. Turn east onto Highway 26/287. At the U.S. FOREST SERVICE sign for the Brooks Lake Recreation Area, turn onto Brooks Lake Road and drive 5 miles to the lodge. Transportation from the airport is not provided, but you will be picked up at the Brooks Lake Road Turnoff by snowmobile when Brooks Lake Road becomes undrivable in the winter.

See color photos on pages 143 and 144

TOGWOTEE MOUNTAIN LODGE

P.O. Box 91
Moran, WY 83013
Tel: 800-543-2847; 307-543-2847
Fax: 307-543-2391
www.togwoteelodge.com

Closest airport: Jackson Hole, WY (40 miles)
Activities: cross-country and downhill skiing, snowboarding, snowshoeing, dogsledding, horseback riding, hiking, mountain biking, fishing, rafting, climbing/mountaineering, orienteering, hot-air ballooning, wildlife watching
Season: mid-June through September; early December through early April
Guides/Instruction: horseback riding guides and instruction, on-site naturalist, children's programs
Services: massage, conference facilities
Accommodations: 35 lodge rooms, 54 cabins; capacity 450
Rates: $99–$159 per room, double occupancy (summer); $109–$249 per person, including breakfast, dinner, and airport transportation (winter)

High above Jackson Hole in a Bridger-Teton National Forest mountain pass, the self-contained Togwotee Mountain Lodge has the amenities of a resort town without the inflated prices and the crowds. The area's national parks and ski slopes are within easy driving distance, but you'll come home to a relatively isolated base.

The native word *Togwotee* means "from here you can go anywhere." When you're looking out your window onto endless Rocky Mountain peaks, the geographic possibilities do seem limitless. But the translation also applies to a broader lodge philosophy: Wherever you want to go, whatever you want to do, your hosts will make sure it happens.

AT THE LODGE: Every building on the property was built from native wood and stone. Guest rooms in the 1921, three-story main lodge are

basic, clean, motel-style units with queen beds, private baths, views of the Tetons, and cable TV. The top-floor suites have a microwave and fridge. Aside from subtle wood detailing, there's nothing in the room décor that shouts out "mountain lodge!" The cabins, however, ooze character. Nestled in the woods and spread out just enough to ensure privacy, their knotty pine walls surround pine-log furniture. Outside, there are grills and picnic benches on the decks. All cabins have kitchenettes, full baths, separate living rooms, two bedrooms, and two televisions. Some have fireplaces. There are shared hot tubs between the cabins.

THE SPORTS: The activities can include just about anything. If it's not available on-site, the lodge will connect you with a local outfitter. Wintertime activities include cross-country skiing (20 kilometers of groomed and tracked trails), downhill skiing and snowboarding (at Jackson Hole), and snowshoeing. The lodge will also arrange dogsled tours. In the summer, you can hike or bike on trails that follow creeks through the pine forests to open alpine meadows, or climb to the 10,200-foot summit of Angle Mountain to straddle the Continental Divide. Guided mountain biking and horseback riding trips are available for riders of every level. There's a kid-sized trout fishing pond on-site and ample fly-fishing terrain nearby; guide service is available. Local companies offer rafting and float trips on the Snake River, orienteering seminars, and hot-air ballooning. The lodge is only 17 miles from Grand Teton National Park and 44 miles from the south entrance to Yellowstone National Park, where the lodge runs naturalist-guided tours. Day-trippers are allowed to partake of the on-site activities without an overnight stay.

BACKCOUNTRY BONUS: Horse packing excursions up to a week long can be arranged by the lodge's activities staff. Prices depend on the destination. Packages usually include gear, guides, and meals.

MEALTIME: After happy-hour appetizers in the Red Fox Saloon, you'll retreat to the Grizzly Steakhouse for a hearty, mountain-style dinner. Some summer evenings there are Western cookouts with live entertainment. The food is good, plentiful, and not too fancy. Vegetarians can be accommodated. In the winter, breakfast and lunch are also served; in summer only breakfast and dinner. Sack lunches with huge sandwiches, chips, fruit, cookies, and drinks are available on request. The lodge will cook any fish you catch, as long as it has already been cleaned.

FINE PRINT:

Pets: leave 'em home
Kids: bring 'em on
Credit cards: MasterCard, Visa, American Express, Discover
Heads-up: bears, mosquitoes in early summer; snowmobiles and ATVs in winter—lots of them.
Nearest medical: Dubois, WY (38 miles)
Weather: Extremely variable. Spring and summer temperatures can range from daytime 80s to nighttime 20s. In winter, lows to 10 below. The area gets 15 inches of yearly rainfall and 500 inches of snow. Lodge elevation is 8,600 ft.

GETTING THERE: Take a left at the airport exit and drive north on Highway 26/89/189. At the Moran Junction, bear right onto Highway 26/287. Drive southeast along the valley floor until you start to climb Togwotee Pass. The lodge is on the left, 16.5 miles past the Moran Junction. Transportation from the airport is included in winter stays.

See color photo on page 144

SOUTH: Florida

STEINHATCHEE LANDING RESORT

P.O. Box 789
Steinhatchee, FL 32359
Tel: 800-584-1709; 352-498-3513
Fax: 352-498-2346
www.steinhatcheelanding.com
slr@inetw.net

Closest airport: Gainesville, FL (70 miles)
Activities: canoeing, kayaking, horseback riding, hiking, fishing, scalloping, road biking, snorkeling, diving, wildlife watching
Season: year-round
Guides/Instruction: canoeing and horseback riding guides and instruction, hiking guides, on-site naturalists
Services: conference facilities
Accommodations: 31 cottages; capacity 120
Rates: $145–$433 per cottage (one to three bedrooms), including breakfast and some activities

Long before the mouse ears and the faux jungle cruise arrived, Florida was a place where alligators didn't run on electric power. Entertainment meant dangling a fishing line off a quiet dock, taking long walks through the cypress groves, and listening to the crickets chirp. That version of the Sunshine State still exists at Steinhatchee Landing, a 35-acre riverfront resort built in 1990 to look and feel like Old Panhandle, circa 1920.

Kids love it here, as does the family pooch, who can splash in the river, yap at the wild turkeys, and wreak havoc on the manicured lawn. But those seeking solace need not turn the page—there are plenty of secluded nooks along the river and in the surrounding parks. This is a something-for-everyone destination.

AT THE LODGE: The one- to three-bedroom cottages were built on the site of Fort Frank Brooke, which was burned to the ground in 1840 on the order of soon-to-be-president General Zachary Taylor—an act carried out as a precursor to the Civil War. The Victorian and Key West cracker-style buildings have tin roofs and broad screened porches, some with swings or rockers. Anachronistic amenities like stereos, TVs, VCRs, washer/dryers, and refrigerators belie the old-fashioned exteriors. All cottages have full kitchens and outdoor grills. Some have fireplaces, hydrotherapy baths, or antique pine floors and trim reclaimed from an 1836 hotel. Porches have views of the Steinhatchee River, King's Creek, the vegetable garden, or the landscaped grounds, where you'll also find an outdoor hot tub, a riverfront pool with a screened picnic pavilion, and a 100-seat Gothic wedding chapel.

THE SPORTS: Guests have access to the lodge's rental canoes, kayaks, and bikes, in addition to complimentary trail maps. From rise to gulf, the Steinhatchee River spans 11 miles, emptying into the Gulf of Mexico 2.5 miles past Steinhatchee Landing. The lodge's staff will drive you upriver to Steinhatchee Falls for the portage-free, 7-mile paddle home. They'll also arrange for outside outfitters to take you fishing, scalloping, and diving. The most common catches are sea trout, redfish, flounder, mackerel, grouper, and red snapper. Scallops

and crabs are also abundant. Look for cleaning stations at any of the six village marinas and at the lodge. Divers usually head for offshore reefs and nearby caves—the mapped cave system at Peacock Springs State Park, 35 miles from the lodge, is the world's largest. Snorkelers can expect to see stingrays, trout, sea bass, shellfish, and the occasional manatee. One area guide offers spear fishing for grouper and snapper. Along the river, trails are set aside for hiking, biking, or horseback riding. Cycling terrain is paved and flat. There's a dude ranch across the river that offers horseback riding instruction and trail rides on level terrain. Hiking opportunities outside the property include Jena Wildlife Management Area (18,000 acres), Big Bend Wildlife Management Area (31,000 acres), Steinhatchee Falls Wildlife Management Area (29,000 acres), and several state parks, many of which are within a 10-minute drive. The lodge also offers naturalist-guided sunset pontoon cruises and a farm-animal petting zoo for kids.

MEALTIME: Beyond the basic continental breakfast and the sodas in your fridge, you're on your own for sustenance. You can find hearty Southern breakfasts at the Bridge End Café, and outstanding barbecue and seafood dishes at Fiddler's Restaurant, where they'll let you choose from the menu or bring in any fish or scallops you pulled from the river. Both restaurants are a few minutes from the lodge. The other option is to bring your own groceries. Each cottage has a full kitchen, complete with microwave, dishwasher, cookware, and flatware. There are also outdoor grills.

FINE PRINT:

Pets: welcome in some cottages if under 28 pounds; security deposit required
Kids: bring 'em on
Credit cards: MasterCard, Visa, American Express
Heads-up: sand gnats, occasional mosquitoes
Nearest medical: Steinhatchee, FL (0.5 mile)
Weather: Variable, with summer temperatures ranging from the mid-50s to upper 90s and winters ranging from the mid-20s to the mid-80s. There's about 50 inches of annual rainfall. Lodge elevation is 13 feet.

GETTING THERE: From Gainesville, take Highway 26 to Fanning Springs, then Highway 19 to Tennille Crossing. Turn left onto Highway 51 and drive 8 miles to the resort. Airport transportation is available for $100.

See color photo on page 145

Georgia

THE LODGE ON LITTLE ST. SIMONS ISLAND

P.O. Box 21078
Little St. Simons Island, GA 31522
Tel: 888-733-5774; 912-638-7472
Fax: 912-634-1811
www.littlestsimonsisland.com
LSSI@mindspring.com

Closest airport: Brunswick, GA (30 minutes)
Activities: hiking, fishing, horseback riding, canoeing, road biking, kayaking, birding, wildlife watching
Season: year-round
Guides/Instruction: hiking, fishing, horseback riding, and canoeing guides, boating instruction, on-site naturalists, children's programs
Services: conference facilities
Specialty: environmental education
Accommodations: 13 rooms and two suites in five cottages; capacity 30
Rates: $325–$600 per room, double occupancy, all-inclusive (meals, activities, gear); lodge and island buyouts also available

Little St. Simons Island owes its pristine condition to wind, salt, and a forward-thinking pencil magnate. Philip Berolzheimer bought the land in 1908 to harvest the cedars for his Eagle Pencil Company. On discovering that natural elements had rendered the wood too flimsy for manufacture, however, he opted instead to preserve the 10,000-acre barrier island as his personal eco-retreat.

The property opened to visitors in 1979, but a 30-guest maximum limit and strict environmental policies keep impact to a minimum. Resident naturalists keep a close watch on the loggerhead sea turtle population. Birders have counted more than 280 shorebird species. Alligators, armadillos, fallow deer, and dolphins can still be spotted in the salt marshes, forests, and tidal creeks. Still owned by the Berolzheimer family, this is one of the few remaining private islands on the 100-mile-long Georgia coast. Guests are treated like personal friends of the pencil king himself.

AT THE LODGE: In the shade of live oaks dripping with moss, five separate cottages house the guest rooms. The 1917 Hunting Lodge is the only original building. An Adirondack-style structure, it houses two rooms, both decorated with antique wicker and pine-bough furniture and Berolzheimer family heirlooms. This lodge also contains the dining room, where meals are served family style. The 1929 Helen House cottage was named after the original owner's daughter. Like all of the cottages, Helen House has a fireplace, private deck, and screened porch. Michael Cottage, built in the 1930s, is set at the edge of the forest. It's standout feature is the outdoor shower built for two. The Cedar House and River Lodge, both built in the 1980s, have large sitting rooms and outdoor decks. Don't waste time looking for a phone, fax, or television set in any of the rooms. It won't be long before you'd rather spend your days communing with the birds than the outside world.

THE SPORTS: If you visit during the May through October loggerhead nesting and hatching season, you can join naturalists on their daily turtle walks. You might even spot a hatchling making its way along the beach. The Audubon Society has designated this shorebird reserve an Important Bird Area, a less-than-clever term for the astoundingly diverse avian population that gets visiting birders all atwitter. Some rare finds include the piping plover and the American oyster catcher. During the spring and fall migration, huge flocks of red knots soar overhead. Naturalists lead interpretive guides all over the island, but you can also explore the 15 miles of hiking trails on your own. Just over 2 miles on the Beach Road takes you to a 7-mile stretch of white sand beach. A short walk down the Half Moon Trail leads to fishing on Eagle's Nest Creek. Guides and gear are available for fly-fishing, spin casting, and surf casting. Expect to catch redfish, sea trout, and flounder. All of the island's trails are open to bikes and horses, too. Guided tours leave from the stables and are suitable for riders of any skill level. Paddlers can grab a house canoe and explore Mitchell Marsh an hour before high tide. From there, follow the incoming tide down Mosquito Creek to the pull-out at the South End Road bridge. The walk home takes about 30 minutes. Guided canoeing trips are also available, as is gear for all of the above.

MEALTIME: The food didn't have to be this good; visiting nature lovers would have settled for granola and PB&J. But mealtime here is always a newsworthy event. It starts with peach-pecan pancakes or grits with Tasso gravy, and maybe some homemade buttermilk biscuits and pumpkin muffins for regional flare. Picnic lunches of fried chicken or local blue crab cakes with red pepper sauce are the perfect complement to the salty ocean air. You can also have homemade wraps, sandwiches, soups, and snacks packed for the trail, or bring back your catch to have it cleaned and prepared. When the cast-iron dinner bell clangs, it's time to gather around the Hunting Lodge's long oak tables for a family-style feast. First, citrus salad with toasted coconut. Then crispy flounder with ginger-peach sauce and basmati rice with lime zest, or maybe grilled cinnamon duck breast with red currant sauce. Then finish with key lime pie or a prickly pear sorbet. These meals and a smattering of tasty snacks are included in a stay. In fact, there's hardly enough time between feedings to work up a hunger. Not that you'll mind.

FINE PRINT:
Pets: leave 'em home
Kids: bring 'em on
Credit cards: MasterCard, Visa, American Express, Discover
Heads-up: mosquitoes (netting and bug spray provided)
Nearest medical: Brunswick, GA (45 minutes)
Weather: Expect summer highs in the 80s and winter lows in the low 40s. The lodge is just above sea level.

GETTING THERE: Take Interstate 95 to Highway 17 toward Brunswick, GA. Follow the signs to St. Simons Island. Once you reach the island, follow the signs to the Hampton River Club Marina. The lodge is accessible only by boat. Shuttle service costs $75–$90 for the first guest, $10 for each additional guest.

See color photos on pages 145 and 146

MOUNTAIN TOP LODGE AT DAHLONEGA

447 Mountain Top Lodge Road
Dahlonega, GA 30533
Tel: 800-526-9754; 706-864-5257
www.mountaintoplodge.net
mountaintop@alltel.net

Closest airport: Atlanta, GA (90 miles)
Activities: hiking, mountain and road biking, canoeing, rafting, kayaking, fishing, horseback riding
Season: year-round
Guides/Instruction: none
Services: conference facilities
Accommodations: 13 rooms; capacity 30
Rates: $80–$150 per room, double occupancy, including breakfast

If everyone understood the healing power of a fresh baked chocolate chip cookie after a long day on the trail, lodge owners everywhere would make it a standard amenity. The folks at Mountain Top Lodge at Dahlonega definitely get the cookie concept. They also up the ante with a complimentary evening sherry. And when 40 acres of blooming dogwoods are all that stand between you and national forest trails that extend far beyond state lines, there's plenty of cause for nightly celebration.

AT THE LODGE: The bed-and-breakfast is spread between two rustic cedar buildings, the mansard-roofed Main Lodge and the smaller, more cabinlike Hillside Lodge. All of the common space is in the nine-bedroom Main Lodge, where a woodburning stove warms the large space beneath the Great Room's cathedral ceiling. There's also a guest kitchen, a TV room, an upstairs game and library loft, and two dining rooms. Each of the four Hillside rooms has its own entrance and a private deck. These rooms are much more secluded than the others, even though they're just across the lawn. All rooms have private bathrooms, two with Jacuzzi tubs. The décor is country, peppered with antiques.

THE SPORTS: Hundreds of miles of hiking trails run through the Chattahoochee National Forest and Blood Mountain Wilderness Area. Most notably, the Appalachian Trail has its southern terminus at Springer Mountain, just outside Dahlonega. Mountain bikers should head for the Bull Mountain Loop, a 14-mile stretch of singletrack that climbs through the thick mountain laurel to the summit before offering up a shocks-jarring descent. Lumpkin County is home to the infamous Six Gap Century, where cyclists brave 10,700 feet of vertical grade on the hilly byways of the North Georgia Mountains. You can tackle the steepest section of the course—a 7-mile, 7-percent ascent up Hogpen Gap. The Chattooga National Wild and Scenic River, of *Deliverance* fame, is a classic whitewater run. Local outfitters also offer guided canoeing trips on Class I and II sections of the Etowah and Chestatee Rivers. Anglers can reel in trout on the Etowah and dozens of nearby creeks. There's boat fishing for striped and largemouth bass at Lake Lanier. Guided and unguided horseback rides are available nearby. The lodge doesn't stock its own gear or guides for any of the above, but everything you need can be found in Dahlonega, 5 miles away.

BACKCOUNTRY BONUS: Gold City Corral (706-867-9395; www.goldcitycorral.com) in Dahlonega offers overnight horse packing campouts in the North Georgia Mountains. Mountain Top offers packages that combine this trip with a lodge stay.

MEALTIME: The family-style breakfast starts with fresh squeezed orange juice. Then the gut-splitting entrées roll in. You might see a garden frittata with fresh veggies, herbs, and cheese; or cinnamon-baked French toast. Orange-glazed ham or bacon, stone-ground grits, homemade biscuits, muffins, and broiled grapefruit or gingersnap peaches are often on the menu. Meat is served on the side, so vegetarians need not make special requests. All other dietary restrictions can be accommodated with advance notice. If you can't force yourself out of bed for the 9 A.M. seating, you can order a breakfast basket with cereal, muffins, biscuits, fruit, and juice. Coffee and tea are always available in the guest kitchen, which is home to the famous chocolate chip cookies. If you request it ahead of time, a basic sack lunch (sandwich, chips or pasta salad, fruit, dessert, drink) will be ready to go when you are. Otherwise, the closest lunch and dinner options are in Dahlonega. Ask at the lodge for restaurant recommendations.

FINE PRINT:
Pets: leave 'em home
Kids: 12 and older
Credit cards: MasterCard, Visa, American Express, Diner's Club
Nearest medical: Dahlonega, GA (5 miles)

Weather: Mild, with most days in the mid-50s to upper 60s. You might see 85°F at the peak of summer, but winters very rarely dip below freezing (just often enough to sustain the 4 inches of yearly snowfall). Expect rain throughout March. Lodge elevation is 1,500 feet.

GETTING THERE: Take Route 75/85 from Atlanta. Stay on Route 85 (75 will branch off) to Route 400. After about 50 minutes, it ends at Route 60. Turn left and continue to the first stoplight. Turn left onto Route 52 west (Morrison Moore Connector) and drive 4 miles to Siloam Church Road. Turn right at the sign for Mountain Top Lodge, follow it to another lodge sign marking the right turn onto Ellijay Road East, then turn left at a third sign onto Mountain Top Lodge Road, which climbs to the top of the mountain and ends at the lodge.

See color photo on page 147

North Carolina

THE COTTAGES AT SPRING HOUSE FARM

P.O. Box 130
Chimney Rock, NC 28720
Tel: 877-738-9798
www.springhousefarm.com
thecottages@springhousefarm.com

Closest airports: Asheville, NC (one hour), and Charlotte, NC (90 minutes)
Activities: hiking, fishing, horseback riding, canoeing, kayaking, rafting, downhill skiing, snowboarding, hot-air ballooning, wildlife watching
Season: year-round
Guides/Instruction: fishing guides
Services: spa, conference facilities
Accommodations: five cottages; capacity 10
Rates: $220 and up per room, including breakfast and snacks; weekly rates start at $1,254

When Zee and Arthur Campbell turned this 92-acre farm into a bed-and-breakfast in 2000, their priority was preservation of the grounds. To accomplish that goal, they turned the surrounding hardwood forest into a private wildlife sanctuary to protect the resident wild turkeys and deer. And they kept the original farmhouse intact. Dating back to 1826, the Albertus Ledbetter House has since been given national historic status. Guests are welcome to take a tour of the two-story, gable-sided structure, whose hand-detailed interior has not been altered since the 1830s.

Yet the main attraction at Spring House Farm is the solitude, not the history. Each of the five cottages is tucked into the woods for optimum privacy. After fixing yourself a hearty breakfast, you can walk the property's hiking trails, cast for trout in the pond, wander home for a snack, take a nap by the fire, soak in the front porch hot tub, and look forward to repeating the routine the next day.

AT THE LODGE: Each two-person cottage has its own theme. All have stone fireplaces, claw-foot tubs, hot tubs, private decks, full kitchens, and VCRs. Flying Bridge cottage has a four-person hot tub overlooking the trout pond. Its sun-room has a rope bed hammock. There's a gas grill on the deck and a canoe for floating on the pond. The one-bedroom Compleat Angler has a sliding barn door and covered porch. The best cottage for wildlife watching is The Bimini Twist, which is surrounded by forest. Tall windows and a hilltop perch give The Reach cottage 360-degree views of Hickory Nut and Pinnacle Mountains and the valley below. The Outrigger is a log-cabin-style cottage on a ridge overlooking rhododendrons. Water to all of the buildings comes from a single well. The lodge is a member of two international eco-tourism organizations.

THE SPORTS: The on-site trail system is kept cool year-round by the hardwood canopy. There's plenty of terrain to occupy guests for a one- or two-night stay. Beyond that, hikers can take the 20-minute drive to Chimney Rock Park where the Skyline Trail climbs to the Exclamation Point gorge lookout before leveling off along a cliff top and ending at wooded Fall Creek. From there, the Cliff Trail takes

you back to the starting point for a two-hour loop. To paddle on something bigger than the on-site pond (but also to paddle in the company of many), drive 20 minutes to Lake Lure, where you can rent kayaks, canoes, paddleboats, and pontoon boats. The much more secluded, if smaller, creek and pond on-site at Spring House are stocked with trout. Guide service is available with advance notice. Horseback trail rides can be arranged through a nearby outfitter. In the summer, there's whitewater rafting about an hour away. In winter, skiers can head for Beech and Sugar Mountains, about 90 minutes away. Hot-air balloon rides leave from the farmhouse's front yard.

MEALTIME: Every cottage has its own grill and kitchen, stocked with eggs, bread, jam, and other necessary accoutrements for a hearty country breakfast and midday snacks. Doing it yourself is part of the hideaway experience; you can hole up inside your cabin and avoid humanity for the duration of your stay. Though sack lunches aren't usually provided, Zee and Arthur will make lunch on request. For dinner, you can pack in your own groceries or buy what the lodge keeps in stock: chicken, pork chops, filet mignon, salmon, pizza, salad, and baked potatoes. They'll even pick up lobster with 24 hours' notice. If you would rather drive to dinner, the closest restaurants are in Marion (20 minutes) and Asheville (1 hour). Ask your hosts for dining recommendations.

FINE PRINT:

Pets: leave 'em home

Kids: bring 'em on

Credit cards: MasterCard, Visa, American Express

Nearest medical: Marion, NC (20 minutes)

Weather: Moderate. Summer days rarely top 90°F; winter nights can drop to 20°.

GETTING THERE: From Asheville, take Interstate 40 to exit 81. Turn right onto Sugar Hill Road and drive about 5 miles. Keep to the right when the road forks, then continue 6.3 miles to Donna's Excel Station. Turn right onto Ham Creek Road and drive less than a mile to Haynes Road. Turn left onto Haynes; the Cottages at Spring House Farm is on the left.

EARTHSHINE MOUNTAIN LODGE

Route 1, Box 216-C
Lake Toxaway, NC 28747
Tel: 828-862-4207
www.earthshinemtnlodge.com

Closest airport: Asheville, NC (30 miles)
Activities: hiking, mountain and road biking, canoeing, rafting, fishing, climbing, orienteering, horseback riding, wildlife watching
Season: year-round
Guides/Instruction: hiking guides, horseback riding instruction (for kids), on-site experts, children's programs
Services: conference facilities
Specialty: families, pioneer- and Cherokee-themed kids' programs
Accommodations: 13 lodge suites; capacity 40
Rates: $170 per adult, double occupancy, including meals and activities; $50–$110 per child

Forget Disneyland; any kid who has stayed here can tell you Earthshine is the happiest place on earth. The strange thing is, their moms and dads agree. While the little ones are busy scaling the 31-foot climbing wall, rock hopping through creeks, and feeding snacks to Nubies the goat, the grown-ups are free to gallop through Pisgah National Forest on horseback and take uninterrupted naps beneath the trees. At the end of the day, everyone thinks they got the better end of the deal.

The lodge is the brainchild of co-owners and co-builders Marion Boatwright and Kim Maurer-Heinish, whose earthy dream was to unite families and friends through experiences in nature. They've succeeded beyond anyone's expectations. Since it opened its doors in 1990, Earthshine has become a favorite site for reunions, retreats, and weddings, not to mention family getaways. What sets it apart is genuine warmth, an amenity too many vacation spots are without.

AT THE LODGE: Though it was built in 1989, the log-cabin-style lodge looks, at first glance, like it has weathered a century or more. It's an effect that connects the solid, one-and-a-half story cedar building to the 100-year-old homestead's history. Perched on an Appalachian ridge on 70 acres of land abutting Pisgah National Forest, the lodge offers expansive views of mountains and meadows from every room. Guests stay in family-sized suites with lofts, private decks, and (thank goodness) no televisions. Handmade quilts cover the log beds. Rocking chairs and stone fireplaces make you feel like Laura Ingalls Wilder, which is appropriate, since you probably spent part of the day shearing sheep, picking berries, or feeding chickens.

THE SPORTS: Though there are hundreds of miles of hiking and biking trails just off the grounds, the headlining sports are for kids. In addition to the ever-popular climbing wall ($25, ages 5 and older), there's a pony ring and a "learning" barnyard with goats, sheep, chickens, and ducks. Summertime water games include lawn slides and squirt gun wars. Scheduled trips to the pond involve the use of nets and microscopes. Living-history programs involve kids in pioneer and Cherokee activities like splitting shingles, making candles, and twisting bark into rope. Grown-ups have access to guided, two-hour trail rides

($40), trout and catfish fishing (there are catfish tournaments twice a week), three-season rafting, and flatwater canoeing. Anyone over 10 can give the ropes course ($30) or treetop swing ($50) a try. A favorite family hike is the walk on Flat Creek, where a rock slide empties into a natural pool. At the end of the day, everyone reconvenes for moonlit hikes, scavenger hunts, folk dancing, and storytelling.

MEALTIME: Food preparation is a team sport at Earthshine Mountain, with guests helping to bake the bread, pick the herbs, and press the cider. On the breakfast table, you might see blueberry pancakes one morning, scrambled eggs and grits the next. Lunch can be anything from a pita sandwich to a baked potato bar. Fresh trout makes frequent appearances on the dinner menu, as do ribs, salmon filets, and oven-roasted turkey. Meals are casual home-style buffets with just enough flare to keep the adults interested yet not discourage the kids. Snacks available throughout the day include fresh fruit and granola. The hors d'oeuvres hour features regional favorites: hush puppies with clam dip, pecan-crusted cheese balls, deviled eggs, and pimento-stuffed celery. Packed lunches and vegetarian options are always available, and the kitchen will clean and prepare whatever fish you catch.

FINE PRINT:
Pets: leave 'em home
Kids: bring 'em on!
Credit cards: MasterCard, Visa, Discover
Nearest medical: Lake Toxaway, NC (10 minutes)
Weather: Summer days rarely top 90°F; winter lows can dip to 15°. The area gets about a foot of snow each year. Lodge elevation is 3,100 feet.

GETTING THERE: From the airport, take NC 280 east to Brevard, then U.S. 64 west about 11 miles to Silversteen Road. Turn right and follow the signs for 2.3 miles to the lodge. The lodge provides airport transportation for $70.

See color photo on page 147

PISGAH INN

P.O. Drawer 749
Waynesville, NC 28786
Tel: 828-235-8228
Fax: 828-648-9719
www.pisgahinn.com
pisgahinn@aol.com

Closest airport: Asheville, NC (40 minutes)
Activities: hiking, climbing, mountaineering, road biking, rafting, canoeing, fishing, birding
Season: April 1 through October 31
Guides/Instruction: none
Services: conference facilities
Accommodations: 51 rooms; capacity 110
Rates: $80–$130 per room

Folks who've sampled the entirety of the Blue Ridge Parkway have said the prettiest sight on the route was the sunrise they watched from their bed at the Pisgah Inn. As wake-up calls go, little compares to the slow climb of soft orange light filtered through pines.

In full daylight, the views are equally worthy of superlatives. The inn's perch at the highest point on this 469-mile scenic corridor positions it perfectly for gape-mouthed gawking. Since it first opened its doors to the traveling public in 1919, millions have come here to do just that.

AT THE LODGE: None of the original lodge remains—the last pieces were disassembled for safety reasons in 1990. The existing inn was built in 1964, around the same time that the parkway was extended to the Mount Pisgah area (though it started as a Depression-era public works project, the corridor wasn't completed until the late 1980s). Most of the rooms are basic, motel-style units that would be fairly ordinary if not for the balconies and porches that open up to expansive views of Pisgah National Forest and beyond. Standard rooms have TVs, and porches or balconies with rocking chairs. Deluxe rooms are slightly larger, with in-room coffeemakers, small refrigerators, and bigger windows for better views. The Pisgah Suite is twice the size of a deluxe room. Sixties-style plaid sofas surround the stone fireplace and big-screen TV. Sliding glass doors open to a double balcony with panoramic mountain views. Reservations for the suite are accepted as much as two years in advance.

THE SPORTS: Hiking is the main activity here. You can find a few paths to follow, and plenty of wild berries to pick, without getting into your car. Ask for trail maps at the front desk. One of the more interesting hikes, the Graveyard Fields Loop, requires a short drive to milepost 418.8. This is a gentle, 90-minute stroll to Yellowstone Falls and a "graveyard" of fallen tree trunks that were victims of a 1925 fire. Hikers and climbers can access Looking Glass Rock by turning off the parkway at milepost 412 and heading south on U.S. 276 to Fire Road 475. There's a parking area 0.4 mile down the road on the right. Take the trail 3.1 miles through hardwood forest to the large granite dome. Whatever your destination, be sure to bring your binoculars—more than 300 bird species have been counted in the area. Cyclists are restricted to paved roads, but the absence of dirt is the least of your concerns here: Narrow shoulders, dark tunnels, steep hills, and summer traffic make you a target on two wheels. If you plan to ride, wear as much protective gear as you can carry.

MEALTIME: In general, people come here to look out the windows, not at their plates. But the food is much better than you might expect from a remote tourist stop that could get by on its vistas alone. Breakfast features all the country standards, from pancakes to steak and eggs with homemade biscuits. Anything on the lunch menu (burgers and sandwiches, steaks and salads) can be packed to take on the trail. For dinner, you can nibble on cheese sticks and chicken tenders before moving on to the main event. Entrées include fried chicken, garlic fettuccine, ham steak, grilled fish, and various cuts of beef, including (weekend nights only) a tasty, 10- or 14-ounce prime rib. The house specialty is fresh mountain trout baked in lemon butter or charbroiled and filleted at your table. Be sure to save room for homemade cobbler à la mode.

FINE PRINT:

Pets: leave 'em home
Kids: bring 'em on
Credit cards: MasterCard, Visa
Heads-up: watch for skunks at dusk
Nearest medical: Asheville, NC (20 miles)
Weather: Summers are cool, with highs in the upper 70s. Winter temperatures fall well below zero. Waynesville gets 40 to 60 inches of yearly rain- and snowfall. Lodge elevation is 5,000 feet.

GETTING THERE: From Asheville, head south on the Blue Ridge Parkway to milepost 408.6.

Tennessee

BLACKBERRY FARM

1471 West Millers Cove Road
Walland, TN 37803
Tel: 800-648-2348; 865-380-2260
Fax: 865-681-7735
www.blackberryfarm.com
info@blackberryfarm.com

Closest airport: Knoxville, TN (20 miles)
Activities: fishing, horseback riding, hiking, biking, canoeing, rafting, hot-air ballooning
Season: year-round
Guides/Instruction: fly-fishing and horseback riding guides and instruction, children's programs
Services: spa, conference facilities
Accommodations: 44 rooms in five houses and cottages; capacity 88
Rates: $495–$1,190 per room, double occupancy, all-inclusive (meals, activities, gear)

As a Christmas gift to Tennessee in 2002, Blackberry Farm proprietor Sandy Beall and other area landowners donated 769 wooded acres to a state conservation group. The gift created a much-needed buffer zone next to Great Smoky Mountains National Park on land that could have been sold for many millions and subdivided for development.

Any guest who has seen Blackberry's annual Christmas tree decked in fly-fishing gear knows that the holidays have always been a big deal at this family-farm-turned-luxury-inn. So have gestures of kindness. It would take a mountain-sized trophy case to hold all of the farm's accolades. This lodge is the epitome of Southern elegance and hospitality.

AT THE LODGE: Feather beds, thick robes, and custom bath accoutrements that make you feel like human potpourri—these are just a sampling of the details that put Blackberry Farm in the deluxe class. Not plush enough? Book one of the suites with a fireplace and whirlpool tub. The Holly Glade Cottage Suite features a covered porch and rocking chairs. The room décor is fresh from the English countryside, replete with floral prints. Guest quarters are spread among five houses and cottages. The Main House and Guest House rooms have views that stretch across the lawn to distant mountains and meadows. All rooms have phones and TVs, but the down-time diversion of choice is rocking on the Main House front terrace. An 1870s farmhouse is where you'll find the full-service spa, where you can indulge in over-the-top treatments like Blackberry Mist ($150), which culminates in a berry-infused steam canopy and a vanilla lotion rubdown.

THE SPORTS: Guests have access to two stocked trout ponds and a creek filled with bass, bream, catfish, and trout—all on the farm's property. Next door, Great Smoky Mountains National Park has 700 miles of fly-fishing streams. The lodge stocks top-end fishing gear and employs Orvis-endorsed guides who can teach anglers of all skill levels a new trick or two. The farm's own fleet of Rocky Mountain horses will take you through meadows, over creeks, and deep into the woods without leaving the 2,500-acre estate. Guided two-hour trail rides cost $95 per person. Half-day trips are also available. Of the 11 miles of on-site hiking trails, one-third is paved. Serious hikers would do better to explore the 800-square-mile national park. Though the farm stocks mountain bikes, its 2.5 miles of bike paths are paved as well. To get off-road, try the ridgeline trail that runs from Blackberry Farm to the park border. All gear, including binoculars and tennis racquets, is free to guests, as is Camp Blackberry, where kids are led on hikes, hayrides, and other guided adventures on holidays and during Family Month in July. Call the concierge two weeks before your stay to arrange all activities, including hot-air balloon rides and rafting, which can be scheduled through nearby outfitters.

MEALTIME: Anyone who thinks of catfish as the culinary equivalent of macaroni and cheese hasn't had it pan-seared in a light potato crust and served with creamy spiced grits and buttermilk pie. Transforming simple Appalachian ingredients into gourmet dishes is the key to "foothills cuisine." Blackberry's chef is known throughout the Smokies and beyond for his mastery. Your day might start with buttery biscuits and homemade jam or cornmeal pudding with maple cream cheese. Picnic lunches are far from ordinary—the sweet-tea-brined fried chicken is often served with pineapple coleslaw and basil-marinated corn on the cob. Be sure to make it home in time for the afternoon Tennessee Tea. And if you've had a successful day of fishing, give the kitchen your catch; it may end up on the candlelit dinner table dressed in pecans and rice. On the off chance you should experience anything resembling hunger between meals, there's a guest pantry stocked with snacks.

FINE PRINT:
Pets: leave 'em home
Kids: 10 and older, except holidays and Family Month in July
Credit cards: MasterCard, Visa, American Express, Discover
Heads-up: bears
Nearest medical: Maryville, TN (13 miles)
Weather: Summer highs to 90°F; winter lows to 23°. Lodge elevation is 1,100 feet.

GETTING THERE: Turn right out of the airport and take Highway 129 south toward Maryville. Take Highway 321 north about 14 miles toward the Smoky Mountains. Drive past the entrance and exit to the Foothills Parkway and take the next right onto West Millers Cove Road. Drive 3.5 miles to the BLACKBERRY FARM sign on your left.

See color photo on page 148

CHARIT CREEK LODGE

250 Apple Valley Road
Sevierville, TN 37862
Tel: 865-429-5700
Fax: 865-774-0045
www.charitcreek.com
reservations@charitcreek.com

Closest airport: Knoxville, TN (2.5 hours)
Activities: hiking, mountain biking, horseback riding, fishing, rafting, canoeing
Season: year-round
Guides/Instruction: none
Services: none
Accommodations: two cabins, two lodge rooms; capacity 48
Rates: $54 per adult, including dinner and breakfast; $44 per child

A true wilderness retreat knows how to take pride in its don't-haves. At Charit Creek Lodge, they don't have electricity (their light comes from kerosene lanterns), they don't have phones (the only thing ringing at mealtime is the dinner bell), and, most notably, they don't have traffic (access is by foot, bike, or horseback only).

Run by the same folks whose wildly popular LeConte Lodge (see page 96) fills up months in advance, this lesser-known cluster of rustic cabins is set in a river gorge at the convergence of two creeks. The lodge is surrounded by 125,000-acre Big South Fork National River and Recreation Area, which provides it with its long list of do-haves—among them, a never-ending soundtrack of trickling water and occasional visits from the neighborhood deer.

AT THE LODGE: Every building on the property began as a structure on a 19th- or early-20th-century homestead. The main lodge was built around an 1819 hunting cabin, which remains as one of the two small guest rooms. All rooms are lit by kerosene lamps and warmed by woodburning stoves. There's no electricity, phone, or TV on-site, and the flush toilets and solar-heated showers operate seasonally. The rooms sleep up to 12 in double-sized bunks. Each of the two one-room log cabins has a screened-in porch with rockers and a detached bath. Groups of 6 or more can reserve a private room or cabin. Horseback riders have access to the lodge's stable, which can accommodate 11 horses for $6 each, including hay.

THE SPORTS: The most direct of the four hiking paths to the lodge is the Charit Creek Hiking Trail, a 0.8-mile descent that takes hikers to the base of a bluff, past a seasonal waterfall, across a wooden bridge, and down to the lodge. The Twin Arches Loop Trail runs 0.7 mile to the base of North Arch, where you can choose between a 1-mile and a 3-mile route that converge at the bridge. Longer choices are the scenic Slave Falls Trail and the Bandy Creek Campground Trail, which runs from the campground to the Charit Creek trailhead. Horseback trails include the Charit Creek Horse Trailhead, just 2 miles from the lodge, and two longer paths that run from the campground. Hikers and mountain bikers are allowed on the horse trails, but horses must keep to their own paths. Once you get there, the dayhiking opportunities include 130 miles of trails lined with mountain laurel and wildflowers. There's fly-fishing nearby (bring your own gear; the catch is bass and trout), and 80 miles of the Big South Fork River that are open to rafting and canoeing (trips are run by local outfitters). You can also play volleyball and horseshoes in the lodge's front yard.

BACKCOUNTRY BONUS: Custom, overnight horseback trips with a lodge stay and/or creekside camping can be arranged through Southeast Pack Trips (931-879-2260; www.southeastpacktrips.com). Prices depend on the accommodations and destination, but all itineraries include meals, gear, and wranglers.

MEALTIME: Classic country meals are served family style at tables that seat up to 10. There's a woodburning stove in the corner of the lantern-lit dining room. The menu includes soup, baked beef with gravy, or chicken and dumplings, mashed potatoes, green beans, or carrots, fried apples, cornbread, and chocolate chip cookies. Vegetarians can be accommodated with advance notice. For breakfast, there's Canadian bacon, scrambled eggs, biscuits, grits, pancakes, a powdered soft drink, coffee, and hot chocolate. Multinight guests also get a sack lunch with a sandwich on homemade bread, trail mix, and dessert.

FINE PRINT:
Pets: welcome
Kids: bring 'em on
Credit cards: none
Heads-up: poison ivy, gnats, some mosquitoes, ticks
Nearest medical: Jamestown, TN (15 miles)
Weather: Expect summer highs to 90°F; winter lows to 20°. There's 40 to 50 inches of annual rainfall and 12 to 20 inches of snow. Lodge elevation is 1,000 feet.

GETTING THERE: Take Interstate 40 west to the Jamestown–Crossville exit, then U.S. 127 north 36 miles to Jamestown. Leave town on 154 north and continue 15 miles to the Big South Fork National River and Recreation Area. Take one of the trails to the lodge.

See color photo on page 148

LECONTE LODGE

250 Apple Valley Road
Sevierville, TN 37862
Tel: 865-429-5704
www.leconte-lodge.com
reservations@leconte-lodge.com

Closest airport: Knoxville, TN (one hour)
Activities: hiking
Season: late March through late November
Guides/Instruction: none
Services: none
Accommodations: seven cabins, three small lodges; capacity 67
Rates: $83 per adult, including breakfast and dinner; $67 per child

Founder Jack Huff built this simple, mountaintop lodge in 1926, just four years before the surrounding half-million acres of the Great Smoky Mountains were tagged for federal protection. To this day, LeConte remains the only guest lodge in what is now the most visited national park in America—10 million people each year hike, fish, and ride horses on the park's 800 miles of densely forested trails.

Of course, anyone who's hiked elbow-to-elbow in the foothills can attest that popularity is not the park's finest feature. That's one reason LeConte Lodge books up months in advance. Its namesake peak is 1 vertical mile above Gatlinburg—at 6,593-feet, the tallest summit in the Smokies. Since the daytripping masses rarely get this far, those who do are treated to a genuine wilderness experience.

AT THE LODGE: The rustic, hand-hewn log and wood frame cabins have cedar siding and cedar-shingled roofs. Each sleeps 4 to 13 on double-sized bunk beds. There are propane heaters, kerosene lanterns (no electricity), clean linens, and warm Hudson's Bay blankets. Flush toilets are adjacent the lodges and cabins. There are no showers, but you're welcome to use the house basins for a sponge bath. Communication with the outside world is by two-way radio and an emergency-only cell phone. Food and clean linens are carried in by llama a few times a week; they pack out laundry and trash. The lodge office has a common room with books, games, and sofas. Its outdoor deck has rocking chairs—not a bad venue for taking in the views of the valley and surrounding peaks.

THE SPORTS: Five trails lead from Gatlinburg to the lodge. The shortest and steepest is the Alum Cave Bluff Trail, a 5.5-mile climb from Newfound Gap Road (Highway 441) with a 2,560-foot elevation gain. Highlights are spruce-lined Alum Cave Creek and the Alum Cave Bluff overlook. The cables at the top of the trail tend to get icy. The Rainbow Falls Trail climbs 3,820 feet in 6.7 miles. It follows a gravely old horse trail that starts at the parking lot on Cherokee Orchard Road. The Bullhead Trail starts at the same place but stretches the climbs to a gentler 7.1 miles. Both routes run past Rainbow Falls. The Trillium Gap Trail starts at the Grotto Falls parking lot on Roaring Fork Motor Nature Trail. It climbs 3,300 feet in 6.5 miles, passing scenic Roaring Fork Creek on the way. Note: this is the trail used by the lodge's llamas for the thrice-weekly restocking trips. The longest route is the Boulevard Trail, which starts at the Newfound Gap lot and follows the Appalachian Trail for 2.7 miles before branching off to the lodge. It's a rolling ridge trail that climbs just 1,080 feet in 7.8 miles. Once you're at the lodge, there are plenty of dayhiking opportunities. For sunset, take the quarter-mile path to Cliff Tops. Early risers can walk ¾ mile from the lodge to Myrtle Point to catch the sunrise.

MEALTIME: Dinner is exactly what you'll crave after a long day on the trail: hot, country-style comfort food. The menu includes soup, baked beef with gravy, or chicken and dumplings, mashed potatoes, green beans or carrots, fried apples, cornbread, and chocolate chip cookies. Vegetarians can be accommodated with advance notice. For breakfast, there's Canadian bacon, scrambled eggs, biscuits, grits, pancakes, a powdered soft drink, coffee, and hot chocolate. Meals are served family style in the large, open dining room at tables that seat 10 to 16. Guests staying for more than one night get a basic lunch with a sandwich, trail mix, and dessert.

FINE PRINT:

Pets: leave 'em home

Kids: bring 'em on (reminder: the shortest access route is a rugged 5.5-mile hike)

Credit cards: none

Heads-up: black bears

Nearest medical: Sevierville, TN (15 miles)

Weather: Expect ice on the trails in March, April, November, and sometimes in between. Temperatures are consistently 15° to 20° cooler than in Gatlinburg—there's never been an 80° day recorded here. The area gets up to 100 inches of rain each year, and 90 to 100 inches of snow. Lodge elevation is 6,593 feet.

GETTING THERE: Take Highway 129 to Maryville–Alcoa, then Highway 73/321 to Townsend. At the Y, take Little River Road to Gatlinburg. Park at any of the five trailheads and hike to the lodge.

See color photo on page 149

Virginia

FORT LEWIS LODGE

HCR 3, Box 21A
Millboro, VA 24460
Tel: 540-925-2314
www.fortlewislodge.com
ftlewis@tds.net

Closest airport: Roanoke, VA (65 miles)
Activities: fishing, hiking, mountain and road biking, canoeing, caving, wildlife watching
Season: April through October
Guides/Instruction: none
Services: conference facilities
Accommodations: two cabins, 16 rooms; capacity 45
Rates: $165–$210 per room, double occupancy; includes breakfast, dinner, some activities

Colonel Charles Lewis built this fort in 1750 to keep the Shawnee from storming the southern pass of the Shenandoah Mountains. Or so the story goes. But you might wonder, as you cast into the quiet Cowpasture River or sip lemonade on the front porch of the main lodge, if he actually chose this spot because it's a particularly nice place to fish.

The 3,200-acre property is cut through by a 3-mile stretch of bass-rich river, surrounded by meadow and forest as far as you can see. There's no formal instruction or gear—this is a hands-off kind of place. You come here to enjoy the surroundings, eat well, sleep in beautifully renovated cabins and rooms, and wander the grounds as you please.

AT THE LODGE: The cedar, board-and-batten main lodge houses the common room and large Shaker-style guest rooms. A spiral staircase climbs the attached glazed-tile silo, where three round bedrooms are topped by a lookout with views of cliffs that drop down to the river. For more privacy, you can stay in one of the historic hand-hewn log cabins, each of which has a stone fireplace and rocking chair porch. The Riverside House is the most recent addition. Spacious rooms look onto the vegetable garden and the river, with a backdrop of the mountains. It's a few minutes' drive from the main lodge, but a short walk to the property's best fishing. The dining room and upstairs game room are in the recently restored, 19th-century Lewis Grist Mill, where guests gather on the porch for a cocktail hour at Buck's Bar before dinner.

THE SPORTS: Anglers will be happy to find a large population of smallmouth bass and kid-sized rock bass in the Cowpasture River. Rainbow trout are stocked in the early spring. The river is suited to both fly-fishing and spin casting, but it's all catch-and-release. Bring your own gear and know-how, as there's nary a fly-rod on-site. This applies to all other activities as well—this is not an outfitter, just a fine angling venue. Adjacent to the property are miles of hiking trails in the Allegheny Mountains. The logging roads are open to mountain bikers, and there's highly technical singletrack nearby. Cyclists have access to rarely traveled, hilly country roads. The wide, calm river is perfect for an easy float. There's almost no current along this stretch of river, so if you drop a canoe in the water, you'll work hard to make it move. Just in front of the lodge is a 5-foot-deep swimming hole, where you can take a dip or practice skipping stones. A few miles outside the property, spelunkers can explore limestone caves. Return to the main lodge at the end of the day to soak in the hot tub on one of the decks.

MEALTIME: While you're busy sipping wine at the Buck's Bar social hour, owners John and Caryl Cowden will be putting the finishing touches on your barbecue dinner. The grill is John's domain. By the time the dinner bell rings, you'll be dizzy with the aromas of roasting beef, chicken, ribs, and seafood, not to mention the country-classic accoutrements Caryl has been prepping in the kitchen. The produce comes from the farm's own garden; breads are baked fresh daily. This is good old-fashioned American backyard cooking, made better because every bite has been grilled to perfection. Like the dinners, the hearty farm breakfasts are included in a stay. Picnic lunches with sandwiches, fruit, cookies, and a drink are available on request.

FINE PRINT:
Pets: leave 'em home
Kids: bring 'em on
Credit cards: MasterCard, Visa
Nearest medical: Hot Springs, VA (30 minutes)
Weather: In-season temperatures range from 50° to 90°. Lodge elevation is 1,600 feet.

GETTING THERE: Head north on Interstate 81 and take Route 220 north to Clifton Forge, then Interstate 64 east to the first exit, Millboro Springs/Route 42 (exit 29). Take Route 42 north for 16 miles to Millboro Springs. Turn left onto 39 west, drive 0.7 mile to Route 678, and turn right. After 10.8 miles, turn left onto Route 625 and look for the lodge sign on the left after 0.2 mile.

See color photo on page 149

West Virginia

CHEAT MOUNTAIN CLUB

P.O. Box 28
Durbin, WV 26264
Tel: 888-502-9612; 304-456-4627
www.cheatmountainclub.com

Closest airport: Clarksburg, WV (one hour, 45 minutes)
Activities: fishing, hiking, cross-country and downhill skiing, snowboarding, snowshoeing, rafting, mountain biking, canoeing, kayaking, climbing, mountaineering, snorkeling, horseback riding, wildlife watching
Season: year-round
Guides/Instruction: fly-fishing and cross-country skiing guides and instruction, hiking guides
Services: conference facilities
Accommodations: 10 rooms; capacity 23
Rates: $500–$800 (entire lodge) per night, $3,500 per week, including activities; full lodge rental only

Shooting bears was the activity of choice in the Cheat Mountain Club's early days. Built at the end of the John Henry steel-driving era, this private hunting and fishing reserve hosted many a gun-toting railroad and lumber kingpin. The sporting opportunities didn't expand much until 1987, when four families bought the lodge, stocked it with a wide range of outdoor gear, and opened it to the public. Now anyone can play mountain adventurer for a week.

A million acres of the Monongahela National Forest surrounds the lodge—isolation is central to the experience. You won't be fighting anyone for fly-fishing space on the Shavers Fork River, which runs 100 feet from the front door. Nor will you have to venture far to ski, bike, or paddle. All the gear and terrain you could want is yours for the asking.

AT THE LODGE: The 1887 spruce log lodge is on the National Register of Historic Places. But a more telling document is the old guest register signed by Henry Ford, Harvey Firestone, and Thomas Edison, all of whom may have swapped stories around the Great Room's massive stone fireplace after a hunt. Dark stained wood-paneled walls give the guest rooms a distinct sporting lodge feel. Quilt-topped beds and Vermont maple antique furniture add period authenticity. All the rooms have views of the Shavers Fork River and surrounding mountains. If that's not entertainment enough, televisions can be provided on request.

THE SPORTS: A stay at the lodge includes access to fly tackle, kayaks, canoes, bikes, and a rack full of cross-country skis and snowshoes. Anglers can expect to land ample rainbows, brookies, and browns—the 2-mile stretch of the Shavers Fork River that passes through the club's property is stocked regularly, as are the ponds by the lodge. Should you get the urge to branch out from the on-site terrain, local outfitters offer day trips to other rivers and tributaries. Better yet, hop on the Cheat Mountain Salamander historic railway. It will take you deep into the forest to the headwaters of Shavers Fork, drop you off in the morning, and pick you up in the afternoon after a day of solitary fishing. Hikers have immediate access to extensive trail systems maintained by The Nature Conservancy and the National Park Service. Red spruce and firs dominate the Cheat Mountain Range, with ferns and wildflowers spilling over the edges of the narrow trails. Most of the club's trails and those in neighboring Monongahela National Forest are open to mountain bikers. The lodge stocks bikes for guests' use. You can drag one of the house canoes onto the Shavers Fork or Greenbrier Rivers for a river trip (with many portages). Or whitewater outfitters will take you rafting on stretches up to Class IV. River snorkeling is an option, too. In January and February, there's a permanent base of snow for out-the-front-door snowshoeing and cross-country skiing (gear is free to guests). Downhill skiing and snowboarding at Snowshoe Mountain is less than an hour away.

BACKCOUNTRY BONUS: The lodge will arrange overnight backpacking, horseback riding, or river trips to add onto a stay.

MEALTIME: Since the lodge is yours for the duration of your stay, you choose the cuisine. The kitchen can accommodate any preference, from hearty home style to healthy gourmet (a word of warning to city dwellers: allow some leeway in your definition of "healthy" and "gourmet"; the chefs here aren't competing for the Manhattan or San Francisco markets). Meals are served at set times, fireside, in the dining room. Previous breakfasts have featured scrambled eggs with county fried ham, homemade donuts, and zucchini bread. For lunch, you might have chicken potpie or an open-faced turkey sandwich with mashed potatoes and gravy. Trail lunches can be requested in advance—anything you want. Dinners often start with broccoli soup or clam chowder and homemade bread before progressing to the main course: local trout (the staff will clean and cook your catch), ribeye steaks, and fried chicken are all solid choices. Vegetarian dishes are available as well. Be sure to save room for homemade apple pie. Meals cost $45 per person, per day.

FINE PRINT:
Pets: leave 'em home
Kids: bring 'em on
Credit cards: none
Heads-up: occasional black bears and bobcats
Nearest medical: Elkins, WV (45 minutes)
Weather: Summer days rarely top 80°, with much cooler nights. Winter temperatures range from 10° to 40° with 180 inches of yearly snowfall. Lodge elevation is 3,800 feet.

GETTING THERE: From Charleston, take Interstate 79 north to exit 99 (Weston–Buchannon), then Route 33 east to Elkins. Get on Route 250/219 toward Huttonsville and continue to Cheat Mountain. At the top of the mountain, look for a green bridge. After you cross it, turn right onto the first dirt road (Fire Road #235). Look for the sign at the intersection. It's a 1-mile drive to the lodge. Transportation from the Clarksburg airport costs $85.

See color photo on page 150

SOUTHWEST: Arizona

EL TOVAR

Apache Street and Center Road
South Rim
Grand Canyon National Park, AZ 86023
Tel: 888-297-2757; 928-638-2631
Fax: 928-638-9810
www.grandcanyonlodges.com
reserve-gcsr@xanterra.com

Closest airport: Tusyan, AZ (8 miles)
Activities: hiking, rafting, cross-country and downhill skiing, snowboarding, snowshoeing, mule trekking, horseback riding, road biking, wildlife watching, flight-seeing
Season: year-round
Guides/Instruction: guided mule trips, on-site naturalist guides, children's programs
Services: conference facilities (limited)
Accommodations: 66 rooms and 12 suites; capacity 198
Rates: $123–$286 per room, double occupancy, including shuttle service around the park

The West was still wild when tourism visionary Fred Hardy talked the Santa Fe Railroad into running a line to the South Rim of the Grand Canyon in 1901. Yet by the time the area's first hotel, El Tovar, opened its doors four years later, the $250,000 project was purported to be as civilized as any stylish Swiss chalet. An on-site greenhouse, henhouse, and dairy made it possible to serve up fresh, gourmet cuisine. And a coal-fired generator powered electric lights, a luxury people didn't expect to find so far from a big city.

Elegance still distinguishes El Tovar from other lodges on this side of Grand Canyon National Park—a 1998 renovation polished nearly a century's worth of accumulated rough edges. And even though a village has been built up around it, the hotel remains a prime access point for canyon adventures. It is situated 20 feet from the rim.

AT THE LODGE: This registered National Historic Landmark was modeled after European hunting lodges and named for the Spanish explorer Pedro de Tovar, who came to Arizona looking for the fabled Seven Cities of Gold (he brought home tales of Hopi villages instead). Native stone and imported Oregon lumber make up the exterior. The Douglas fir boards were corner-notched to make them look like whole logs. Guest rooms have cable television, phones, full private bathrooms, and air conditioning. Sixteen of the rooms and all of the suites have separate sitting rooms; some have porches or balconies. Only four of the suites have full canyon views.

THE SPORTS: In less time than it takes to tie your bootlaces, you can walk from the hotel's front door to the Rim Trail, which skirts the south edge of the canyon. The short, paved path can get uncomfortably crowded in the high season. You can leave most tourists behind by venturing down any of the connecting trails that drop into the canyon. Keep in mind that every step you take on the way down means a harder step up on the way back (most people can't hike rim-to-river and back in a single day). In summer, prepare for extremely hot weather inside the canyon, even if it's somewhat chilly at the rim. In winter, crampons are a good idea; the narrow trails get icy. All told, the park has more than 100 miles of maintained trails. Check with the Backcountry Information Center for conditions (928-638-7888). Bikes are allowed on any road that's open to car traffic. Horses are available at Apache Stables (928-638-2891), just outside the park. Skiers and snowboarders can head for Snow Bowl, near Flagstaff, for downhill or groomed cross-country skiing. One-day mule trips that go partway down the Bright Angel Trail to Plateau Point can be arranged through the park's concessionaire (888-297-2757).

BACKCOUNTRY BONUS: Two-day mule trips take you 10 miles down the Bright Angel Trail, across a suspension bridge that stradles the Colorado River, to an overnight at Phantom Ranch. The return trip is on the 7.5-mile South Kaibab Trail, which hugs the canyon wall for a steep, scenic climb. If you think that sounds like a smashing idea, you're not alone—trips can fill up more than a year in advance. You can make reservations up to 23 months ahead (888-297-2757). The legendary rapids on the 277-mile Colorado River provide your other backcountry option. At least a dozen commercial outfitters will help you tackle them on a 7- to 18-day trip. Visit the U.S. National Park Service web site for a list: www.nps.gov/grca.

MEALTIME: The Grand Canyon's most esteemed entrées grace the tables of the El Tovar dining room. It's no secret either—dinner reservations are required year-round. If you choose to eat all three meals here (not recommended if you're on a budget), you can start the day with polenta corncakes with prickly-pear pistachio butter, cornmeal-crusted trout with eggs, or any number of breakfast standards. Lunch features gourmet sandwiches, salads, and regional choices like Navajo tacos. Sack lunches with sandwiches, fruit, nuts, and a drink can be ordered on request. At dinner El Tovar pulls out all the stops. You might start with hoisin barbecue sea scallops before enjoying salmon tostada with organic greens, limes, sour cream, chile olive oil, and corn salsa. There are also inventive choices for vegetarians. The dining room has two open fireplaces with vaulted ceilings and a century's worth of historic memorabilia on the walls. Casual fare is available at cafeterias and lounges all over the South Rim.

FINE PRINT:

Pets: not allowed in the hotel, but they can board at the park kennel (928-638-0534)

Kids: bring 'em on

Credit cards: MasterCard, Visa, American Express, Discover, Diner's Club

Heads-up: rattlesnakes and scorpions (in the inner canyon), icy trails

Nearest medical: clinic inside the park

Weather: Temperatures range from the mid-80s to the low 20s at the rim. Summer highs at the river can top 100°F. Snow, icy roads and trails, and road closures are possible in the winter. Lodge elevation is at 6,800 feet.

GETTING THERE: From the airport in Tusyan, head north on Highway 64 to the park entrance. Follow the signs to the lodge. Hourly shuttles run between Grand Canyon Village and Tusyan. For rates and schedules, call 928-638-0821.

RANCHO DE LA OSA GUEST RANCH

P.O. Box 1
Tucson/Sasabe, AZ 85633
Tel: 800-872-6240; 520-823-4257
Fax: 520-823-4238
www.ranchodelaosa.com
osagal@aol.com

Closest airport: Tucson, AZ (65 miles)
Activities: horseback riding, hiking, mountain biking, mountaineering, birding, wildlife watching
Season: closed August
Guides/Instruction: horseback riding guides and instruction
Services: massage, conference facilities
Specialty: horseback riding
Accommodations: 19 rooms; capacity 42
Rates: $165–$215 per person, double occupancy, including meals and most activities; single-occupancy and weekly rates available

Grab your star charts. There's little chance of a night sky washout when the nearest city lights are an hour away. From this Sonoran Desert vantage point, tucked between a 130,000-acre wildlife preserve and a remote part of the Mexican border, you'll have unobstructed access to all the constellations you care to count.

When the sun comes up, you can turn your attention to less celestial matters, such as whether your horse will feel the added weight of your ranch-sized breakfast. Rest assured, thousands before you have cast aside such concerns before galloping happily into the hills.

AT THE LODGE: This hacienda has been hosting equine-minded guests since 1920 and boasts a colorful history that dates back long before that. Originally the outpost of a 17th-century Spanish missionary, the cantina is the oldest of the ranch's four adobe buildings. During the Mexican Revolution, Pancho Villa fired cannonballs at the dining room's stucco walls—one cannonball is still on display. Every crevice of the hacienda seems to hold a story. Stick around long enough and you'll hear them all. The individually decorated guest rooms and suites have Mexican antique fireplaces and thoughtfully chosen artwork. Each has a private entrance and a front or rear porch with mountain views. There are no phones or TVs; those in need of entertainment should try the pool or hot tub instead. The guest register reads like a who's who of 20th-century politics and the arts. This one-of-a-kind ranch is exclusive enough to satisfy past presidents and soulful enough to please poets and playwrights.

THE SPORTS: A corral full of much-loved quarter horses meets the needs of riders of all skill levels, but the wranglers allow only those guests with sufficient experience to tackle the challenging, rocky, mountain trails. Guided, two-hour sight-seeing rides are available every day. Half-day trail rides are held every Tuesday, with advanced-only loping rides on Sundays and Thursdays. Individual instruction is also available (not included in the cost of a stay). Weeklong horsemanship clinics are scheduled throughout the year. Guests who don't ride horseback can take the house mountain bikes on a 17-mile trail over mesas and buttes. Hikers and birders have 130,000 acres to explore in the Buenos Aires National Wildlife Refuge—more than 200 bird species have been counted here, and trails start just outside the ranch. Guided walks are available. Nearby peaks over 9,000 feet offer climbers a unique challenge because of the prickly, high-desert terrain. Most ascents are self-guided, but the lodge can set up a pretrip orientation.

MEALTIME: Breakfast, lunch, and dinner are served at two brightly painted Mexican antique tables by the dining-room fireplace, or outside in the courtyard. Occasionally, there's an under-the-stars cookout, too. The

menu changes daily, but the common thread is a Southwest theme. In the past, dishes have included grilled tilapia with fresh mango salsa and lemon piñon rice, grilled lamb chops with apple-pistachio relish, and grilled duck breast with raspberry chipotle sauce. The creativity carries over to dessert, with creations like sweet potato pound cake with homemade butterscotch ice cream and grape pie with vanilla sabayon sauce. Sack lunches with gourmet sandwiches, fruit, granola bars, and a treat are available on request. Special diets can be accommodated with advance notice. Food lovers should plan their visit to coincide with one of the three-day culinary weekends, scheduled several times throughout the year.

FINE PRINT:

Pets: leave 'em home

Kids: 6 and older

Credit cards: MasterCard, Visa

Heads-up: don't back into the cactus

Nearest medical: Tucson, AZ (66 miles)

Weather: Summer highs to 100°F; winter lows to 32°. There's hardly any rain, a foot to a foot and a half each year. But even with 360 days of sunshine, winter nights can be chilly. Lodge elevation is 3,600 feet.

GETTING THERE: Take Highway 86 west to Highway 286 south. Follow the signs to the lodge.

See color photo on page 150

Colorado

SHRINE MOUNTAIN INN

10th Mountain Division Hut Association
1280 Ute Avenue, Suite 21
Aspen, CO 81611
Tel: 970-925-5775
www.huts.org
huts@huts.org

Closest airport: Vail, CO (35 miles)
Activities: skiing, snowshoeing, hiking, biking, fishing
Season: year-round
Guides/Instruction: none
Services: massage
Specialty: hut-to-hut skiing
Accommodations: three cabins; capacity 36
Rates: $25–$39 per person

To prepare its troops for high-altitude combat in Europe, the U.S. War Department set up an army training facility in the Colorado Rockies in the early 1940s. Tenth Mountain Division veteran Fritz Benedict returned to those mountains 40 years later to honor his fallen peers by building backcountry ski huts in their name. With the help of Aspen-area ski buffs, Benedict created a network between Vail and Aspen that contains 15 rustic cabins, all of which are operated by the nonprofit Tenth Mountain Division Hut Association.

Shrine Mountain Inn's three huts are the most accessible of the bunch, located less than 3 miles from the interstate in the mountains near West Ten Mile Creek. Intermediate ski touring trails connect this spot to the other huts that run from Vail to Aspen. For skiers, completing the circuit is a goal akin to hiking the Appalachian Trail or summiting Mount McKinley. But there's certainly no shame in visiting as a weekender.

AT THE LODGE: The three basic but comfortable cabins were built from great big logs of Colorado pine. Jay's is the closest to the highway. Chuck's is 400 feet down the trail and is divided into two separate units, upstairs and downstairs (Chuck's Up and Chuck's Down). Walter's sits 1,200 feet up the ridge, with unbeatable views of the surrounding fourteeners. All three have generator-powered electricity, antique woodstoves, hot and cold water, a kitchen, and two bathrooms with showers or claw-foot tubs. The bedrooms have one to five beds each. There are no phones or televisions; your best bet for evening entertainment is enjoying a group sweat in the sauna situated between Chuck's and Jay's. Compared to your standard military barracks, these huts may seem like Buckingham Palace, but there's an element of do-it-yourself-ness involved: Guests must pack in towels and bedding (or rent a sleeping bag and liner for $10) and prepare their own meals.

THE SPORTS: Cross-country skiing is the main attraction, with trails (not groomed) starting at the front door. Those not doing the hut-to-hut circuit can ski to Shrine Ridge for incredible high-altitude views within day-trip distance. The huts are just 2 miles from the 132,906-acre Eagles Nest Wilderness Area and Gore Range, so hikers and snowshoers need not fear for lack of terrain. Mountain bikers can take advantage of logging roads and the famous singletrack Commando Run between Redcliff and Vail. Road cyclists can pedal 2.7

miles to the paved bike path that parallels scenic Interstate 70 for hours. No gear or instruction is available on-site, but arrangements to rent ski equipment can be made through Paragon Guides (970-925-5775), which offers llama treks as well.

BACKCOUNTRY BONUS: The hut-system ethic is do-it-yourself, with signed trails and detailed maps making that as feasible as possible. From Shrine Mountain Inn, it's 6.8 miles to Fowler/Hilliard Hut. You can make a long overnight loop by continuing to Hornsilver Mountain and turning east on the road that parallels Turkey Creek to the back side of Shrine Pass. For topographical maps that detail the trails and hut sites all the way to Aspen, contact Tenth Mountain (970-925-5775; www.huts.org). If you're not quite ready to go it alone, they can arrange for a guide.

MEALTIME: Your dining options are as follows: pack it in or forage for berries. A motivated angler could probably draw some snack-sized brookies out of West Ten Mile Creek, but it's not a good idea to count on fish for sustenance. Each of the three huts has a kitchen with a propane stove and oven. Keep in mind that you'll be sharing kitchen space with 11 hungry hut-mates. Slovenliness and utensil hogging are not appreciated.

FINE PRINT:
Pets: leave 'em home
Kids: bring 'em on
Credit cards: MasterCard, Visa
Heads-up: mosquitoes can be a problem in mid-July
Nearest medical: Vail, CO (22 miles)
Weather: Summers are cool; winters are as chilly as you'd expect them to be at 11,200 feet. Annual snowfall usually tops 300 inches.

GETTING THERE: Take Interstate 70 from the airport to the Rest Area at the top of Vail Pass. In winter, park there and ski 3 miles to the inn. In summer, you can drive the 3 miles up Shrine Pass Road. Turn left at the outhouse at the top of the pass.

See color photo on page 151

SKYLINE GUEST RANCH

7214 Highway 145
Telluride, CO 81435
Tel: 888-754-1126; 970-728-3757
www.skylineguestranch.com
info@ skylineguestranch.com

Closest airport: Telluride, CO (8 miles)
Activities: horseback riding, fishing, hiking, mountain and road biking, cross-country and downhill skiing, snowboarding, snowshoeing, climbing, mountaineering, hot-air ballooning, rafting, wildlife watching
Season: June through September; December through April
Guides/Instruction: fishing guides, horseback riding instruction
Services: spa, conference facilities
Specialties: mountaineering and horseback riding
Accommodations: 10 rooms and six cabins; capacity 40
Rates: $69–$257 per person, including breakfast (winter) or all meals (summer), activities, airport transportation; three-day minimum in summer

So often it's the owners who set the tone for a lodge experience. Skyline's Farny family is no exception. Whether it's Dave jamming on his accordion, or Sherry starting a campfire sing-along, the mood here is nothing short of giddy. Of course, the Farnys attribute that feeling to the healthy mountain air, not their energetic style of hosting. At 9,600 feet, it's possible that lowland visitors could suffer from oxygen depletion, but it's more likely that the ear-to-ear grins are brought on by the day's climb, trail ride, snowball fight, or balloon flight, and the promise of more adventure to come.

AT THE LODGE: The main lodge was built of roughhewn logs in the early 1950s. In addition to a dining room and library, it has a separate wing for the dorm-sized guest rooms, each of which has a private bath and just enough room for two (no matter, you'll only come here to sleep). The beds are made of logs and covered with thick down comforters. The beautiful log and plank cabins accommodate up to eight guests, and were designed for a gathering of family and friends. Some have fireplaces or potbelly stoves. All have full kitchens or kitchenettes and views of the surrounding peaks. Guests have access to an outdoor hot tub and laundry facilities. The Farnys focus on keeping the environment as pristine as it was when they bought the property in 1968. They've since deeded the land to The Nature Conservancy.

THE SPORTS: The Farnys used to run a mountaineering school, and bagging peaks is still a favorite diversion. They'll happily lead ambitious guests to the top of one of the five nearby 14-footers. Rock and ice climbing excursions are also available. Horseback riding is the Farnys' second specialty. Wranglers lead two-hour-minimum trail rides far into the mountains, paying close attention to individual skill levels and preferences. Anglers can fly-fish in the ranch's three trout-stocked ponds, as well as in nearby lakes and rivers. Hikers and mountain bikers can access hundreds of miles of trails in the surrounding national forest and wilderness areas. Cyclists can push themselves up hilly mountain passes. Paddlers will find Class IV rapids on the Gunnison River, 90 minutes away. In the winter, there's skating and sledding on-site, and the lodge staff will drive you to local ski areas for downhill skiing, snowboarding, and cross-country skiing—Telluride Ski Resort is 10 minutes away. Guests can arrange backcountry ski trips as well. If the local terrain just isn't enough to keep you busy, four national parks are within a few hours' drive.

BACKCOUNTRY BONUS: In the summertime, wranglers lead guests on overnight horse packing trips. You'll ride over high-mountain passes and through elk-inhabited meadows and sleep in a rustic, backcountry cabin.

Meals, gear, and guides are all included. Costs vary according to distance and destination.

MEALTIME: Except for the warm-weather cookouts and trail picnics, meals are served in the main lodge dining room. Breakfasts are hearty and uncomplicated. There's a sack-lunch buffet each morning, so you can choose from an assortment of sandwich ingredients and snacks. Dinners are surprisingly gourmet, with a trained chef serving fresh, regional fare. You might start with caribou tartare or a five-onion tart with wild mushroom clove syrup. Your entrée might be pomegranate- and juniper-glazed venison chop with morel-ribboned grits and braised veggies, or seared black bass with shellfish truffle butter sauce. Vegetarian options are always available. Beer and wine are included in the summer meal plan only; winter guests: bring your own.

FINE PRINT:
Pets: leave 'em home
Kids: bring 'em on
Credit cards: MasterCard, Visa, American Express
Nearest medical: Telluride, CO (8 miles)
Weather: Temperatures range from 10 below to 80 above. There's less than a foot of annual rainfall, but an average 300 inches of snow. Lodge elevation is 9,600 feet.

GETTING THERE: Head south on Highway 145 to the ranch. Airport transportation is provided.

See color photos on pages 151 and 152

TWIN LAKES NORDIC INN

6435 Highway 82
Twin Lakes, CO 81251
Tel: 800-626-7812; 719-486-1830
www.twinlakesnordicinn.com
nordicinn@chaffee.net

Closest airport: Denver, CO (two hours)
Activities: backcountry and cross-country skiing, snowshoeing, hiking, climbing, mountaineering, mountain and road biking, fishing, kayaking, canoeing, rafting
Season: year-round
Guides/Instruction: backcountry skiing guides
Services: conference facilities
Specialty: backcountry skiing
Accommodations: 14 rooms, one apartment; capacity 40
Rates: \$58–\$88 per room, double occupancy, including breakfast

The mountain road from Twin Lakes to Aspen is only 38 miles long, but nothing could feel farther from Aspen's high-priced glitz than this sleepy historic town. Once a bustling stagecoach stop on the route from Leadville (when the 60-mile journey took a week or more), Twin Lakes now has a winter population of 20. People come here mostly for the quiet.

What is now the Twin Lakes Nordic Inn opened as the Twin Peaks Hotel in 1879. It had a brief stint as a brothel in its early days. Throughout the 1900s, a steady stream of innkeepers struggled to keep it afloat, but it wasn't until the current owners dubbed it "Nordic" in 1987 that the skiers started pouring in. Funky as ever, it has been a popular portal to the backcountry ever since.

AT THE LODGE: In any other setting, window shades with pine tree cutouts might qualify as cheesy; but here, against the backdrop of a snowy Mount Elbert, the European ski hut motif fits right in. The classic A-frame lodge, a registered national historic structure, was built of dark stained logs that are now adorned with Nordic skis. Inside, the dining-room and game-room walls are lined with books—at last count, 7,500 of them. The common areas have fireplaces, a phone, and a TV. The rooms are simple, each varying in size and style. Most distinctive is Bessie's, named for the prostitute who is said to have worked there in the late 1880s. All rooms have feather beds, antiques, and views of the surrounding forest. Four rooms have private baths. An on-site apartment rents for $125 per night and sleeps a maximum of five; a two-night minimum stay is required.

THE SPORTS: From November 1 through May 15, a long stretch of Independence Pass starting 12 miles west of the lodge closes to traffic; this closure makes available a vast amount of backcountry skiing terrain. From the lodge, you also have easy access to a skiable stretch of the Colorado Trail, which runs all the way from Denver to Durango. Gear is available in Leadville. And there's just as much to do here when the snow melts. Hikers, bikers, and horseback riders can take the 3-mile path along the south shore of Twin Lakes to the Interlaken ghost town, to explore the shell of another 1879 lodge that didn't fare quite so well as the Nordic. Most of the hiking trails in the surrounding San Isabel National Forest are open to mountain bikers. Great single-track rides start at the Twin Lakes dam. Call the Greater Leadville Chamber of Commerce for detailed maps (719-486-3900). When Independence Pass isn't frozen, cyclists can take it all the way to Aspen. Topping out at 12,095 feet, it's the highest paved road in the country. For climbers set on bagging Mount Elbert, Colorado's tallest peak at 14,433 feet, the inn makes a perfect base camp. Other area fourteeners with nearby trailheads include Mount Massive, La Plata Peak, Oxford, Belford, Missouri, Princeton, Yale, Harvard, and Columbia. There are topographical maps (for looking, not taking) in the lodge's sitting room. A quick rundown of other area activities: paddling on the lakes (rentals available), fly-fishing for trout (guides in town), and early-summer rafting on the Arkansas River (outfitters nearby).

MEALTIME: A no-frills breakfast is included for all overnight guests. Basic box lunches (sandwich, fruit, dessert) can be ordered to take on the trail. The dining room's mostly German dinner menu features entrées that are authentic, if not quite gourmet. The apple strudel and coffee are exceptional.

FINE PRINT:
Pets: welcome
Kids: bring 'em on
Credit cards: all major cards
Nearest medical: Leadville, CO (21 miles)
Weather: In winter, nighttime temperatures often dip far below zero. The hottest summer day rarely tops 75°F. Average yearly snowfall is 200 inches. The lodge is 9,225 feet.

GETTING THERE: From Denver, take Interstate 70 west and exit at Copper Mountain. Take Highway 91 to Leadville, then Highway 24 south 15 miles. Turn left (west) onto Highway 82 and drive 6 miles to the village.

New Mexico

BEAR MOUNTAIN LODGE

P.O. Box 1163
Silver City, NM 88062
Tel: 877-620-2327; 505-538-5204
Fax: 505-534-1827
www.bearmountainlodge.com
innkeeper@bearmountainlodge.com

Closest airport: El Paso, TX (160 miles)
Activities: birding, hiking, road biking, fishing, horseback riding
Season: year-round
Guides/Instruction: birding and hiking guides, on-site naturalists
Services: conference facilities (limited)
Specialty: birding
Accommodations: 11 rooms; capacity 33
Rates: $115–$200 per room, double occupancy, including breakfast

When the former owner of what was then the Bear Mountain Guest Ranch donated the property to The Nature Conservancy in 1995, she did so with one caveat: that it remain open to the bird-loving public. Not only did the group comply, they extended her mission by staffing the lodge with wildlife experts who can tell a cliff swallow from a purple martin in a single, fleeting glance. To explore this wilderness in the presence of these experts gives nature a new dimension—it's one thing to be overwhelmed by beauty, another entirely to be able to admire it by name.

AT THE LODGE: Previously a boys' school, a country club, a cougar hunting lodge, and a guest ranch, the 1928 hacienda-style building underwent significant renovations in 1999 and reopened as a wilderness lodge in 2001. Guest rooms are spread among three buildings, each of which has hardwood floors throughout. All rooms have balconies (upstairs) or porches (downstairs) with views of the property's 20 bird feeders. Some of the large, private bathrooms have whirlpool tubs and vintage ceramic block tile. Upstairs rooms have sleeper sofas. There are phones, but no TVs. The Great Room's hand-hewn beams, hand-carved pine staircase, and stone fireplaces were added during the face-lift. Much of the Mission-style furniture was commissioned from a local woodworking shop that used small trees cut during a forest management project.

THE SPORTS: Pack your binoculars—more than 300 bird species migrate through the conservancy's nearby Gila Riparian Preserve. Without leaving the property you've got a great chance of spotting a flock of Mexican jays or a mountain chickadee, which you'll know by its trademark hiss. The area's most conspicuous mammal is the javelina, a wild mountain pig with poor eyesight and a bad attitude. Naturalists lead guided hikes and birding, photography, art, and archaeology workshops throughout the year. Six short hiking trails run through the lodge's 178 acres, which is bordered by 3.3 million acres of Gila National Forest and another 750,000 acres of Gila

Wilderness, the nation's first designated wilderness area. The trails run from 4,000 to 11,000 feet in elevation over varied terrain. The Continental Divide Trail is within walking distance from the lodge. Mountain bikers can expect 200-plus miles of mostly intermediate and advanced singletrack and fire roads lined with alligator juniper, piñon pine, and gray oak. Cyclists can ride the course of the annual Tour of Gila Bicycle Race, a rolling, mountainous route on lightly trafficked roads. Anglers can fly-fish for trout in the wilderness area's 250 miles of streams. There's also a horseback outfitter nearby. Bring your own gear for all of the above.

MEALTIME: In addition to the home-style standard flapjacks and eggs, the morning menu features tasty Spanish tortillas with roasted red pepper almond sauce, quiche, and fresh baked goods. Breakfast is the only meal included in a stay, but lunch and dinner are available for $8.50 and $12. The sack lunches contain a sandwich, baby carrots, chips, and homemade cookies, thoughtfully packed with a frozen bottle of water so the carrots keep their crunch. Dinner starts with an antipasto plate, soup, salad, and bread. Your entrée could be beef kabobs with couscous, chicken tacos with black beans, baked polenta with eggplant and grilled Italian sausage, or a veggie stir-fry and pork tenderloin. Vegetarian dishes are always available. The dining room, which is open to the kitchen, has a guest library with overstuffed chairs, perfect for nursing an overstuffed belly. For between-meal munchies, you can grab fresh fruit and homemade cookies from the kitchen at all hours, or drive 3 miles to a restaurant in Silver City.

FINE PRINT:
Pets: leave 'em home
Kids: 10 and older
Credit cards: MasterCard, Visa, American Express
Nearest medical: Silver City, NM (3 miles)
Weather: Summer highs in the upper 80s, winter lows in the mid-20s. The area gets about 17 inches of rain and 11 inches of snow each year. Monsoon season (hot weather, heavy but brief afternoon downpours) runs from July through August. Lodge elevation is 6,200 feet.

GETTING THERE: Take Highway 85 north to Interstate 10 west. At Deming, New Mexico, exit to Highway 180 north. In Silver City, keep to the right at Mr. Ed's Do-It Center and turn right onto Alabama Street, which becomes Cottage San Road. Drive 2.8 miles and turn left at the BEAR MOUNTAIN LODGE sign.

See color photo on page 152

HACIENDA DEL CEREZO

100 Camino del Cerezo
Santa Fe, NM 87501
Tel: 888-982-8001; 505-982-8000
Fax: 505-983-7162
www.haciendadelcerezo.com
hacienda@rt66.com

Closest airport: Santa Fe, NM (12 miles)
Activities: horseback riding, hiking, mountain biking, rafting, kayaking, fishing, downhill skiing, snowboarding, snowshoeing
Season: year-round
Guides/Instruction: horseback riding guides
Services: massage, conference facilities (limited)
Specialty: horseback riding
Accommodations: 10 suites; capacity 20
Rates: $600, double occupancy, all-inclusive (meals, activities, wine); two-night minimum

Stephen Kirschenbaum doesn't let just anyone ride his prized Arabians. The owner of this exclusive, high-desert hideaway would rather risk disappointing a guest than subject his purebred babies to an inexperienced rider. But if you've put in enough trail time to know your way around a saddle, prepare to be impressed by a peerless trip through the arroyos to the Rio Grande.

In all other respects, the guests make the rules. They usually go something like this: Treat me as if the continued availability of oxygen depends on my absolute happiness; feed me so well that I burst the seams of my dungarees at every meal; point me toward a hiking trail that'll make me redefine my notion of heaven; and at all other times, leave me alone to enjoy this place in peace.

AT THE LODGE: At some point on the 5-mile drive down the unpaved road to the hacienda, you're bound to wonder if you somehow missed a turn. Worry not, it's a common reaction to the quick transition from Santa Fe pavement to middle-of-nowhere dirt. Though this place is just 12 miles outside the city, when you're standing on its grounds, you see nothing but mountains. Every room has a view across the 336-acre property to the Sangre de Cristo or Jemez range, but you're still within driving distance from the opera. Each suite has its own motif, from Crucitas (decorated with the crosses symbolic of colonial Santa Fe) to Sombrero (an homage to vaquero culture). Dark wood beams, some with intricate carvings, run across the ceilings. Rooms are warmed by custom-built, wood-burning kiva fireplaces and radiant heating underfoot. Every suite has an enclosed, private patio, a separate sitting area with satellite TV, a closet big enough to sleep in, and a large bathroom with black-walnut vanities, a two-person whirlpool tub, etched shower glass, and a bidet. The lodge itself is a pueblo-style adobe with a black-bottom infinity pool positioned to reflect every detail of the sunset. True to its architectural heritage, the building's three sides surround a central courtyard adorned with aspens, piñons, and fruit trees. The Hacienda is Southwest elegance at its finest.

THE SPORTS: The Hacienda del Cerezo stable has its own wrangler to lead qualified riders on a variety of desert trails. A detailed lineage of the resident mares is happily furnished on request. Hikers have hundreds of miles to choose from in the contiguous 150,000 acres of open land and the mountains beyond. Mountain bikers have access to more singletrack than most city dwellers dare to dream about. Rent a bike in town and get directions to the Windsor Trail, which runs as far as you can ride. From early spring through fall, you can raft or kayak a Class IV stretch of the Rio Grande known locally as The Box. Outfitters between Santa Fe and Taos have all the gear and guidance you may need. Aspiring anglers can find fly-fishing guides nearby. Downhill skiers and snowboarders can get to the Santa Fe Ski Area in 40 minutes, Taos in 90. What-

ever activity you choose to pursue, the folks at the Hacienda will help you make it happen.

MEALTIME: Ladies and gentlemen are asked to kindly remove their cowboy hats before dinner. Otherwise, there's no dress code for the candlelit dinners in the Great Room, where an evening gown wouldn't look at all out of place. The china is a replica of a 1930s Santa Fe Railway design, with 1937 "First Love" silverware to match. But the food consistently outmatches the tabletop finery every single time. The four-star chef might start you off with a Stilton and goat cheese beignet with warm apple compote and toasted walnuts, before serving grilled swordfish steak over saffron risotto with tapenade. Dessert could be a zinfandel poached pear tartlet or warm chocolate molten cake with frozen white chocolate mousse and mango puree. Lunches are served on the stone terrace overlooking a garden or on your private patio. Trail lunches are also available, with a meat wrap, pasta or couscous, salad, fruit, cheese, cookies or cake, candy, bottled water, juice, and wine. If you catch any fish while you're out, bring it back to be cleaned and cooked for you. Every dietary specification can be met on request.

FINE PRINT:

Pets: leave 'em home

Kids: bring 'em on

Credit cards: American Express

Nearest medical: Santa Fe, NM (14 miles)

Weather: Summer days can reach 95°F; winter nights can drop to 10°. Lodge elevation is 6,542 feet.

GETTING THERE: Take Airport Road to NM 599, exit Camino La Tierra to Paseo La Tierra to Horcado Road to Camino de Cerezo.

See color photo on page 153

KOKOPELLI'S CAVE BED-AND-BREAKFAST

3204 Crestridge Drive
Farmington, NM 87401
Tel: 505-325-7855
Fax: 505-325-9671
kokoscave@hotmail.com

Closest airports: Farmington, NM (3 miles), and Durango, CO (one hour)
Activities: hiking, mountain biking, fishing, downhill skiing, snowboarding, wildlife watching
Season: March through November
Guides/Instruction: on-site geologist
Services: conference facilities (limited)
Accommodations: one cave; capacity six
Rates: $220 per room, double occupancy, including continental breakfast

This one-of-a-kind cave hotel was blasted out of the New Mexico sandstone by owner Bruce Black in 1980. But before you sound the gimmick alarm, you should know that the retired geologist's original intent was to create an underground office where he could be surrounded by his stratified subjects. It wasn't until years later, when he saw his rock-walled hovel dressed up with plush carpeting, stylish furniture, and indoor plumbing that he thought, *Hey, this would make a nifty bed-and-breakfast.*

Kokopelli's has been functioning as such since 1997, succeeding on much more than the "cool factor" of sleeping in a cave that is 70 feet underground. It's comfortable enough to have earned a loyal following without its quirky location. And a quick peek out the cliff-side bedroom window reveals its major geographic appeal—miles and miles of Four Corners–area wilderness that stretch as far as you can see.

AT THE LODGE: The 1,650-square-foot subterranean luxury apartment has every convenience a modern cave dweller could demand—Jacuzzi tub, waterfall shower, fireplace, telephone, TV/VCR. Rough, natural sandstone (with petrified wood and plant fragments) forms the walls and ceiling. Thick carpeting covers the floors. The open bedroom, living room, kitchen, and den are divided by a large central pillar. Sliding glass doors in the 8-by-8-foot entryway and the bedroom open to small balconies that jut out from a cliff face that drops 250 feet to the La Plata River. The in-house views span three states, with the Shiprock monument visible to the west, Arizona's Carrizo Mountains just beyond, and Colorado's San Juan range to the north. Climb to the cliff tops for panoramic vistas of the entire Four Corners region.

THE SPORTS: Even if you do nothing but watch caveman-themed videos while you're here, be sure to take a walk atop the cliffs at sunset. Long shadows stretch from the tall rock formations across the wide, dusk-tinged desert, and silver foxes dart between the piñon and juniper trees as the sandstone turns blazing shades of orange and red before all the sky goes black. That sight alone, all 360 degrees of it, is worth the trip. For daylight hours, there are 400 acres of hiking and mountain biking terrain in the immediate area, and Durango, Colorado (where just about every parked car has a high-end bike on its rack), isn't far away. Skiers and snowboarders can reach the Purgatory slopes in about 90 minutes. In the Southwest few waters can top the San Juan River for fly-fishing, and trout-stocked Jackson Lake is a couple of miles from the cave. Gear and guides are available in Farmington. Anyone interested in geology should ask for a rock-by-rock tour of the cave. The Ojo Alamo sandstone dates back about 65 million years, and if you know what you're looking for, you can follow the cross beds and fluvial current indicators all the way around the central pillar.

MEALTIME: The cave kitchen is stocked with cookware and a few do-it-yourself, continental breakfast basics and snacks: cereal, oatmeal, milk, juice, hot beverages, fruit, bread, and popcorn. There's a gas grill outside and a microwave oven, fridge, and stove inside. Grocery stores and restaurants are nearby in Farmington. If you make arrangements in advance, catering is also available.

FINE PRINT:
Pets: leave 'em home
Kids: 12 and older
Credit cards: MasterCard, Visa, American Express
Nearest medical: Farmington, NM (3 miles)
Weather: Summer highs can top 90°F; winter lows dip just below 20°F. The area gets 7 to 10 inches of precipitation each year. Lodge elevation is 5,500 feet.

GETTING THERE: From Durango, Colorado, take Highway 550 south to Highway 516. In Farmington, turn right onto 30th Street and right again onto Crestridge Drive. You'll check in at the manager's house (3204 Crestridge Drive). She'll guide you the last few miles to the parking area. The short jaunt to the cave involves a 100-foot vertical descent on a sandstone trail, lots of stairs, and a climb up a three-step wooden ladder. Pack accordingly. Airport transportation from Farmington is free. From Durango, the cost is $50.

Utah

CAMELOT ADVENTURE LODGE

P.O. Box 621
Moab, UT 84532
Tel: 435-260-1783
www.camelotlodge.com
Camelot@camelotlodge.com

Closest airport: Grand Junction, CO (3.5 hours)
Activities: camel trekking, mountain biking, hiking, rafting
Season: year-round
Guides/Instruction: camel trekking, hiking, and boating guides; on-site naturalist
Services: none
Accommodations: five rooms; capacity 10
Rates: $110 per person, double occupancy, including meals

When angry, camels have been known to regurgitate half-digested food globs midgrowl. But they are otherwise entirely lovable creatures, insist Terry and Marcee Moore, who operate the only camel trekking business in North America at their Camelot Adventure Lodge. This part of Utah was home to many a roaming dromedary thousands of years ago, and the Moores have been reintroducing the species to the area around the lodge since the spring of 2000.

But Camelot isn't limited to one-humped adventures. The rustic lodge is sandwiched between red rock bluffs and the Colorado River, 18 rugged miles from town, in prime hiking and mountain biking country. From the vantage point of the dining-room window, all you see is deep pink sticky sandstone. It's a sweeping view of the classic Southwest landscape that has drawn fat-tire fanatics for decades.

AT THE LODGE: The red stucco, adobe-style lodge blends so well with the surroundings that it's hard to spot it from the road. Since there's no shortage of sunshine here, the owners took full advantage by installing a solar power system when the lodge was completed in 2000. There's a backup generator, but energy conservation is still a priority (note to the vain: no electric styling products, please). Rooms are subtly Southwest-style suites with private bathrooms and individual access to a shared deck. Three rooms have queen beds; the others have two twins. There's no television, but all rooms have views of the river or 1,000-foot-tall red buttes. The house phone is a cellular attached to a big antenna on the roof. Your cell phone won't work here.

THE SPORTS: The lodge is surrounded by 30,000 acres of public parkland that includes Dead Horse Point State Park and Canyonlands National Park. Mountain bikers can access slickrock just outside the lodge. The trails are moderate to challenging, but there's ample bumpy-road riding for anyone who is just getting used to knobby tires. There are no rentals here; bring your own bike or rent at one of the many bike shops in Moab for about $35 a day. On-site guides take guests hiking on "secret" trails that run through slot canyons and washes, on sandstone, over sand dunes, and along the banks of the Colorado

River. Expect to see petroglyphs and Anasazi ruins. One of the favorite hikes is the six-hour Claret Cup Valley trail, which starts at the lodge and follows an abandoned horse trail that drops several hundred feet before connecting to a sheep trail along the river. The name comes from the claret cup cactus, which blooms blood red in the springtime. For $61, guests can take a jet boat trip to Dead Horse Point State Park for a hike to the petrified trees. Last, but certainly not least, there's camel trekking. A two- to four-hour desert trek costs $35 per person, per hour.

BACKCOUNTRY BONUS: Multiday raft trips down the Colorado River put in just outside the lodge. The minimum is a three-day trip down Cataract Canyon, ending with a scenic flight from the takeout to Moab, for $750 per person (all-inclusive). Make reservations through the lodge.

MEALTIME: Marcee's home-style breakfasts and dinners are hearty and made from scratch. In the morning, she might serve frittatas and pumpkin bread with cantaloupe, strawberries, and organic coffee. The dinner menu may feature Cornish game hens, grilled steaks, or baby back ribs served with a mandarin spinach salad, and homemade fruit pie. All special meal requirements (vegetarian, nondairy, food allergies) can be accommodated with advance notice. Breakfast and dinner are served at the dining-room farm table next to a picture window overlooking the Colorado River; you'll share your meal with the camel wranglers and other guests. Sack lunches include a sandwich, fruit, veggies, a sports bar, cookies, soda, chips, and whatever else you request.

FINE PRINT:

Pets: leave 'em home
Kids: bring 'em on
Credit cards: none
Heads-up: summer temperatures frequently top 100°F
Nearest medical: Moab, UT (18 miles)
Weather: Spring and fall have moderate weather, 40s to

70s, with occasional sprinkles. Winters are mild (rarely below 20°F), with very little snow; but summers can be miserably hot. Lodge elevation is 4,000 feet.

GETTING THERE: From Moab, it's a 90-minute drive on the 18-mile dirt road that transits Hurrah Pass. If you don't have a four-wheel-drive vehicle, transportation arrangements can be made through the lodge.

See color photo on page 153

WEST: Alaska

BIRCH POND LODGE

P.O. Box 370
Willow, AK 99688
Tel: 907-495-3000
Fax: 907-495-7663
www.birchpondlodge.com
birchpnd@pobox.alaska.net

Closest airport: Anchorage, AK (75 miles by road, 35 miles by floatplane)
Activities: hiking, canoeing, kayaking, cross-country skiing, snowshoeing, ice skating, fishing, flight-seeing, rafting, mountaineering, dogsledding, wildlife watching
Season: closed mid-April through mid-May
Guides/Instruction: paddling, hiking, and cross-country skiing guides and instruction
Services: none
Accommodations: two cabins, one lodge suite; capacity 10
Rates: $220 per person, double occupancy, including meals and activities; two-day minimum

There are eco-lodges, and then there are *eco-lodges.* The former uses the label as a trendy euphemism for bare-bones rustic. The latter goes to great lengths to minimize the impact of its existence without ignoring comfort or quality. Birch Pond Lodge is the real deal, from its building materials (including Alaskan white spruce trees that were killed by beetles and would have been left as kindling for the next big forest fire) to its philosophy of human-powered everything (not just hiking, paddling, and other nonmotorized sports, but also hand-dug foundations and hand-cranked ice cream).

To watch owner Bill Royce flash a huge grin as he taps a birch for syrup is to realize he's not in this just for the trees. The part-time Anchorage attorney gets downright giddy when he's showing off his 100-acre project, where creeks trickle into birch- and spruce-rimmed lakes, and thickly insulated cabins hold heat like giant thermoses. Protecting this place is an exercise in happiness. Staying here is, too.

AT THE LODGE: Royce built the pine-paneled Loon Cabin in 1988 as his own private skiing retreat. Its windows frame views of Rainbow Lake and the Talkeetna Mountains. Thick insulation and a woodburning stove keep it cozy throughout the harsh winters. Sized for two, the cabin has a private deck with built-in seats, a hammock, a ski rack, a propane-heated outdoor shower, and a sauna. The outhouse is gussied-up with propane heating, a candelabra, and a lakeview window. The hexagonal, two-person Beaver Lodge Cabin was built from beetle-killed birch logs in 2001. It showcases eco-technology's finest amenities: on-demand hot water and a composting toilet. Three large windows and a cedar deck offer views of Mount Susitna, 28 miles away. The 1993 main lodge has a second-floor suite designed for families. Its 14-foot cathedral ceilings make the 700-square-foot space feel even bigger. A full bath is downstairs. The main lodge also houses a library stocked with Alaskan natural and cultural history books.

Solar power is used whenever possible, supplemented with a generator that charges 12-volt batteries. A wind-powered system and additional solar panels are in the works.

THE SPORTS: With 22,000-acre Alaska State Park adjacent to the property, you won't run out of playtime terrain. In summer, paddle lake-to-lake on the lodge's canoes and kayaks; guides give informal instruction before leading you through the best of the region's 130 lakes. Three miles of on-site hiking trails include a short path to a hilltop view of Mount McKinley, 100 miles to the north. You can also head into the neighboring Talkeetna Mountains, where guides lead alpine hikes to mountain ridges and old gold mining sites. Most of the hiking here is cross-country, with significant altitude gains; but the terrain isn't technical. You'll visit raptor nesting areas and may spot deer, bear, lynx, marmots, and moose. The lodge can connect you with local outfitters who offer guided salmon and trout fishing, river rafting, mountaineering, and flight-seeing, which can include a glacier landing on Denali. In winter, the lodge's hiking trails are groomed for cross-country skiing, with an additional 10 miles of ungroomed trails for skiing and snowshoeing. One section of Birch Pond is cleared for ice skating and pickup hockey. Guides also lead skiing trips across the lakes and into the state park for views of the Northern Lights. Dogsledding trips are available through a local guide who has Iditarod experience. Since the lodge is small, all activities can be customized to suit the preferences of individual guests.

BACKCOUNTRY BONUS: The lodge offers two- to three-day canoe or kayak trips down a 25-mile, Class I stretch of the Little Susitna River. You'll portage and paddle through 18 Alaska State Park lakes before taking out at the lodge. Another possible add-on is a multiday Talkeetna alpine backpacking trip. With hundreds of miles of trails that run to old gold mines, high-mountain lakes, and tarns, the route can be tailored to your interests. Guides, tents, cookware, and food are provided. Bring your own boots, backpack, and sleeping bag.

MEALTIME: When they say the food is regional, they're not just talking homegrown produce. Local ingredients include the reindeer sausage served with your eggs and the just-caught salmon at dinner. Other breakfast specials are sourdough-beer pancakes, gourmet frittatas, and Belgian waffles with real whipped cream. A light breakfast of fresh baked breads, fruit, juice, and yogurt can be delivered to your cabin on request. Lunch is usually a hearty soup, salad, and sandwich, with homemade chocolate chip cookies (box lunch versions are also available). Though catch-and-release fishing is encouraged on the property's ponds, if you bring back a fresh catch, the staff will gladly clean and cook it. After hors d'oeuvres, dinner is served around a large pine table in the main lodge. There's a heavy emphasis on Alaskan salmon and produce from the Matanuska Valley. All dietary preferences can be accommodated, but you'll be discouraged from honoring any eating restrictions that don't allow for homemade ice cream.

FINE PRINT:
Pets: leave 'em home
Kids: no minimum age, but activities are geared toward grown-ups
Credit cards: MasterCard, Visa, American Express
Heads-up: bears, moose, mosquitoes (summer), extreme terrain
Nearest medical: Willow, AK (5 miles)
Weather: Summer temperatures average 50° to 75°F, with winter temperatures ranging from 30 above to 30 below. The area gets about 15 inches of yearly rain and 3 to 4 feet of snow. Lodge elevation is 200 feet.

GETTING THERE: Take Glenn Highway north 35 miles to the junction with Parks Highway. Take Parks Highway 40 miles to the town of Willow. You'll be met there by Birch Pond staff, who will take you the remaining 5 miles to the lodge. Ground transportation costs $50. Floatplane transportation costs $100 per person (two-person minimum).

See color photo on page 154

KENAI BACKCOUNTRY LODGE

P.O. Box 389
Girdwood, AK 99587
Tel: 800-334-8730; 907-783-2928
Fax: 907-783-2130
www.alaskawildland.com
info@alaskawildland.com

Closest airport: Kenai, AK (35 miles)
Activities: hiking, kayaking, rafting, wildlife watching
Season: June 1 through late September
Guides/Instruction: hiking and kayaking guides, resident naturalists
Services: none
Accommodations: six tent cabins, two log cabins; capacity 16
Rates: $825 for two nights, $1,250 for three nights, per person, double occupancy, all-inclusive (meals, guided hiking/kayaking, airport transportation); 10 percent of profits is donated to local conservation groups

A trip to Kenai Backcountry Lodge starts with a six-hour float trip on the Kenai River, which spits you out onto glacier-fed Skilak Lake. There you're surrounded by the bear/caribou/wolf/moose-inhabited Kenai National Wildlife Refuge. A little bit of paddling brings you to the south shore of the lake, where you pull up to the dock at the Kenai Backcountry Lodge—finally. It takes a full day on the water to reach the lodge.

After that a rest may be in order, and home-

made cookies, perhaps, and a contemplative sit in the wood-fired sauna with its view of the western sky. If you're aware that this eco-conscious operation has drawn applause from greenies across the continent, it won't be because you've sacrificed any comfort for the cause. A stay at Kenai Backcountry Lodge is an act of hands-off heroism; you can support your friends the tree huggers without enduring any nasty bark scratches yourself.

AT THE LODGE: The Sitka spruce main lodge was built in the 1930s to house hunters, who have long since moved on to rifle-friendly regions. The traditional, wood-heated log structure has a cathedral ceiling and a lofted, west-facing sitting area that overlooks the mountains. An on-site hydroelectric generator powers the main building. Guests stay in canvas, Yukon-style platform tent cabins or rustic log cabins, both of which have wall heaters, propane lights, sliding glass doors, handmade log furniture, and thick down comforters. All rooms have views of the lake. None have phones, televisions, or bathrooms—hot showers and flush toilets are located in a shared bathhouse. The sauna sits within easy cold-plunge distance of the lake, which doubles as a parking lot of sorts, since the lodge can be accessed only by boat.

THE SPORTS: When Franklin Roosevelt set aside the 1.9 million acres surrounding the lodge as a moose preserve, all sorts of lucky critters got to piggyback on the deal. The area now supports a healthy population of black and brown bears, caribou, wolves, wolverines, bald eagles, and ravens (to name a few), and you're bound to spot a few of them on the Cottonwood Creek Trail that starts just outside the lodge. The path parallels the creek for a 2,300-foot elevation gain to the blueberry bushes atop the Knuckle Hills. It passes from boreal forest through hemlock forest to alpine tundra, with a few waterfalls along the way. Day packs are provided by the lodge; boots and rain gear are not. Many guests have pinpointed this hike, especially when accompanied by one of the resident naturalist guides, as the highlight of their stay. In case you're wondering why there's no mention of fishing on the activities list, the reason is simple: the fishing is lousy. But that's no reason to stay off the water. Single and double kayaks are available when the lake is calm. Guides lead kayaking/hiking trips to parts of Skilak Lake where bald eagles often come to feed.

MEALTIME: Alaskans like their meals to be plentiful and plenty filling, and this lodge does its best to honor the tradition. Each morning, after a hearty breakfast, the staff puts out a pack-your-own lunch buffet with lunch meats, cheeses, fruits, veggies, salads, snacks, and sodas. Salmon, halibut, and prime rib feature prominently on the dinner menu, but vegetarians can be accommodated with advance notice. Everything served here is made fresh, including the breads and desserts. Meals are served next to the woodstove in the main lodge dining room, which is surrounded by windows facing out onto the preserve.

FINE PRINT:
Pets: leave 'em home
Kids: bring 'em on
Credit cards: MasterCard, Visa
Heads-up: bears, wolves, wolverines, mosquitoes, biting flies
Nearest medical: Soldotna, AK (30 miles)
Weather: Temperatures can range from 30° to 80°F, with sun, rain, sleet, or snow any time of year. Lodge elevation is near sea level.

GETTING THERE: If you'd rather skip the approach by river, or if your timing doesn't allow it, exit the airport via Airport Drive. Turn left onto the Kenai Spur Highway. Drive 10.5 miles to the Sterling Highway. Turn left and drive 20 miles to Skilak Lake Road. Turn right and drive 11 miles to the Upper Skilak Lake boat landing. A private boat will meet you there (included in the cost of a stay).

See color photos on pages 154 and 155

LAKE CLARK BEAR LODGE

33881 Sterling Highway
Sterling, AK 99672
Tel: 800-544-2261; 907-262-8797
Fax: 907-262-8797
www.greatalaska.com
greatalaska@greatalaska.com

Closest airport: Anchorage (200 miles, fly-in only)
Activities: wildlife watching, fishing, flight-seeing, hiking
Season: June 1 through September 10
Guides/Instruction: naturalist guides, bear experts, fishing guides and instruction
Services: none
Specialty: bear viewing
Accommodations: six tent cabins; capacity 12
Rates: $995 for two days, one night; $1,495 for three days, two nights; double occupancy; all-inclusive (meals, activities, bush plane transport)

You'll catch your first glimpse of the bears from the air, a few hairy brown hunchbacks loping across a meadow as your bush plane approaches the beach. They look massive, even from above. And tonight they'll be a stone's throw from your tent.

The brown bears that live near Lake Clark Bear Lodge are bigger than the grizzlies of the lower 48, and they consider the grounds around the lodge compound to be their very own all-you-can-eat buffet. From the safety of a platform lookout or positioned behind a

well-armed guide, you'll spend the long summer days watching ursine antics and exploring the surrounding parkland. This is wildlife watching at its best.

AT THE LODGE: The domed tent cabins have twin beds, propane heat, and portable toilets—luxurious by backcountry camping standards. Even showers are available. Raised on platforms with wood floors and solid doors, the tents are sturdy enough to withstand the weather (and other natural elements). There's no electricity, but 15-hour days leave little need for artificial light. Tents are positioned between the bay and the mountains. From your bed you can hear ocean waves and watch wind rustle the spruce and alders. Climb the central platform, which has two telescopes, for bear viewing between walks; or point the scope toward Mount Iliamna, the 10,020-foot active volcano that rises up from the edge of the property.

THE SPORTS: Savvy guides toting Winchester rifles will lead you into black and brown bear country. A few close encounters from 100 yards away should satisfy most adrenaline junkies. Photographers, pack your telephoto lenses. If you're planning to get close enough for a 50mm shot of a brown bear in action, you may not live to see the print. These coastal browns can weigh up to 1,500 pounds; they've got a lot of snacking to do, and they don't appreciate your getting in the way. When you're not bear watching, opportunities to explore the surroundings are ample: The lodge lies at the base of 4-million-acre Lake Clark National Park; miles of sandy beach make excellent hiking terrain; and salmon run in two nearby creeks. Naturalist guides will lead the way.

BACKCOUNTRY BONUS: This is more of a front-country foray than a backcountry bonus; but since you can't get much deeper into the wilderness than the bear lodge, consider pairing your stay with a less remote destination. Lake Clark Bear Lodge is a satellite of **Great Alaska Adventure Lodge** on the Kenai Penin-

sula, where salmon are as legendary as the guides who always seem to know where they're biting. The lodge sits on 25 acres at the confluence of the Kenai and Moose Rivers, and has all the plush perks you might long for at the bear camp. Nightly rates start at $995 per person.

MEALTIME: Simple favorites like steak and spaghetti are flown in daily, along with plenty of fresh produce. If you happen to catch salmon or halibut, expect them to show up grilled at chow time, too. An afternoon of beachcombing might even yield an appetizer of mussels or clams. Meals are served in a large tented dining room. To stave off unwelcome critters (and to keep humans from ever becoming a menu item), no food can leave the tent. You'll break from your daytime exploits long enough to reconvene here for lunch, which usually includes deli meats, cheeses, smoked salmon, and fresh fruit. Not your typical middle-of-nowhere nosh.

FINE PRINT:
Pets: leave 'em home
Kids: 13 and older
Credit cards: MasterCard, Visa, American Express
Heads-up: bears (of course)
Nearest medical: Anchorage, AK (200 miles)
Weather: Prepare for everything from 75°F and sunny to 40° with torrential rain and winds. Closed during the snowy season. Lodge is 10 feet above sea level.

GETTING THERE: You'll be picked up from Anchorage International Airport and flown into the camp by a six-passenger Cessna 207. The scenic 50-minute flight is included in the price of a stay.

See color photo on page 156

KACHEMAK BAY WILDERNESS LODGE

China Poot Bay
Box 956
Homer, AK 99603
Tel: 907-235-8910
Fax: 907-235-8911
www.alaskawildernesslodge.com
info@alaskawildernesslodge.com

Closest airport: Homer, AK (10 miles)
Activities: birding, canoeing, kayaking, hiking, fishing, tide pooling
Season: mid-May through late September (book a year ahead for July and August)
Guides/Instruction: paddling, hiking, and fishing guides; archaeology, birding, and anthropology tours
Services: spa
Specialty: natural history
Accommodations: three cabins; capacity 12
Rates: $2,800 per person for five days, all-inclusive (meals, guides, boat travel from Homer)

A few minutes into the boat ride from Homer, you might spot a pensive red-faced cormorant nesting on a cliff top, or a boldly colored harlequin duck slurping down a clam. Whatever your first exposure to China Poot Bay's enormously diverse wildlife, it's bound to have you clinging to your binoculars for the duration of your stay. You can count on owners (and resident bird buffs) Michael and Diane McBride, along with their ever-expanding staff of naturalist guides, to add insightful narrative tidbits to your daily encounters. And you can expect to spend your evenings sharing stories and blue mussels by the fire with the few like-minded travelers lucky enough to have snagged a room here, too. Year after year, Kachemak Bay Wilderness Lodge has drawn heartfelt kudos from the world's most discriminating travel experts. It won't take you long to figure out why.

AT THE LODGE: Each private cabin has a bay-view deck, woodburning stove, a homemade quilt, and a living room decorated with wildflowers and 19th-century antiques. The dark wood walls and low ceilings of the main lodge create a cozy common space, where you can cuddle up next to the big stone fireplace or mosey on over to watch the action in the open kitchen before retreating to the glass-walled dining room. Paths from the cabins lead to a Finnish sauna, a hot tub surrounded by ferns, and a solarium with a telescope for star- or harbor seal–gazing. On warmer nights, seafood dinners are held at the barbecue pavilion by the dock.

THE SPORTS: Make like a Pacific kittiwake and glide across the bay, inches above the calm water. Your vantage point will be from a kayak or canoe, and any fish you bag will be with the assistance of a rod, not a beak. But still, you're likely to feel a special kinship with the feathered locals after joining them for a day on China Poot. The million acres of Kachemak Bay State Park give hikers plenty of options, from tackling the tall surrounding peaks to sauntering around the tide pools in search of anemones to poke. Many guests opt for the mellow, hour-long walk to China Poot Lake, happy home to many a sockeye salmon. Archaeology-savvy guides can take you to ruins left by predecessors of the Tanaina Indians. The on-staff biologists and forest ecologist can turn an ordinary forest walk into an intensive *Jeopardy* training session. If brown bear watching or charter fishing for halibut hold any appeal, the lodge staff can set up trips with nearby outfitters. When you return to the lodge, indulge in a massage to get you recharged for the next day's adventures.

BACKCOUNTRY BONUS: On the off chance that some guests would think this remote lodge isn't quite remote enough, the owners built a backcountry wilderness cabin that's a short floatplane trip away. **Loonsong Mountain Lake Chalet** is situated in what a local might call the "real" Alaska, straight down to the wolverines sniffing at the boots you set to dry

The Birches on Moosehead Lake, Maine, see page 14

The Lodge at Moosehead Lake, Maine, see page 16

Old Inn on the Green and Gedney Farm, Massachusetts, see page 18

The Bartlett Inn, New Hampshire, see page 20

Nereledge Inn, New Hampshire, see page 22

Adirondack Rock and River Lodge, New York, see page 26

Elk Lake Lodge, New York, see page 27

The Point, New York, see page 29

Trail's End Inn, New York, see page 31

Blueberry Hill Inn, Vermont, see page 33

Blueberry Hill Inn, Vermont, see page 33

On the Loose Expeditions Yurts, Vermont, see page 35

Big Bay Point Lighthouse, Michigan, see page 37

Pinewood Lodge, Michigan, see page 40

Bluefin Bay on Lake Superior, Minnesota, see page 45

Idaho Rocky Mountain Ranch, Idaho, see page 48

Big EZ Lodge, Montana, see page 51

The Bungalow Bed and Breakfast, Montana, see page 53

Chico Hot Springs Resort, Montana, see page 55

Mountain Meadows Guest Ranch, Montana, see page 57

Papoose Creek Lodge, Montana, see page 59

Papoose Creek Lodge, Montana, see page 59

Pine Butte Guest Ranch, Montana, see page 61

Potosi Hot Springs Resort, Montana, see page 63

Rainbow Ranch Lodge, Montana, see page 65

Triple Creek Ranch, Montana, see page 68

Triple Creek Ranch, Montana, see page 68

Bitterroot Ranch, Wyoming, see page 70

Boulder Lake Lodge, Wyoming, see page 72

Brooks Lake Lodge, Wyoming, see page 74

Brooks Lake Lodge, Wyoming, see page 74

Togwotee Mountain Lodge, Wyoming, see page 76

Steinhatchee Landing Resort, Florida, see page 79

The Lodge on Little St. Simons Island, Georgia, see page 82

The Lodge on Little St. Simons Island, Georgia, see page 82

Mountain Top Lodge at Dahlonega, Georgia, see page 84

Earthshine Mountain Lodge, North Carolina, see page 89

Blackberry Farm, Tennessee, *see page 93*

Charit Creek Lodge, Tennessee, *see page 94*

Leconte Lodge, Tennessee, see page 96

Fort Lewis Lodge, Virginia, see page 98

Cheat Mountain Club, West Virginia, *see page 100*

Rancho de la Osa Guest Ranch, Arizona, *see page 104*

Shrine Mountain Inn, Colorado, see page 106

Skyline Guest Ranch, Colorado, see page 108

Skyline Guest Ranch, Colorado, see page 108

Bear Mountain Lodge, New Mexico, see page 111

Hacienda del Cerezo, New Mexico, see page 114

Camelot Adventure Lodge, Utah, see page 118

Birch Pond Lodge, Alaska, see page 121

Kenai Backcountry Lodge, Alaska, see page 123

Kenai Backcountry Lodge, Alaska, see page 123

Lake Clark Bear Lodge, Alaska, see page 125

Kachemak Bay Wilderness Lodge, Alaska, see page 128

Tutka Bay Wilderness Lodge, Alaska, *see page 177*

The Ahwahnee Hotel, California, *see page 180*

Costanoa Lodge and Camp, California, see page 182

Otter Bar Lodge and Kayak School, California, see page 188

Point Reyes Seashore Lodge, California, see page 190

Rock Creek Lodge, California, see page 192

Safari West Wildlife Preserve and African Tent Camp, California, see page 194

Sorensen's Resort, California, see page 196

The Palms Cliff House Inn, Hawai, see page 201

The Palms Cliff House Inn, Hawai, see page 201

Sheraton Molokai Lodge and Beach Village, Hawaii, see page 203

Mount Ashland Inn, Oregon, see page 206

Steamboat Inn, Oregon, see page 209

Timberline Lodge, Oregon, see page 211

Freestone Inn, Washington, see page 214

Freestone Inn, Washington, see page 214

Paradise Inn, Washington, see page 216

Run of the River, Washington, see page 218

Sun Mountain Lodge, Washington, see page 220

Inconnu Lodge, Canada, *see page 226*

Island Lake Lodge, Canada, *see page 228*

Island Lake Lodge, Canada, see page 228

Killarney Lodge, Canada, see page 230

King Pacific Lodge, Canada, see page 232

Lake O'Hara Lodge, Canada, see page 234

Lake O'Hara Lodge, Canada, *see page 234*

Mount Assiniboine Lodge, Canada, *see page 235*

Sentry Mountain Lodge, Canada, see page 242

Tuckamore Lodge, Canada, see page 245

Danzante, Mexico, see page 252

Hotel Eco Paraíso Xixim, Mexico, see page 255

Hotel Eco Paraíso Xixim, Mexico, see page 255

Las Cañadas Cloud Forest Ecovillage, Mexico, see page 256

Las Cañadas Cloud Forest Ecovillage, Mexico, *see page 256*

Picocanoa Adventure Lodge, Mexico, *see page 260*

Maho Bay Camps, St. John, Virgin Islands, see page 265

Maho Bay Camps, St. John, Virgin Islands, see page 265

Mount Plaisir Estate, Trinidad, West Indies, see page 267

Stonefield Estate Villa Resort, St. Lucia, West Indies, see page 270

outside your door. As Michael puts it, "With my head on the pillow, I have seen rainbow trout swim by." Giant spruce logs frame a 7-foot-tall bubble window that looks onto an alpine lake. There's no electricity, but with two bedrooms, a full bathroom, a kitchen, and personal chefs housed in a cabin across the lake, this hardly qualifies as rustic. Oh, and there's the sauna. This worthy, four-day add-on to a stay at the lodge costs $1,750 per person, all-inclusive. Hiking and wildlife watching opportunities abound.

MEALTIME: Days begin at 7:30 with a hot pot of coffee or tea and fresh juice delivered to your doorstep. Breakfasts at the main lodge are big and hearty, with an emphasis on fresh breads baked in an old wood oven. The veggies on your plate are almost always home grown, and berries are plucked from nearby bushes. Seafood entrées are the norm, though the specific catch depends on what happens to be swimming in the bay. Dungeness crab makes a frequent appearance. Dishes are always accompanied by carefully chosen wines. Vegetarians, fear not; your needs are catered to here without a hint of resistance from the chef.

FINE PRINT:
Pets: leave 'em home
Kids: bring 'em on
Credit cards: none
Nearest medical: Homer, AK (10 miles)
Weather: Don't expect temperatures to top 70°F; even in midsummer, days and nights are cool. Bring layers, including a rainproof one.

GETTING THERE: Fly or drive to Homer (one-hour flight or five-hour drive from Anchorage); a boat will pick you up from there.

See color photo on page 156

TUTKA BAY WILDERNESS LODGE

P.O. Box 960
Homer, AK 99603
Tel: 800-606-3909; 907-235-3905
Fax: 907-235-3909
www.tutkabaylodge.com
tutka@xyz.net

Closest airport: Homer, AK (14 miles)
Activities: wildlife watching, kayaking, fishing, hiking, flight-seeing
Season: mid-May through mid-September
Guides/Instruction: hiking guides, on-site naturalists, kayaking guides and instruction
Services: conference facilities
Accommodations: three cottages, two suites; capacity 22
Rates: $580–$650 per person for two nights, all-inclusive (meals, activities)

Roughing it doesn't get much cushier than this. Sure it's a wilderness lodge, but owners Nelda and Jon Osgood have done everything they can to protect you from the big, bad elements. Let's start with the location. While the rest of coastal Alaska gets regular poundings from Pacific rainstorms and surf, the 7-mile-long Tutka Bay fjord hides in quiet waters behind the weather-blocking Kenai Mountains. At the lodge, many of the spruce-sided buildings are connected by boardwalks that make any boot-to-dirt contact a matter of choice. Inside, urban amenities like massage shower heads and in-room VCRs make it easy to forget you're in a faraway place that can be reached only by floatplane or helicopter. But the reason to come here is not the indoors; guests come for the easy access to forests, islands, inlets, and bays where sea otters play within inches of kayaks, and bald eagles soar overhead.

AT THE LODGE: The cottages, made of rough-cut local spruce, are clustered in a Sitka spruce forest around the main building, which houses the dining solarium and a lounge

stocked with books on natural history and local lore. Rooms have private decks overlooking Tutka Bay and its backdrop of old-growth trees. Though you wouldn't expect it in such a remote setting, electricity powers small fridges, VCRs, coffeepots, and even hair dryers (for those who'd never dream of hitting the trail without a heat-styled coif). Originally built in 1984, the lodge has undergone constant upgrades and renovations—Jon is meticulous about maintenance and considers the lodge to be a never-ending art project. One of the nicer touches is a shared wood-fired sauna.

THE SPORTS: The 200-foot-long floating dock makes a convenient launching spot for sea kayakers. The lodge requires guests to attend a safety class before allowing them to explore the bay alone. Most paddlers head for the protected waters of the nearby Herring Islands, where sea stars, anemones, and urchins are visible from the surface. Guided trips are available, and all gear is included in the cost of a stay. The activity director can arrange deep-sea halibut fishing trips with local guides from May through September. The average catch weighs 30 to 60 pounds, but 100-pound trophies have been documented. Gear, bait, instruction, and fish cleaning are included. Hikers have 400,000-plus acres of Kachemak Bay State Park to explore. Trails run from shoreline to treeline, through Sitka spruce forests and alpine meadows thick with wildflowers, berries, and critters. Your wildlife checklist should include mountain goats, moose, black bears, sea ducks, loons, hummingbirds, and sea otters—just to start. The lodge property has a 2-mile network of private nature trails that runs along the coast past moss- and fern-covered trees. Ask the activity director for trail maps to nearby peaks. There are hikes to accommodate all energy levels.

BACKCOUNTRY BONUS: Though the lodge no longer offers overnight extensions, their full-day bear-viewing trip should satisfy any backcountry itch. The floatplane fly-out trip to Katmai National Park and Preserve starts with a 75-minute scenic flight west of the lodge. You'll spend four hours on the ground observing massive coastal brown bears before returning home. Advance reservations are required; the cost is $550 per person.

MEALTIME: Nelda's cooking gives new meaning to the term "home style." Her halibut seviche and polenta pudding have drawn national praise. Breakfasts of sourdough hotcakes with wild blueberry sauce are the norm. Lunches are packed, but don't expect your mama's PB&J. More typical is a halibut salad sandwich and peanut butter cookies. If you bring back halibut or salmon, the kitchen staff will not only clean and prepare it, they'll also ship it off to Homer to be vacuum packed, frozen, and packaged for shipping. As souvenirs go, that has to rank among the best.

FINE PRINT:
Pets: leave 'em home
Kids: bring 'em on
Credit cards: MasterCard, Visa
Heads-up: biting insects
Nearest medical: Homer, AK (16 miles)
Weather: Temperatures generally stay between 45° and 70°F. The region gets plenty of rain (40 inches a year) and an average of five feet of snow. The lodge is at sea level.

GETTING THERE: Take a taxi from Homer Airport 5 miles to Homer Harbor (approximately $12). A water taxi (prearranged by the lodge) will take you the remaining 9 miles to Tutka Bay in about 30 minutes.

See color photo on page 157

California

THE AHWAHNEE HOTEL

1 Ahwahnee Road
Yosemite National Park, CA 95389
Tel: 209-372-1407
Fax: 209-372-1463
www.YosemitePark.com

Closest airport: Fresno, CA (95 miles)
Activities: hiking, climbing, mountaineering, cross-country and downhill skiing, snowboarding, snowshoeing, fishing, horseback riding, rafting, road biking, wildlife watching
Season: year-round
Guides/Instruction: on-site naturalists
Services: massage, conference facilities
Accommodations: 99 rooms, 24 cottages; capacity 325
Rates: $357–$864 per room, double occupancy

In a John Muir–era Yosemite, coming to the park and sleeping in anything but a tent would have been a sacrilege. For that reason, the architects of the Ahwahnee Hotel had a bear of a task: How do you design a hotel that can match the scale of Yosemite's setting without creating a gaudy and intrusive structure?

After 11 months of construction, however, the six-story, $1.25 million Ahwahnee opened its doors in 1927 to immediate applause, even from skeptics. The granite façade blended comfortably with its surroundings. The high ceilings and long, graceful windows of the massive lobby had a humbling effect of the sort one gets when walking through a grove of the park's tallest trees. Even the name was well chosen. *Ahwahnee* comes from the Miwok word for Yosemite Valley, which translates as something like "large, gaping mouth." As you step inside the building and your lower jaw hits your chest, you might wonder if the hotel's name derives from something other than the local geography.

AT THE LODGE: Another architectural puzzle was how to achieve the look of all-natural building materials without introducing wood—an obvious fire hazard. The answer: concrete, which was poured into molds cast from rough-hewn logs, then dyed the color of redwood. Concrete, along with steel and granite, constitute the hotel's exterior. Inside, enormous stone hearths, elaborate chandeliers, and Native American artifacts decorate almost every room. Many of the newly restored guest rooms have views of a Yosemite all-star lineup: Half Dome, Yosemite Falls, and Glacier Point. All rooms have king or two double beds, phones, guest robes, and anachronistic amenities like hair dryers and televisions. The separate cottages, equipped with small refrigerators and private, stone patios, are set beneath dogwoods and pines on the hotel grounds. For anyone keeping track, the hotel is a National Historic Landmark.

THE SPORTS: Almost a thousand miles of trails wander through Yosemite National Park, and thousands more lie just outside it, yet most visitors congregate at the same few Yosemite Valley trailheads. Granted, you can't overpromote the beauty of Bridalveil Fall, but sharing the view with dozens of day-trippers can mar the

experience. If you're hiking from the valley, try to select a trail that's long enough to discourage the masses (like the 8.2-mile Chilnualna Fall Trail). Better yet, drive to a less frequented part of the park—the Hetch Hetchy area's waterfalls and peaks are much more seldom seen than their valley counterparts. For climbers, the allure of Half Dome and El Capitan compensate for the crowds at the base. But there's plenty of granite to go around. Look to one of the many park guidebooks or consult the Yosemite Mountaineering School for guidance. Come winter, the school doubles as a cross-country ski center. The park offers 350 miles of skiable trails and roads, including 25 miles of groomed track and 90 miles of marked trails at Badger Pass, Crane Flat, and beneath the giant sequoias of Mariposa Grove. Park naturalists lead two-hour snowshoe walks from the Badger Pass ranger station for $3. Ski gear and snowshoes can be rented at Curry Village or Badger Pass, where you can also ski or snowboard. Fishing is another favorite Yosemite diversion. Rainbow and brown trout inhabit the 58 year-round streams. The fishing season runs from late April through mid-November, and fishing licenses are required. For anyone hoping to explore the park on horseback, two-hour to all-day trail rides depart from the stables in Yosemite Valley, Wawona, and Tuolumne Meadows.

BACKCOUNTRY BONUS: Rewarding yourself with a stay at the lodge after conquering the 211-mile John Muir Trail from Mount Whitney would be the ultimate rags-to-riches wilderness experience. For those who don't want to cover quite so much mileage, a more feasible backcountry add-on is the Glacier Point Ski Hut overnight trip. The Yosemite Mountaineering School and Cross-Country Ski Center offers a guided 10.5-mile skiing trip on intermediate, groomed terrain through the Yosemite backcountry to a rustic Sierra backcountry hut with views of Yosemite Valley, Half Dome, and the Yosemite High Country. The stone and log building has wood heat, indoor plumbing, and a bunk room that sleeps 20. The cost is $160–$192 per person, including meals. Rentals are extra. Previous cross-country skiing experience is required for most trips.

MEALTIME: There are British prep schools with less stringent dress codes than that at the Ahwahnee Dining Room. This is definitely not the place drop in after a hike, unless your trail attire includes a sport coat or below-the-knees dress. High-beamed ceilings with top-to-bottom windows help air out any potential stuffiness, however, and the award-winning cuisine is worth dressing up for. Breakfast gives a boost to the flapjacks-and-omelets wilderness standard with dishes like the Ahwahnee Wrap (scrambled eggs, cheese, veggie hash, and salsa in a flour tortilla). Lunch can be anything from a classic burger to a grilled portobello on a sun-dried tomato roll. Dinners start with creative appetizers like seared himachi with citrus, black mushroom, and Koji miso broth, and get better from there. Thanksgiving dinner is a major event and a tradition for so many families—even at $75 per person—that it's nearly impossible to get a reservation. For a much more dressed-down version of the dining-room fare, eat at the Ahwahnee Indian Room Bar. Cafeteria food is available at several Yosemite Valley locations, and sack lunches with sandwiches, fruit, cookies, and drinks can be ordered at the lodge.

FINE PRINT:
Pets: leave 'em home
Kids: bring 'em on
Credit cards: MasterCard, Visa, American Express, Discover, Diner's Club
Heads-up: black bears
Nearest medical: Yosemite, CA (less than a mile)
Weather: Summer days are usually in the 80s but can hit 100°F, especially in the valley. Nights are much cooler. Winter temperatures range from the mid-20s to the high 40s, with a few nights hovering around zero. Most of the 3-plus feet of yearly rain comes in the fall. Winter snow accumulation rarely exceeds 2 feet. Lodge elevation is about 4,000 feet.

GETTING THERE: Drive north on Highway 41 (through the park's south entrance) to Yosemite Valley, which takes about three hours. The road is fairly straight until the park entrance, which is about an hour from the valley floor. The last stretch of the road is winding as it dips and climbs between 3,000 and 6,000 feet in elevation. Signs point you to the lodge.

See color photo on page 157

COSTANOA LODGE AND CAMP

2001 Rossi Road at Highway 1
Pescadero, CA 94060
Tel: 800-738-7477; 650-879-1100
Fax: 650-879-2275
www.costanoa.com

Closest airports: San Jose, CA, or San Francisco, CA (one hour)
Activities: hiking, mountain and road biking, kayaking, horseback riding, surfing, windsurfing, fishing, diving, wildlife watching
Season: daily, April through October; weekends only, November through March
Guides/Instruction: hiking, kayaking and mountain biking guides and instruction, on-site naturalists, children's programs
Services: spa, conference facilities
Accommodations: 40 lodge rooms, 12 wood cabins, 90 canvas cabins, 47 tent sites, 19 RV sites; capacity 400 plus
Rates: $30–$240 per night, including breakfast (some rooms) and guided hikes; all-inclusive packages available

On a walk through a gusty meadow between the Pacific and a redwood-covered hillside, assistant manager Eric Malone stops to gush, "There's just so much killer open space!" That, in a nutshell, is Costanoa's greatest offering. Just an hour's drive from the congested Bay Area, this refuge sits amid thousands of acres of state parkland on a piece of property so closely watched by eco-groups and the California Coastal Commission, it's a wonder the lodge was allowed to exist at all.

In fact, it almost wasn't. Concerned that this would become yet another snobby coastal resort, community members insisted on strict environmental guidelines and budget-friendly accommodations to offset the pricier ones. The result is a something-for-everyone, outdoors-oriented base camp where comfort, not excess, is the rule.

AT THE LODGE: Built in 1999, the lodge and wood cabins have local Douglas fir siding, beams, and trim. Rooms are furnished with down bedding, bathrobes, Bose radios, mini-fridges, phones with voicemail and data ports, and decks, patios, or balconies. Some have fireplaces. Lodge rooms have private baths, but the cabins share bath facilities that feature thoughtful touches like skylights, a central courtyard with a fireplace, and heated floors to keep your feet toasty on a midnight trip to the loo. The above rooms include continental breakfast, daily maid service, and hot tub access, as do some of the canvas cabins. These sturdy tents on platforms have all the amenities of a hotel room, but you'll fall asleep to the sound of wind whipping against the walls (light sleepers may not consider this a plus). If you don't mind the short walk to the bathroom, the wood or canvas cabins are the way to go. Costanoa also built a camping village on an exposed meadow overlooking the Pacific, where there's no protection from ocean gusts, and little distance between you and your neighbors. The only reason to pitch a tent here is if all the nearby park campgrounds are full.

THE SPORTS: The lodge's own small network of hiking and mountain biking trails connects to 20,000-plus acres in Big Basin and Butano Redwoods State Parks and Año Nuevo State Reserve, and the Pacific Ocean is just across the highway. More than 50 miles of hiking trails and 30 miles of biking trails are accessible from the property. The lodge's Adventure Guide details 16 area hikes, from its own Whitehouse Bridge Loop, which takes you to the knolls above the camp for sweeping ocean views, to a challenging 11-mile loop in Butano that climbs through the forest to a ridgetop. Trails also run along the coast, where you'll find tide pools and sand dunes. Bike trails

include a 20-mile single- and double-track loop that ends with a speedy descent through the redwoods. There's scenic road riding, too. Unless you're here on an adventure package, bike rentals are not included. Trek 6500s with front shocks rent for $15 per hour or $45 per day. On-site horseback riding tours on Tennessee walking horses are available for riders of all skill levels. Guided sea kayaking is offered year-round on a coastline that features sea caves, calm bays, and large rolling waves. There aren't many beginner spots; paddlers should have wet-exit experience. The seasonal estuary and marshland trips are novice friendly. Surfers will find big waves nearby, and smaller ones in Santa Cruz. Anyone with a death wish can try Maverick's, just up the coast. Gusty conditions make some of the coves great for windsurfing and kiting. Anglers with their own gear can surf-cast here. Divers should head for Santa Cruz. The resident wildlife includes over 200 bird species, bobcats, and coyotes. Naturalists lead hikes every weekend. In summer, there's hiking, tide pooling, and crafts for kids. There's a full-service spa year-round ($80 to $114 for Swedish or Shiatsu massage).

MEALTIME: The included breakfast is frills-free continental: muffins, bagels, fruit, juice, coffee. You can order extras like granola and bagel toppings for a few dollars more, or made-to-order eggs and frittatas for $16–$23. The deli case in the general store and café contains chicken, tri-tip, fish, pasta, and side dishes that can be heated on demand or packed to go. There are picnic areas with grills throughout the property. A separate menu of gourmet lunch and dinner options, like tarragon pecan-crusted salmon and roast nine-spice leg of lamb with tomato-mint marmalade, is also available, but county regulations prevent the lodge from operating a full-service restaurant. You place your order, pick it up when it's ready, and seat yourself in the café. For sit-down service, try the New Davenport Cash Store, 12 miles south in the tiny town of Davenport. The menu features classic California cuisine (e.g., pan-seared halibut with summer veggie ragout); entrées cost $15 to $20. You can also find taquerias nearby. Back at the lodge, there's fresh pie and a freezer full of Ben & Jerry's ice cream.

FINE PRINT:

Pets: leave 'em home

Kids: bring 'em on

Credit cards: MasterCard, Visa, American Express, Discover

Heads-up: poison oak, ticks

Nearest medical: Santa Cruz, CA (30 minutes)

Weather: Management will tell you, "There's no bad weather, only wrong clothing." Translation: pack layers—it's mighty chilly underneath that coastal fog. The best time to visit is during Indian summer, September through November. Temperatures range from the low 40s to mid-70s year-round, with 25 inches of average yearly rainfall. The lodge sits 10 feet above sea level.

GETTING THERE: *From San Jose,* take Highway 17 west to Highway 1 north. Drive 25 miles to the lodge. *From San Francisco,* take Highway 280 south to Highway 92 west to Highway 1 south. Drive 30 miles to the lodge.

See color photo on page 158

DEETJEN'S BIG SUR INN

48865 Highway 1
Big Sur, CA 93920
Tel: 831-667-2377
www.deetjens.com

Closest airport: Monterey, CA (30 miles)
Activities: hiking, kayaking, surfing, windsurfing, horseback riding, fishing, mountain and road biking, birding, wildlife watching
Season: year-round
Guides/Instruction: hiking guides, on-site naturalists
Services: none
Accommodations: 20 rooms; capacity 49
Rates: $75–$195 per room, double occupancy

You can pay upward of $1,000 per night for the privilege of sleeping along this stretch of coastline. That price might buy you an oceanview infinity pool and a fancy pillow mint, but it's sure to come up short on soul. Within the weathered walls of Deetjen's historic redwood cottages, novels have been written, sputtering romances have been rekindled, celebrities and fugitives have hidden from the world. Eccentrics have found solace, bohemians have found good company, and countless travelers have enjoyed a great meal and a warm bed.

Grandpa Deetjen would be proud. Before he died in 1972, he willed the inn to a nonprofit foundation so that its unique character would be preserved. Tucked into a canyon and cut through by a creek, Deetjen's is surrounded by parkland. To this day, it remains one of the best finds on the California coast. Journals in each cabin chronicle the impressions of previous guests. One wrote, "I never thought I'd sleep in a bed where so many neurotics and bad poets slept before me. I hope it doesn't affect my sleep, because it is—otherwise—very peaceful here."

AT THE LODGE: The buildings are constructed of reclaimed redwood, much of it taken from Monterey's Cannery Row in the early 1930s by Helmuth "Grandpa" Deetjen, who built the inn in the board-and-batten style of his native Norway. Rooms are cozy (read: small) and tastefully decorated with antiques. Some have fireplaces, decks, courtyards, and canyon views. All have towering redwoods and oodles of ambiance. There's a pay phone outside, but none in the rooms. No TVs or radios either, as you'd expect of an inn that's on the National Register of Historic Places. Light sleepers, take note: The rustic rooms are far from soundproof, which is great if your only ambient noise is the creek, but not so great if you're downstairs from heavy-footed neighbors. In some of the cottages, you can rent both rooms to ensure privacy and a solid snooze.

THE SPORTS: There are three state parks within 10 miles of the inn. To the south, Julia Pfeiffer Burns State Park has a beautiful 6-mile loop trail that follows a creek beneath the redwoods. It's also home to the only waterfall in California that pours directly into the Pacific Ocean. To the north, Pfeiffer Big Sur's 821 acres contain miles of trails that climb peaks to ocean overlooks. A little farther, at Andrew Molera State Park, ancient redwoods give way to eucalyptus stands that line the beach. The park is a popular spot for horseback riding and birding. If you plan to do anything but hike, be sure to bring your own gear. The innkeepers can direct you to nearby kayak launches. They'll also tell you where to look for steelhead and trout. Surfers, windsurfers, and kiteboarders need only drive along the highway to find the hot spots. The beaches catch north swells in the winter, south swells in the summer. The area is sparsely populated, so there's no attitude, even on the best breaks. Cyclists can ride Highway 1, but tight turns and narrow or nonexistent shoulders make it as scary as it is scenic. Mountain bikers can expect steep, technical terrain. At press time, the inn was working on procuring hiking guides and a house masseuse. Stay tuned.

MEALTIME: Guests have described dinner at Deetjen's as an act of foreplay. The combination of candlelit tables and gourmet edibles is undeniably romantic, but it's the Old World aura that sets this inn apart. The restaurant is divided into four intimate rooms, where fireplaces, soft music, and the right bottle of wine set the tone. A favorite starter is the heirloom tomato salad, lightly dressed and topped with shaved Parmesan. Entrées include pan-seared duck breast with couscous and berry-apricot coulis, grilled New York steak with parsley potatoes and red wine butter, fresh fish with a gingered cucumber salad, and numerous vegetarian options. Dishes are simple and filling, with an emphasis on organic local produce. Dress is casual. Reservations are recommended. The restaurant is also open for breakfast, where the house-special eggs Benedict comes with a heaping side of home fries. You can also opt for pancakes, old-fashioned oatmeal, a granola and yogurt parfait, or French toast stuffed with blackberry–Grand Marnier cream cheese. For lunch, stop at the Big Sur Center Deli for trail-friendly takeout.

FINE PRINT:

Pets: leave 'em home
Kids: 12 and older
Credit cards: MasterCard, Visa
Heads-up: poison oak, occasional mud slides
Nearest medical: Big Sur, CA (5 miles)
Weather: It's the rare day in Big Sur when it's warm enough to walk around sans sweater. Average summer afternoons are in the mid-60s to mid-80s, but early-morning lows can be as low as 30°F because of the fog. The area gets about 62 inches of annual rainfall. Lodge elevation is 600 feet.

GETTING THERE: The lodge is just off Highway 1, 26 miles south of Carmel. Look for the sign that says BIG SUR INN, between the Henry Miller Library and the Coast Gallery.

GOLD MOUNTAIN MANOR

1117 Anita Avenue
P.O. Box 2027
Big Bear City, CA 92314
Tel: 800-509-2604; 909-585-6997
Fax: 909-585-0327
www.goldmountainmanor.com
info@goldmountainmanor.com

Closest airport: Ontario, CA (80 minutes)
Activities: hiking, downhill and backcountry skiing, snowboarding, snowshoeing, mountain and road biking, fishing, windsurfing, horseback riding, wildlife watching
Season: year-round
Guides/Instruction: hiking and trail running guides
Services: spa, conference facilities
Accommodations: four rooms, three suites
Rates: $125–$225 per room, double occupancy, including breakfast and afternoon hors d'oeuvres

Few sights bring as much joy to a Los Angeles resident as a smog-free, clear blue sky. That's why it's imperative that you take the time to pull off the highway on your way up Gold Mountain, look down on the hazy basin, and appreciate the fact that you're no longer in it.

The transition from cranky urbanite to mellow mountain dweller should be complete by the time you reach Big Bear Lake. Any residual stress will disappear as you drive the last few miles along the pine-rimmed shoreline of Big Bear Lake to the lodge. What separates this lodge from others in the area is attention to detail: the homemade milk bath powder at the edge of a claw-foot tub, heated towel racks for the fluffy house robes, the chopped wood and kindling stacked in your fireplace. Innkeepers Trish and Jim Gordon have perfected the art of relaxation.

AT THE LODGE: The historic log mansion dates back to 1928, when it was built as a private mountain hideaway for Hollywood movie investor Alexander Buchanan Barret and his new bride, Bessie (one of the rooms still bears her name). Antiques from the era are scattered throughout the maple-floored common room, where high-beamed ceilings help reduce the risk of clutter. The suites have two-person Jacuzzi tubs; other rooms have claw-foot tubs. All have an antique queen-sized bed made of hand-hewn logs or brass, a private bath, a woodburning fireplace, and views of the surrounding Ponderosa pines. There are no phones or televisions, but no one seems to miss them. The obvious pick for an over-the-top romantic getaway is the wood-paneled Presidential Suite, which has a large river rock fireplace embedded with 20-million-year-old fossils and relics from Big Bear's mining days. After a candlelit, fireside bubble bath, fall into the cushy poster pine bed in the fan-cooled adjoining room, where you can still peek out at the fireplace through the doorway.

THE SPORTS: There's skiing and snowboarding (groomed and backcountry) at two nearby ski areas, and a freestyle park with a halfpipe. Thousands of acres of hiking and snowshoeing terrain start one block from the manor's front door. Trish and Jim will take you hiking or running on their favorite San Bernardino National Forest trails, which include a portion of the Pacific Crest Trail. Routes range from easy strolls through wildflower-filled meadows to peak climbs as high as 10,000 feet. If you don't mind canine company, house pups Mat and Cappie will happily tag along. Cyclists can take a 30-mile spin around the lake. Mountain bikers have access to world-class downhill terrain that draws racers to the ski resorts in the off-season. Boats and gear can be rented at the lake for guided or unguided trout fishing. Windsurfers can take advantage of the gusty fall days when most boaters opt to stay off the water. Local outfitters are available for horseback instruction and guided trail rides. The lodge will connect you with gear and guidance for all of the above activities, but no rentals are available on-site.

MEALTIME: The Culinary Institute of America–trained chef shuns ordinary breakfast fare. After your first morning, you may think it can't get any better than fresh fruit bruschetta, blueberry donut muffins, and a Santa Fe Scramble. But you'll wake the next day to a plate of croissant French toast with caramelized bananas and kiwi, served with a side of fruit-and-granola yogurt parfait. Meals are served in the dining room half the year and outside on the veranda when the weather warms up. All dietary requests can be accommodated. Breakfasts are usually hearty enough to satisfy guests until the afternoon hors d'oeuvres hour (which may include spicy shrimp Napoleons, caramelized onion boxes, Jim's California rolls, and Parmesan crisps with sun-dried tomato and basil), but Trish or Jim will order you a sack lunch from a local deli on request. For dinner, you'll have to head into the town of Big Bear Lake, a five-minute drive from the lodge. Ask to see the notebook of restaurant menus in the common room.

FINE PRINT:
Pets: leave 'em home
Kids: bring 'em on
Credit cards: all major credit cards
Nearest medical: Big Bear Lake, CA (4 miles)

Weather: The elevation (6,800 feet) keeps summer days reasonably cool. Expect temperatures in the mid-50s to mid-80s. The winter range is 15° to 45°F with 120 inches of annual snowfall.

GETTING THERE: From Ontario Airport, take Interstate 10 east to Highway 30, go north to Highway 330, and continue north on 330 to Big Bear Lake. At the lake, keep to the left for 9.4 miles on North Shore Drive. Turn left onto Anita Avenue. Gold Mountain Manor is the fourth house on the left.

OTTER BAR LODGE AND KAYAK SCHOOL

14026 Salmon River Road
Forks of Salmon, CA 96031
Tel: 530-462-4772
Fax: 530-462-4788
www.otterbar.com
otterbar@aol.com

Closest airport: Arcata, CA (2.5 hours)
Activities: kayaking, hiking, mountain biking, snorkeling, wildlife watching
Season: mid-April through September
Guides/Instruction: kayaking instruction, teen programs
Services: spa, conference facilities
Specialty: whitewater kayaking instruction
Accommodations: four lodge rooms, three cabins; capacity 14
Rates: $1,890 per week, double occupancy, all-inclusive (meals, kayak lessons)

If Otter Bar was just a wilderness lodge, or just a kayak school, or even just a place to grab a beer, experiencing it would be well worth the long drive from civilization. Since it ranks among the best in all three categories, it's a mandatory stop on any lifetime adventure tour.

What sets it apart is the quality of the staff, who can transform a reluctant neophyte into an Eskimo roll aficionado in a single session, or add the perfect cartwheel to an experienced paddler's bag of river tricks. The instructors are unflinchingly professional but always up for a good chuckle, the kind of folks you want to take home with you. Not that any of them would be inclined to leave their idyllic post on 30 acres of riverbank in Klamath National Forest. To play with them again, like so many of their guests, you'll find yourself going back year after year.

AT THE LODGE: In the beginning, there was just the lodge. Kayaks were an afterthought. Maybe that's why this pine-rimmed compound is so spectacular—to attract weekenders to a part of the state most Californians couldn't locate on a map, it had to be. Hardwood paneling extends from floor to ceiling, with high, rectangular windows encircling the perimeter like frames in a strip of celluloid. The owner, who designed the 1964 lodge, wanted light to pour in from every direction. Ongoing renovations keep the four lodge bedrooms and three newer cabins up-to-date, with amenities you wouldn't expect to find in the middle of a forest, like in-room VCRs (Otter Bar generates its own electricity). Rooms have views of the pines and/or ponds, and private decks where you sit and listen to the river rush by. Being a guest at Otter Bar is like staying at a luxury bed-and-breakfast with its own 1.7-million-acre backyard.

THE SPORTS: Otter Bar has been called the best kayaking school in the country by so many whitewater experts that the designation no longer turns heads. Instructors group students by skill level for lessons in everything from basic strokes to advanced hole riding, with special clinics for rodeo tricks and springtime high-water trips. Two weeks a year are set aside

for kids ages 10 to 14. Gear is provided for beginners; intermediate and advanced students usually bring their own. A snorkel and mask could come in handy for hanging your head overboard to observe schools of salmon. A total novice can expect to spend the first two days learning the basics in the safety of a spring-fed pond. By day seven you'll be ready for a graduation trip on the Klamath River. Off-the-water options include hundreds of miles of hiking and mountain biking terrain (bikes available for guests' use; singletrack and logging roads). Keep an eye pointed treeward to catch sight of resident eagles and hawks.

BACKCOUNTRY BONUS: One night of each weeklong beginner session is spent on a kayak/camping overnight. Bring your own sleeping bag and ground pad. Nearby Trinity Alps and Marble Mountain Wilderness Areas offer numerous additional backcountry activities.

MEALTIME: Chow time never disappoints. Trained chefs serve meals outdoors on an elegant candlelit table (or in the dining room in colder weather). In addition to fresh juices, fruits, and organic coffee, the breakfast selection will include berry scones, coffee cakes, and other homemade baked goods alongside entrées like Spanish tortillas and veggie frittatas. On river days, lunch is a make-it-yourself sandwich bar packed in and set up by the guides. The dinner buffet varies according to what's in season but always features locally grown produce and a multiethnic variety of main dishes. Dishes have included Thai shrimp curry with a tofu veggie stir-fry, Middle Eastern chicken breasts with tomato chutney, and homemade pasta primavera with homegrown tomatoes and basil sauce. There's always something to accommodate vegetarians, devoted carnivores, and chocolate addicts (try the chocolate decadence cake with strawberries in Grand Marnier). Good wines are included.

FINE PRINT:

Pets: leave 'em home

Kids: 14 and older (except during special sessions for 10- to 14-year-olds)

Credit cards: MasterCard, Visa

Heads-up: some poison oak

Nearest medical: Hoopa, CA (75 minutes)

Weather: In spring, nighttime temperatures can get as low as 50°F, which is enough to make any thin-skinned Californian shiver. Summer highs can top 100°F but usually stay in the 80 to 90° range. Lodge elevation is 1,200 feet.

GETTING THERE: From the airport, drive south on Highway 101 to Highway 299. Go east 45 minutes to the town of Willow Creek. Turn left at Highway 96, which takes you to Somes Bar. At Somes Bar turn right onto Salmon River Road. Drive 17.5 miles to the lodge.

See color photo on page 158

POINT REYES SEASHORE LODGE

10021 Coastal Highway 1
P.O. Box 39
Olema, CA 94950
Tel: 415-663-9000
www.pointreyesseashore.com
lodgekeeper@pointreyesseashore.com

Closest airport: San Francisco, CA (45 miles), or Oakland, CA (40 miles)

Activities: hiking, mountain and road biking, surfing, kayaking, canoeing, horseback riding, birding, wildlife watching, hang gliding

Season: year-round

Guides/Instruction: on-site naturalist

Services: massage, conference facilities

Accommodations: 21 rooms, two cottages; capacity 52

Rates: \$135–\$295 per room, double occupancy, including breakfast

Point Reyes National Seashore. Tomales Bay State Park. Golden Gate National Recreation Area. Muir Woods National Monument. Samuel P. Taylor State Park. Gulf of the Farallones National Marine Sanctuary. Audubon Canyon Ranch. Tule Elk Preserve. The list goes on and on.

One good reason to stay here is that all of these protected lands lie just outside the lodge. Another is that the lodge is less than an hour's drive from the Bay Area's most congested cities. But the best reason is that after a day of hiking and biking and surfing and paddling in those parks and monuments and sanctuaries and preserves, you can nose-dive into a feather bed, doze off by a blazing fire, and wake up knowing you can do it all over again.

AT THE LODGE: Details like curved handrails and arched doorways give the Douglas fir lodge a turn-of-the-19th-century feel, though it was built in 1988. Rooms look onto extensive English gardens and the creek at the edge of the manicured lawn. The Mount Wittenberg Ridge rises beyond the creek; you can look out your bedroom window and see cows grazing on its slopes. Many rooms have fireplaces, decks, whirlpool tubs, feather beds, and Shoji screens in the bathrooms. The two country cottages have their own kitchens, outdoor private hot tubs, and gardens. Rooms and cottages all have in-room phones. There are TVs in the cottages and the lodge's game room.

THE SPORTS: Fat-tire aficionados know Mount Tamalpais as the birthplace of mountain biking. It was here, in the 1970s, that daredevils turned two clumps of knobby rubber into a major outdoor industry. Since then, most of the skinny trails on this mountain (and in most parts of the county) have been restricted to hikers and horses, but you can still ride the fire roads on this lush coastal landmark to pay homage to the sport's founders. There's lots of quiet, hilly riding for road cyclists, too. What most folks come to this part of the North Bay for, however, is the hiking. Point Reyes National Seashore's 65,000 acres of designated wilderness contain 140 miles of trails, some starting at the lodge's back door. Staff at the lodge really know their hiking trails and can send you over grassy meadows into forests so thick you can hike beneath the trees in a light rain and come out dry. Ferns spill onto the edges of paths that climb to rocky, tree-covered bluffs and peaks that overlook the ocean from heights of up to 1,400 feet. From the lookouts, you can sometimes spot migrating gray whales. The area is also home to at least 425 species of birds (125 of which have been spotted on the lodge grounds). Nearby stables offer guided trail rides in the national seashore. Rides range from one hour in flat pastures to a six-hour climb over the ridge to Wildcat Camp and down to the beach at Alamere Falls. Paddlers can explore peaceful Tomales Bay in their own kayak or canoe. Or rent a kayak near the lodge to explore the islands and national park shoreline. Surfboard rentals are available at Stinson Beach, 25 minutes south of the lodge. The half-dozen nearby surfing spots have fast, snappy waves that usually top head-high in the winter. Thick wetsuits are a must.

MEALTIME: The breakfast buffet contains continental standards: locally baked pastries, fresh fruits, juices, granola, cornflakes, yogurt, bagels, toast, coffee, assorted teas. There's also afternoon tea and coffee with fresh baked cookies. The fireside dining room has a two-story stone fireplace and wood floors with Oriental rugs and local art. For lunch, order a picnic basket with cheeses from local dairies, fresh baked goods, award-winning local wines, organic produce, and fresh seafood (including locally farmed oysters). Come dinnertime, you'll probably end up at one of the two restaurants next to the lodge. Olema Farmhouse is more casual than Olema Inn. Both serve commendable seafood dishes and excellent wines.

FINE PRINT:
Pets: leave 'em home
Kids: bring 'em on
Credit cards: MasterCard, Visa, American Express, Discover
Heads-up: poison oak
Nearest medical: Point Reyes Station, CA (2 miles)
Weather: The seaside location means warmer winters and cooler summers than in inland Northern California

cities. Summer mornings can be cold and foggy, but they usually clear by midday. Temperatures range from the mid-50s to low 80s. Annual rainfall is 45 inches. Lodge elevation is 45 feet.

GETTING THERE: *From San Francisco,* take Highway 380 to Highway 280 north. Exit 19th Avenue and take it to the Golden Gate Bridge. Cross the bridge to Highway 101 north. Exit at San Anselmo/Sir Francis Drake Boulevard and drive west on Sir Francis Drake Boulevard about 20 miles to Highway 1. Turn right onto Highway 1. The Lodge is on the immediate left. *From Oakland,* take Highway 880 north to 980, to 80. Highway 80 becomes Highway 580. Take 580 west across the Richmond–San Rafael Bridge, exit at Sir Francis Drake Boulevard and drive 20 miles to Highway 1. Turn right onto the highway; the lodge is on the immediate left.

See color photo on page 159

ROCK CREEK LODGE

HCR 79 Box 12
Mammoth Lakes, CA 93546
Tel: 877-935-4170; 760-935-4170
Fax: 760-935-4172
www.rockcreeklodge.com
info@rockcreeklodge.com

Closest airport: Mammoth Lakes, CA (25 miles)
Activities: backcountry and cross-country skiing, snowshoeing, hiking, climbing, mountaineering, fishing, horseback riding, mule treks, mountain and road biking, kayaking, canoeing
Season: late May through October; late December through early April
Guides/Instruction: backcountry skiing and fishing guides, cross-country and snowshoe instruction, on-site naturalists
Services: conference facilities
Accommodations: 14 cabins; capacity 63
Rates: $85–$150 per night, double occupancy; winter rates include breakfast, dinner, ski pass

To anyone who has endured long lift lines only to weave through crowds on ski-slashed slopes, the devotees of Rock Creek Lodge say . . . Ha! Please forgive their haughtiness, as you, too, may guffaw at commoners once you've sampled the seldom-shussed powder surrounding this lodge. All winter the property is snowed in, so the Mammoth-bound masses are deterred from day-tripping. On-site cross-country trails and easy access to remote corners of the John Muir Wilderness add to the site's appeal.

This is not a luxury lodge, and it makes no claims to the contrary. It offers basic lodging in a four-star setting, and a helpful staff of longtime locals who will happily direct you to the best fishing pond, hiking trail, climbing, and touring terrain around.

AT THE LODGE: Repeat visitors who had to brave the ass-numblingly cold outhouses in previous years will be happy to know that there's now a shared bath facility with indoor plumbing. Some of the newer cabins even have private toilets and showers. That's a huge technological leap for a place that began as a 1920s fishing resort and was left to rot throughout the early 1990s until the current owner resurrected it in 1994. The eight remaining original cabins were built from lumber milled on-site. All have small kitchens and wood-burning stoves with peekaboo windows; some have private decks so close to Rock Creek you could almost fish from bed. As this is a no-frills establishment, bring your own sleeping bags, towels, and toiletries (sorry, no complimentary soap square).

THE SPORTS: Rock Creek Canyon's backcountry terrain is among the finest in the High Sierra. But it's unwise to venture out without a fair amount of avalanche knowledge. The lodge offers a four-day avalanche awareness course for $610, including room and board. Or you can ski with a guide. With rentals, lessons, and 14 groomed kilometers on-site, cross-country skiers don't have to venture off the grounds. Snowshoes can be rented at the lodge, too. Best of all, the unfortunate phenomenon known as Sierra Cement is not a problem here—expect light, fluffy flakes à la Aspen. And the fun doesn't end when the snow melts. Hikers can take trails through the John Muir Wilderness to open meadows and waterfalls, or walk a nearby section of the Pacific Crest Trail. Climbers have access to classics like the Northeast Buttress of Bear Creek Spire and the North Face of Mount Dade. There's guided reel and spin fishing on lakes and streams. Nearby stables offer beginner trail rides on steady horses; outfitters in Bishop feature more challenging high-desert rides and give instruction. Mountain bikers will find plenty of fire roads and fairly technical singletrack. Lightly trafficked, the high-desert roads are well suited to cycling. Paddlers have access to Rock Creek Lake or the million-year-old Mono Lake, where kayaks are available for rent. At the end of the day, everyone can reconvene at the Finnish sauna.

BACKCOUNTRY BONUS: Nearby outfitters offer multiday horse and mule packing trips and guided ascents of the Little Lakes Valley peaks, many of which top 13,000 feet. Contact the Rock Creek Pack Station (760-872-8331) and Sierra Mountain Center (760-873-8526) for information.

MEALTIME: The lodge's general store stocks enough basics to sustain you through a stay, but serious cooks should buy groceries en route. The cabin kitchens have their own cookware. Sack lunches with sandwiches on homemade bread, chips or pretzels, fruit and veggies, and fresh baked cookies can be ordered in advance. There's a cleaning station for fish, which you can have frozen or cooked for you on request. At the restaurant, breakfast and lunch consist of standards like pancakes and burgers. At dinnertime, chef–lodge manager Jan Huffstutler pulls out all the stops, with dishes like curried zucchini soup with coconut milk and lime, homemade rosemary and garlic focaccia, and pork tenderloin with cranberry Cabernet sauce. The menu varies according to the availability of fresh ingredients, but breads are baked daily, and vegetarian options are always available. Ski-in moonlight dinners are served throughout the winter.

FINE PRINT:

Pets: summer only; $20 per pet, per night
Kids: bring 'em on
Credit cards: MasterCard, Visa
Heads-up: bears, mosquitoes
Nearest medical: Mammoth Lakes, CA (25 miles)
Weather: Unpredictable. Summer days can reach 80°F, but nights can drop to freezing. Winter temperatures range from 40 above to 15 below. The area gets about 160 inches of yearly snowfall, but almost no rain. Lodge elevation is 9,373 feet.

GETTING THERE: Head south on Highway 395 to the Tom's Place exit. Turn right and drive up the canyon 8 miles. The lodge is on the left, across the creek. In winter, you'll be shuttled by snowmobile from the parking area to the lodge (or you can ski in—about 2 miles).

See color photo on page 159

SAFARI WEST WILDLIFE PRESERVE AND AFRICAN TENT CAMP

3115 Porter Creek Road
Santa Rosa, CA 95404
Tel: 800-616-2695; 707-579-2251
Fax: 707-579-8777
www.safariwest.com
info@safariwest.com

Closest airport: San Francisco, CA (79 miles)
Activities: hiking, wildlife watching, canoeing, horseback riding, road biking, hot-air ballooning
Season: year-round
Guides/Instruction: guided safaris and hikes, wildlife conservation courses, on-site naturalists, children's programs
Services: spa, conference facilities
Specialty: exotic wildlife
Accommodations: 31 tent cabins, one cottage; capacity 190
Rates: $225–$300 per room, double occupancy, including breakfast

Waaaay "out of Africa," giraffes and zebras roam an unlikely game park set on 400 acres in the Sonoma wine country. This is not a zoo. It is not a theme park. It's a genuine wildlife preserve with a conservation ethic that should have every gazelle in the Maasai Mara applying for a visa.

The brainchild of lifelong animal enthusiast Peter Lang, this handpicked menagerie began in 1978 as a small collection of exotic species. The winged and four-legged residents now number nearly 400, and guides lead daily safaris through the property. It may not have the scale or allure of the Serengeti, but it's the closest you'll get to the real thing without leaving the continent.

AT THE LODGE: The lodge's roomy canvas safari tents were manufactured in South Africa. Not at all rustic, they have hardwood floors, pillow-top beds, and private baths with flush toilets and hot showers (no phones or TVs). Screened windows open to views of a lake or the woods. You're likely to wake up to a chorus of squawks and chirps, but barriers keep unwelcome wildlife from wandering into your tent. Most guests opt for this safari-style lodging, but there's also the option of a two-bedroom cottage with a private bath, kitchenette, and outdoor sitting area.

THE SPORTS: This is one of just six facilities in North America to have been granted membership in the American Zoo and Aquarium Association. Its focus is on preservation, research, and education, not just-for-kicks tourism. Safari guides lead 2½-hour tours twice daily in winter, three times a day the rest of the year. You'll start with a 30-minute jaunt in an open-air jeep before venturing out on foot. Inside the oak woodland forest, you'll see waterbucks, cheetahs, wildebeests, and African crowned cranes, among others. The giraffes may stop their chomping long enough to give you a curious glance, but otherwise your presence isn't likely to cause a stir. The facility also regularly runs photo safaris and sunset tours. Bring your own hiking boots, camera, and binoculars. Trips cost $58 for adults, $28 for kids ages 3 to 12. Group rates are also available. Between safaris, you can walk the property's 14 miles of wooded hiking trails or paddle a canoe on two of its ponds. The staff will arrange bike rentals, horseback riding, balloon rides, and wine country tours through outfitters outside the preserve. The Russian River and Napa and Sonoma State Parks are nearby, and avid cyclists should note that the back roads running between the wineries rank among the world's most scenic stretches of pavement.

MEALTIME: The cuisine is a blend of California wine country and authentic African safari, with dishes like warm duck breast salad and open-fire-roasted meat. Meals are served buffet style in the safari-themed Elephant Room or the Savannah Café, or on a veranda overlooking the so-called Sonoma Serengeti. In the outdoor eating area, large wooden tables are set beside a boma fire pit. The wine and beer list features both local and South African selections. For lunch, you can eat in or order a sack lunch with grilled chicken, fresh salads, fruit, and cheese. All dietary restrictions can be accommodated. Breakfast is included (continental most of the week, an all-out feast prepared by Peter on Sundays). Lunch and dinner cost $15 to $25 per adult, $12 to $15 per child. An ample selection of wine country restaurants is nearby.

FINE PRINT:
Pets: leave 'em home
Kids: bring 'em on
Credit cards: all major cards
Heads-up: poison oak, mosquitoes, blackflies, rattlesnakes, ticks
Nearest medical: Santa Rosa, CA (7 miles)
Weather: Much milder than Kenya, with temperatures ranging from the low 50s to the low 80s. Average yearly rainfall is about 28 inches. Lodge elevation is about 500 feet.

GETTING THERE: Drive over the Golden Gate Bridge to U.S. 101 north. After about 54 miles, take the River Road/Guerneville exit (also marked Calistoga/Mark West Springs Road). Exit the freeway and turn right onto Mark West Springs Road to head east toward Calistoga. Continue for 7 miles. At Franz Valley Road, turn left into the entrance to the preserve.

See color photo on page 160

SORENSEN'S RESORT

14255 Highway 88
Hope Valley, CA 96120
Tel: 800-423-9949; 530-694-2203
www.sorensensresort.com
info@sorensensresort.com

Closest airport: Reno, NV (90 minutes)
Activities: cross-country skiing, snowshoeing, hiking, fishing, mountain and road biking, kayaking, rafting, climbing, mountaineering, llama trekking, horseback riding, birding
Season: year-round
Guides/Instruction: fishing and cross-country skiing guides and instruction; birding and natural history guides
Services: massage, conference facilities
Accommodations: 32 cabins; capacity 95
Rates: $95–$275 per room, some including breakfast

When John and Patty Brissenden bought this dilapidated Gold Rush–era rest stop in 1982, they didn't realize the extent of their rescue mission. The Brissendens ultimately initiated a 10-year effort to wrestle 25,000 acres of land from cattle ranchers and put it under federal protection. The U.S. Forest Service now governs that property, and visitors can hike beneath quaking aspens to lupine-filled meadows that otherwise would have been grazed bald and crisscrossed with power lines.

But it's not just the surrounding forest that makes Sorensen's a wholly satisfying wilderness retreat. The Brissendens' preservation ethic is matched by their commitment to service. Thoughtful details like in-room trail guides and organized birding walks make it easy to get outdoors. Cozy comforts like woodburning stoves and warm quilts make it just as easy to stay indoors. And the prospect of enjoying the valley's spring wildflowers and later its fall foliage makes it all too tempting to keep coming back.

AT THE LODGE: This 1876 homestead started hosting West-bound migrants in the early 1900s, but the original rough cabins were pretty run-down when the current owners purchased them. Even so, they managed to salvage some of the original structures as building materials for the current cabins, each of which has a unique design. The most distinct is a replica of a 17th-century Norwegian home; it was built in Europe and shipped overseas, replete with ornately carved details. Other cabins have grass roofs—not thatch, but actual sod. The cabins accommodate from two to six guests. All have down quilts, original artwork, old-fashioned bathtubs, and private decks; some have woodburning stoves. The only phone on-site is a pay phone. And don't even think about looking for a TV. Instead, you might saunter to the wood-fired sauna or stare out a window at the pines. All of the rooms have forest views.

THE SPORTS: You can start by flipping through your in-room copy of the Sierra's preeminent what-to-do-outdoors guide, *Alpine Trailblazer,* by Jerry and Janine Sprout. Then choose your own adventure, or tag along on one of the many organized trips. In the snowy season, trips might include a full-moon tour on cross-country skis, or a guided snowshoe trek that traces the route of a legendary mid-1800s Alpine mail carrier who tramped through backcountry snow, sleet, and ice. Though the resort doesn't stock rentals, every piece of equipment you could think to take outdoors is available at the nearby Hope Valley Outdoor/Cross-Country Ski Center. The resort's trails are marked but not groomed. In warmer weather, guided excursions may include birding walks led by a local naturalist, or llama treks into the High Sierra. Anglers can sign up for a day on the West Fork Carson River with the Horse Feathers Fly-fishing School, adjacent to the resort. The East Fork Carson River has a short summer whitewater rafting season with Class III and IV rapids.

Lake paddlers can rent kayaks at the Hope Valley Outdoor Center, and mountaineers can tackle any of the 20 or so local peaks that top 10,000 feet. Masochistic cyclists can challenge themselves on the infamous "Death Ride," 140 miles of terrain with 17,000 feet of vertical elevation gain. Mountain bikers have several hundreds of miles of singletrack and fire roads to choose from, including the wild ride known locally as "Mr. Toad's." Bring your own bike, and ask at the lodge for details.

MEALTIME: With the exception of the three bed-and-breakfast cabins, meals at the resort are not included. All cabins have kitchens, but if a breakfast of blueberry pancakes topped with real Vermont maple syrup sounds at all appealing, you might consider letting Sorensen's do the cooking for you. Breakfast, lunch, and dinner are served next to a woodburning stove at the cozy café. You can also order packed lunches (turkey, ham, or veggie sandwich with chips, fruit, and a cookie). For dinner, try the beef burgundy stew or pasta primavera, or have the kitchen grill whatever you reeled in that day (clean it first, please). Your morning coffee and afternoon glass of wine are on the house.

FINE PRINT:

Pets: allowed in five of the cabins
Kids: bring 'em on
Credit cards: MasterCard, Visa, American Express, Discover
Heads-up: bears, mountain lions, and cougars (rare), mosquitoes early spring to summer
Nearest medical: South Lake Tahoe, CA (20 miles)
Weather: Summer temperatures are moderate, rarely reaching 90°F. Expect lots of snow in the winter. Lodge elevation is 7,000 feet.

GETTING THERE: Drive south on Highway 395 to Highway 88. At Minden, Nevada, turn right to stay on Highway 88. Continue 20 miles, driving up Woodfords Canyon. The resort is on the left.

See color photo on page 160

TENAYA LODGE AT YOSEMITE

1122 Highway 41
Fish Camp, CA 93623
Tel: 888-514-2167; 559-683-6555
Fax: 559-683-0249
www.tenayalodge.com

Closest airport: Fresno, CA (65 miles)
Activities: hiking, climbing, mountaineering, cross-country and downhill skiing, snowboarding, snowshoeing, fishing, horseback riding, rafting, mountain and road biking, wildlife watching
Season: year-round
Guides/Instruction: hiking guides, children's programs
Services: spa, conference facilities
Specialty: activities planning
Accommodations: 244 rooms, up to five guests each
Rates: $149–$319 per room, single or double occupancy

There's a universal problem with the national park family vacation. You've just endured several painful hours in the minivan and your hundredth round of I Spy, and the answer to "Are we there yet?" is finally a resounding "Yes!" But just as the aspirin kicks in, you're confronted with the toughest question of the day: "So now what?"

In planning activities, Tenaya has the edge over other Yosemite-area lodges. Its poster-sized flyer details 150 activities in the Southern Yosemite Region that don't involve fighting summer traffic inside the park. Its on-site activities staff specializes in organizing age- and ability-specific adventures, anything from riding horses on backcountry trails to learning to bait a hook and cast for trout. And if that's not hands-on enough, its Adventure Club removes the guesswork entirely with two fully planned days of climbing or cycling camp. There's only one remaining question to contend with: "Do we *have* to go home?" For that, you're on your own.

AT THE LODGE: Situated on 35 acres bordering the Sierra National Forest and 2 miles from the south entrance to Yosemite National Park, this 1990 lodge could get by on location alone. Its reputation as a much-lauded luxury resort is just a perk. Light pours into the lobby from tall, sleek windows framed with rough-hewn timber and stone. Natural stone fireplaces and Native American floor coverings decorate the entryway. Rooms have dataport phones, honor bars, hair dryers, movies on-demand, and Nintendo. Some have balconies or patios, fireplaces, pullout sofas, and whirlpool tubs. All were renovated in 2000.

THE SPORTS: In addition to outside-the-park options like evening flashlight hikes and guided walks to a "secret" waterfall, the activities staff can help you plan any number of classic Yosemite diversions. A word of warning about the impossible-to-describe beauty of the famous falls and rock formations located therein: The tendency to speak in Muir-isms to your children is too powerful to contain. Here's a practice run. You say, "Hey, kids, isn't this park 'a paradise that makes even the loss of Eden seem insignificant?'" At this point, they roll their eyes and retreat down the trail. You enjoy a few moments of well-earned solitude. In the high season, you'd be wise to avoid such heavily traveled standards as the paved half-mile trail to Lower Yosemite Fall. Instead, try something outside the valley. The Hetch Hetchy area sees much less traffic and has no shortage of impressive waterfalls. At press time, the Tenaya Lodge Adventure Club was offering two camps—climbing and cycling; but plans were in the works to add at least a dozen more, including backpacking, fishing, canoeing, orienteering, and whitewater sports. The camps are open to anyone over the age of seven and the cost is $578, including lodging, lessons, gear, transportation, breakfast, and lunch. Daytime kids-only programs are available, too, which could allow you time to sample the lodge's extensive spa menu.

BACKCOUNTRY BONUS: The activities staff will help you add an overnight of backpacking, horse packing, skiing, or any other backcountry experience to a stay at the lodge. Contact the Guest Experience Center for details (800-635-5807, option 2).

MEALTIME: Three on-site restaurants give you the flexibility to eat when you're muddy and stinky or showered and swanky. Hiking garb is appropriate attire for the Parkside Deli, where you can grab bagels, muffins, or a picnic lunch before heading outdoors. Jackalope's Bar and Grill has a separate kids' menu in addition to the expected pub-style burgers and pizzas. If you feel like dressing up, the Sierra Restaurant is a worthy venue for your finest threads. Dishes range from a simple sautéed trout to more unusual entrées like pan-seared, sugar-cane-spiked elk loin with macadamia nut risotto and Riesling-vanilla syrup. Room service is available as well.

FINE PRINT:

Pets: leave 'em home

Kids: bring 'em on

Credit cards: MasterCard, Visa, American Express, Discover, Diner's Club

Heads-up: bears, poison oak at lower elevations

Nearest medical: Oakhurst, CA (12 miles)

Weather: Summer highs in the 80s, lows in the 40s. Winter temperatures range from the 20s to the 50s. The area gets about 40 inches of annual rainfall and 8 feet of snow. Lodge elevation is 5,200 feet.

GETTING THERE: From Fresno, drive north on Highway 41. The lodge is about 12 miles past Oakhurst.

Hawaii

KOKE'E LODGE

Box 819, Koke'e State Park
Waimea, Kauai, HI 96796
Tel: 808-335-6061

Closest airport: Lihue, Kauai, HI (90 minutes)
Activities: hiking, mountain and road biking, birding, fishing
Season: year-round
Guides/Instruction: none
Services: none
Accommodations: 12 cabins; capacity 65
Rates: $35–$45 per cabin

Whoever said that there are no bargains in Hawaii never stayed at Koke'e Lodge. These humble mountain huts set in a redwood grove amid 4,345 acres of parkland give you instant access to the postcard version of the Garden Isle. Deep purple passion fruit grows just outside the cabins, near fragrant tangles of green maile. Trails run through the rain forest to cliff-top ocean overlooks thousands of feet above the Napali coast. And your morning wake-up call comes courtesy of the resident roosters, who will make sure you don't snooze through any potential playtime.

AT THE LODGE: Worlds away from the luxury beach resorts of your travel agent's brochure library, these frills-free wooden housekeeping cabins contain three simple amenities: self-contained kitchens, woodburning stoves, and bathrooms with hot showers. The older, bunkhouse-style cabins rent for less than the newer ones with private bedrooms. Bedding and linens are provided. You can buy firewood at the main lodge, a short walk away. That's also where you'll find the restaurant, cocktail lounge, pay phone, and gift shop (it wouldn't be Hawaii if there wasn't a place to buy macadamia nuts and hula-themed trinkets). Make your reservations early—this place has been known to fill up months in advance.

THE SPORTS: There may not be any surf, but there's plenty of turf. More than 60 miles of hiking trails start near the lodge in Koke'e and Waimea State Parks. You can stop in at Koke'e Natual History Museum (808-335-9975) next door to the lodge to pick up trail maps and books on local flora and fauna, and get an education on the forest and the Alakai Swamp before experiencing them firsthand. For an easy rain forest introduction, take a 15-minute stroll on the interpretive trail behind the museum. A particularly challenging Napali overlook trail is the 6.2-mile Awa'awapuhi Trail, a half-day, out-and-back that starts at mile marker 17 and takes you to a grassy, ridgetop picnic area 2,500 feet above the Pacific Ocean. For a different experience, you can hike into Waimea Canyon on the 5-mile, out-and-back Kukui Trail. The steep descent starts between mile markers 8 and 9, and takes you to a permit-only campsite on the lush canyon floor. Bring ear plugs if you're not a fan of helicopter noise, and bug spray if you'd rather not get devoured by mosquitoes. There's scant mountain biking in the area; cyclists usually keep to the windy highway. It's a beautiful ride, but distracted tourists and an absence of shoulders can make it a scary one. Anglers can take advantage of Hawaii's only trout season, which starts on the first Saturday of August and runs for six weeks (license required). Birders can pick up a guide to indigenous forest birds at the museum and head to the Awa'awapuhi and Nu'alolo Trails for the best viewing opportunities.

MEALTIME: The lodge's restaurant passes the LOCALS EAT HERE test. It's worth driving all the way up from the ocean for a slice of the shredded-coconut pie. The menu emphasizes fresh ingredients and regional specialties like Portuguese bean soup and Kauai corn bread, both of which can be enhanced by a selection from the impressive beer list. Like everything else on the menu, the sandwiches and creative salads can be packed to go. But views of a meadow flanked by pines, cedars, and redwoods make the dining room as scenic a venue as any. The restaurant is open from 9 A.M. to 3:30 P.M. daily. The cabins are stocked with cookware and utensils. Bring your own ingredients (the gift shop carries Maui potato chips, Kauai cookies, trail mix, and gourmet chocolate, but not much in the way of nutritious food).

FINE PRINT:
Pets: leave 'em home
Kids: bring 'em on
Credit cards: MasterCard, Visa, American Express, Discover (checks preferred for prebooking)
Nearest medical: Waimea, Kauai, HI (30 minutes)
Weather: This is not the Hawaii you think you know—temperatures hover between the low 40s and high 60s (warmer if you hike into the canyon) year-round. The area gets 30 to 40 inches of rain each year. Lodge elevation is 3,600 feet.

GETTING THERE: Take Route 50 west to Waimea. Turn right at Waimea Canyon Drive (Route 550) and drive 16 miles via the canyon rim to Koke'e State Park.

THE PALMS CLIFF HOUSE INN

28-3514 Mamalahoa Highway
P.O. Box 189
Honomu, HI 96728
Tel: 808-963-6076
Fax: 808-963-6316
www.palmscliffhouse.com
palmscliffhouse@aol.com

Closest airport: Hilo, HI (15 minutes)
Activities: hiking, horseback riding, diving, snorkeling, surfing, kayaking, fishing, birding, road biking, downhill skiing, snowboarding
Season: year-round
Guides/Instruction: none
Services: spa, conference facilities
Accommodations: eight rooms; capacity 16
Rates: $195–$375 per room, double occupancy, including breakfast

L*anai.* The word itself sounds so lethargic it almost ends in a yawn. And the wraparound lenai that hugs this plantation-white inn is possibly the sleepiest of them all. Squooshy cushions in the wicker chairs, languid breezes blowing from the bay . . . it's enough to make you laze here all day.

If you did, you'd miss out on everything else the quiet side of the Big Island has to offer: waterfalls that tumble into natural pools, colorful reef fish that wiggle past your mask, lava flows that sizzle in the surf. This is the Hawaii that resisted the towel-to-towel beach resort plague. It's worth getting off the lanai for.

AT THE LODGE: John and Michele Gamble were vacationing on the island when they saw this 3.4-acre oceanfront estate and followed the impulse to turn it into a bed-and-breakfast. You'll understand the instant attraction as you drive through the tunnel of Caribbean palms, past the macadamia nut and fruit orchards, to the Victorian-style inn. From the top of the

cliff, you can watch spinner dolphins playing in Pohakumanu Bay. Every suite has a smaller version of the main lanai, perfectly suited to lounging. Many of the rooms have whirlpool tubs and fireplaces (mostly for show—it's rarely cool enough for a fire). All have DVD players, satellite television, ceiling fans, and Italian marble showers. The 4,500-square-foot living room is chock-full of reading nooks and furnished with European and Asian antiques. A separate family room stocks board games, music, movies, and a computer for email addicts.

THE SPORTS: Ease the transition from armchair to hiking trail with the 1-mile rain forest canopy walk past bamboo stands and flowering trees to Akaka Falls, a 420-foot cascade that pounds into a steep ravine. Heartier hikes and horseback rides can be found on the hilly trails of Waipio Valley or in the 217,000-acre Hawaii Volcanoes National Park, where a 4-mile loop trail takes you from the Thurston Lava Tube parking area down forested switchbacks to steam vents on the barren crater floor. Snorkelers can splash among the reef fish south of Hilo along the Kohala Coast, where there's also scuba diving and charter fishing. Sea kayakers can find protected bays and rentals on the Kona side of the island. Surfers should head for Honolii Beach. The birding is best in Kalopa State Park, where you might glimpse an endangered Hawaiian hawk or night heron. Wide shoulders make the two-lane highway that passes by the inn perfect for cycling. Skiers and snowboarders can climb to the "pineapple powder" on Mauna Kea, the 13,796-foot extinct volcano that boasts 100 square miles of skiable terrain in January and February. Access is by four-wheel-drive only. Local companies will gear you up and take you there, even facilitating a one-day combination skiing and surfing trip. Though the innkeepers don't offer gear or guide services, they're happy to refer you to the best outfitters for each activity.

MEALTIME: The gourmet Hawaiian breakfasts start with smooth Kona coffee and fresh tropical juice. Served next are banana pancakes with macadamia nuts, fresh baked cinnamon crumble muffins, smoked chicken and mango sausage, and papaya filled with kiwi. Vegetarians can be accommodated on request. Breakfast is served on the lazy lanai, in the shade of an 11-foot-high ceiling, with the heavy scent of plumeria wafting in after the dishes have been cleared. For lunch and dinner, head for Honumu (half a mile away) or Hilo (15 minutes by car). You can also sign up for one of the inn's cooking classes; the syllabus includes regional specialties like ahi poke, fiddlehead fern soup, and papaya ice cream. Classes cost $90 and last about three hours.

FINE PRINT:
Pets: leave 'em home
Kids: 13 and older
Credit cards: MasterCard, Visa, American Express, Diners Club, JCB
Nearest medical: Hilo, HI (20 minutes)
Weather: Expect daytime temperatures in the 70s and 80s, dropping to the 60s at night. Average yearly rainfall is 100 inches, but most of it comes after dark. The inn sits on a cliff 100 feet above the ocean.

GETTING THERE: Take Highway 19 along the Hamakua coast. Turn onto the inn's driveway just past mile marker 13 (ocean side).

See color photos on pages 161 and 162

SHERATON MOLOKAI LODGE AND BEACH VILLAGE

100 Maunaloa Highway
Maunaloa, Molokai, HI 96770
Tel: 866-500-8313; 808-552-2741
Fax: 808-552-2773
www.sheraton-molokai.com
molokaireservations@sheraton.com

Closest airport: Hoolehua, Molokai, HI (12 miles)
Activities: mountain biking, kayaking, horseback riding, hiking, fishing, snorkeling, diving, surfing, whale watching, mule riding
Season: year-round
Guides/Instruction: mountain biking, hiking, horseback riding, and water sports guides and instruction; children's programs
Services: spa, conference facilities
Accommodations: 22 lodge rooms, 40 tent cabins; capacity 150
Rates: $275–$425 per room, double occupancy; all-inclusive packages also available

Molokai prides itself on its island-wide law that says no building may be taller than a coconut tree. While other Hawaiian islands were busy embracing vertical development, this one developed an impressive network of trails that earned it a reputation as the Fat-Tire Isle. The 54,000-acre Sheraton property alone boasts 75 miles of dirt roads and singletrack that dip and climb across a Martian-looking landscape to cliffs that trace the coastline. Elsewhere on the island, hiking paths cut through the rain forest en route to towering waterfalls at the edge of a surfing beach. Protected bays give kayakers the only access to secluded, white sand beaches. Adventure is Molokai's greatest offering, and this historic-ranch-turned-outfitter-and-lodge is easily the best way in.

AT THE LODGE: Built in 1999 to resemble a 1920s Hawaiian ranch house, the lodge is stocked with modern comforts and shamelessly devoid of grit. No self-respecting Paniolo cowboy would feel at home in such luxury, but you probably won't mind as you step out of your claw-foot tub, wrap yourself in a thick robe, grab a cocktail from the wet bar, and sip it on your private, ocean- or garden-view veranda. Rooms have separate sitting areas, TVs, phones, data ports, and eclectic but tasteful furnishings. Inside the lodge, there's a library, fitness center, and billiard room. Outside is a heated swimming pool, which almost compensates for the 15-minute shuttle ride to the beach. Accessing the Pacific is easier if you're staying at the Beach Village, where the platform-raised, canvas tent cabins are steps from the water. The eco-oriented "tentalows" have solar-powered lights and ceiling fans, open-air bathrooms with flush toilets and pull-chain hot showers, and private wooden decks with lounge chairs and hammocks. As tent life goes, this is plush.

THE SPORTS: If ever there was a place designed for hyperactive outdoors enthusiasts, this is it. The lodge's Molokai Outdoor Activities Desk offers adventures that could keep you busy for weeks. For starters, there's mountain biking. The island's famous red dirt landscape is peppered with dendrite-shaped trees that make zooming across the mostly intermediate trails an otherworldly experience. There's a large selection of rental bikes with optional add-ons like clip-in pedals and water bottle carriages. Ride with a guide or on your own. Open-ocean kayaking is available on guided trips only, but the groups are usually small. From the vantage point of your single or double sit-on-top, you'll see turtles, rays, tropical fish, and maybe a reef shark or two. Other water sports include shoreline casting for bonefish and ulua, snorkeling and diving off white sand beaches, whale watching, and surfing the choppy west-side waves or the more long-board-friendly east side. Rentals are available for all of the above. Hikers can explore the relatively arid west-side trails or shuttle to the other end of the island for a guided Halawa Falls trek. Horseback riding options include a novice trail ride and a rodeo tricks excursion. An outside outfitter offers mule treks down a 1,500-foot cliff that ends at a former leper colony. Archery, paintball, and half-day and full-day children's programs are also available. Unless you've purchased an all-inclusive package, the activities and rentals cost extra. Some prices: $11 a day for snorkel gear rental, $35 to $85 for a guided bike ride, $25 to $45 for a one-day surfboard rental, and $95 for a beach dive. The day spa menu includes Swedish and sports massages, reflexology, aromatherapy, and manual lymph massages for $50 to $145.

MEALTIME: Breakfast, lunch, and dinner are served in the lodge's dining room, Paniolo Bar, or veranda. You can start the day with fresh baked breads and muffins, tropical fruit, and eggs and pancakes or regional specials like poached eggs with island fish and taro hash. The lunch menu features hot sandwiches, soup, chicken, or fish. You can also request a trail lunch with a sandwich, chips, chicken, veggies, and fruit. At the bar, you'll find an impressive tropical cocktail menu. Dinner starts with island appetizers like sashimi, coconut shrimp, or Kalua duck lumpia. Entrées include fresh seafood, meat, or poultry dishes that start at $18. At the Beach Village, meals are made to order at the beachfront, open-air restaurant ($12 to $29 for adults, $6 to $15 for kids). Guests can opt to drive to town for less expensive local fare.

FINE PRINT:
Pets: leave 'em home
Kids: bring 'em on (ages 5 to 12 for the kids' program)
Credit cards: MasterCard, Visa, American Express, Diners Club, JCB
Heads-up: mosquitoes
Nearest medical: Kaunakakai, Molokai, HI (17 miles)
Weather: Winter temperatures range from 50° to 85°F,

and wind and rain are near-daily events. During the rest of the year, the temperatures range from 60° to 90°F with occasional showers. Lodge elevation is 1,300 feet; the beach village is at sea level.

GETTING THERE: Turn right at Hauakea Avenue and drive southwest for a quarter mile. Turn right onto Highway 460 and drive west 12 miles to Maunaloa. The lodge is on the right.

See color photo on page 162

Oregon

MOUNT ASHLAND INN

550 Mount Ashland Road
Ashland, OR 97520
Tel: 800-830-8707; 541-482-8707
www.mtashlandinn.com
stay@mtashlandinn.com

Closest airport: Medford, OR (45 minutes, 25 miles)
Activities: hiking, mountain biking, rafting, kayaking, fishing, climbing, cross-country and downhill skiing, snowboarding, snowshoeing, wildlife watching
Season: year-round
Guides/Instruction: none
Services: none
Accommodations: five suites; capacity 10
Rates: $160–$200 per room, double occupancy; full breakfast and outdoor gear included

From its very beginnings two decades ago, this lodge has literally been a hands-on operation. The use of local materials and handcrafting started with the incense cedar logs that the original owner chopped from the property and hand-peeled to form the walls. It continued with the stained-glass panels that were handmade for the entryway. Today's guests will see it in the furniture and bedding handcrafted by current owners Chuck and Laura Biegert. Almost everything here was constructed on-site, specifically for the inn. The result is a genuine hominess that no designer could replicate.

But don't be fooled by the do-it-yourself roots; there's nothing rustic about this inn. Luxury is the rule, from the in-room hot tubs to the gourmet breakfasts. After a long, hard day on the trails or the slopes, your roughing-it time is done. Snuggle into a thick bathrobe, curl up on the bed, and watch the snow coat the mile-high peaks outside your window.

AT THE LODGE: The four-story, 5,500-square-foot lodge was made entirely from 10- to 14-inch, saddle-notched incense cedar logs that were cut and peeled on-site. Each of the five suites has hand-carved details on the doors, hand-carved log or sleigh beds, and views of Mount Shasta, Mount McLoughlin, or the neighboring forests. Outside, there's a sauna cabin and a large hot tub to soak in under the stars. A major remodeling in 2002 added space to the rooms, plus two-person jetted spas and gas fireplaces. There's no television or in-room phone to detract from the mood. If your romance bells aren't clanging yet, they may be out of order.

THE SPORTS: On a Siskiyou Mountain ridge just 10 minutes from Mount Ashland's 23 ski runs, the inn is a perfectly positioned après-ski spot. Ski and snowboard lessons and rentals are available at Mt. Ashland Ski & Snowboard Resort (541-482-2897; www.mtashland.com), but you don't have to leave the premises to play in the snow. The inn stocks cross-country skis, snowshoes, and sleds; and two golden retrievers will lead the way. Gear is free to guests. In warmer weather, mountain bikers can take the house wheels on a 32-mile ride to Dutchman Peak. The route is mostly over fire roads plus a smattering of singletrack. Fishing and rafting outfitters have the Rogue and Klamath Rivers at their disposal. Climbers can head to Mount Shasta, 30 minutes away. Hikers need not use their cars; the Pacific Crest Trail passes through the inn's backyard, and the property sits on the boundary between Klamath and Rogue River National Forests. The summit of 7,500-foot Mount Ashland is just 3 miles away.

BACKCOUNTRY BONUS: Noah's River Adventures (800-858-2811; www.noahsrafting.com) offers multiday trips on the Rogue River. Class II to IV rapids run through narrow canyons to lodges or campgrounds surrounded by protected old-growth forests where you're more likely to spot otters than humans. Three-day trips, including gear and meals, cost $595 (camping) or $645 (staying at a lodge).

MEALTIME: The breakfast menu changes daily, but expect something like a first course of fresh peach granola parfait with honey yogurt, followed by toasted almond French cheese toast topped with pear compote. The produce is local, the portions are large, and the flavors are never bland. The dining area has a handcrafted trestle table with room for 10, Windsor chairs, and a view of Mount Shasta. No other meals are served at the inn, but the suites have small fridges and microwaves, and Ashland restaurants are 15 miles away. Chateaulin (541-482-2264) on Main Street is a French restaurant and wine shop specializing in local pinot noirs. Their three-course prix fixe menu changes weekly.

FINE PRINT:
Pets: leave 'em home
Kids: 10 and older
Credit cards: MasterCard, Visa, Discover
Nearest medical: Ashland, OR (18 miles)
Weather: Annual snowfall is 16 feet. Winter temperatures can dip to 10°F. Summer highs reach 85°, but nights can drop below freezing. Lodge elevation is 5,500 feet.

GETTING THERE: From Medford, take Interstate 5 south to exit 6. Follow the SKI AREA signs and turn right onto Mount Ashland Road. Drive 5.25 miles. The inn is on the right.

See color photo on page 163

PARADISE LODGE

P.O. Box 456
Gold Beach, OR 97444
Tel: 800-525-2161; 541-247-6022
Fax: 541-247-7714
www.paradise-lodge.com
rrr97@harborside.com

Closest airport: Medford, OR (three hours)
Activities: hiking, rafting, kayaking, fishing, wildlife watching
Season: year-round
Guides/Instruction: rafting guides and instruction
Services: none
Accommodations: six lodge rooms, six cabins; capacity 43
Rates: $115 per person, double occupancy, including meals

One of the few true wilderness lodges left in the continental United States, Paradise Lodge can be reached only by river, helicopter, or trail. It's set in the middle of the Wild and Scenic section of the Rogue River, so the lodge looks much the way it did when homesteader Charlie Pettinger and his pack mules first came here in the early 1900s.

Rafting here means running the Blossom Bar Rapids, a moody, Class IV to V ride made infamous by the 1994 Meryl Streep whitewater thriller *The River Wild.* Once you take out, unload, and dry off, you can celebrate your success with a bottle of the river's namesake ale, then take a seat on the riverside patio and ponder the next phase of your journey.

AT THE LODGE: The main lodge was built between 1959 and 1960, and just about everything at the lodge arrived by river—including the livestock and full-sized freezers. The simple lodge and cabin rooms contain a queen bed, a single bed, and a private bath. Some have additional sleeping space and a fireplace or woodstove. Most of the buildings line the riverfront, with the gardens, orchards, and an airstrip behind. Power comes from a self-contained generator. There are no TVs or phones—perusing the wall-mounted collection of antique weapons, rusted farm tools, and celebrity guest photos is entertainment enough.

THE SPORTS: The well-maintained, 41-mile-long Rogue River Trail runs through the property. Hikers can also take a half-hour walk to a Blossom Bar Rapids overlook to watch the approaching rafters get drenched. Deak's Peak, a strenuous 20 minutes from the lodge, offers a ridgetop, panoramic view of the Paradise region. Hike another half mile amid giant firs and pines and you'll end up at another peak. The trails continue for miles. Anglers can fly-fish or spin-cast for steelhead and salmon on nearby creeks. Rafters and kayakers usually put in at Foster Bar Boat Landing, 7 miles and about four hours upstream. A guided ride costs $70 per adult, $30 per child ages 5 to 11.

BACKCOUNTRY BONUS: A lodge stay can be part of a multiday fishing, rafting, or backpacking trip on the Rogue River or its parallel trail. Contact the lodge's Rogue River Trip Center (800-525-2161) for information.

MEALTIME: Home-style buffet breakfasts, lunches, and dinners are served at a small indoor dining area or outside on the riverside patio. For dinner, expect hearty backcountry favorites like roast beef and hot biscuits with generous servings of homegrown veggies and rich, fresh baked desserts. The kitchen will also clean and prepare your catch, serving it with homemade condiments like a horseradish sauce hot enough to singe your nose hairs with a single whiff. For lunch, you can either eat in or order a trail lunch to go: meat or veggie sandwich, chips, fruit, a homemade brownie, and a drink. Vegetarian options are available at all meals.

FINE PRINT:
Pets: bring 'em on
Kids: if they can get here, they can stay here
Credit cards: MasterCard, Visa
Heads-up: bears, bugs
Nearest medical: Gold Beach, OR (52 miles)
Weather: Summer highs in the 90s; winter lows in the 50s and 60s with lots and lots of rain. Lodge elevation is 350 feet.

GETTING THERE: Hikers can take Interstate 5 north to exit 80 (Glendale), turn left, and drive 3 miles to the old service station on the left. Turn right onto Brown Street, which turns into Rueben Road. Drive 12.3 miles to the wooden sign at the Y. Veer left and drive 12.8 miles. Turn left onto the road marked 32-9-14.2—you'll see a sign with MARIAL spray-painted on the bottom. Continue 15 miles to the trailhead, park, and hike 3.5 miles to the lodge. There's also a 12-mile route. For raft, jet boat, and helicopter access, contact the lodge.

STEAMBOAT INN

42705 North Umpqua Highway
Steamboat, OR 97447
Tel: 800-840-8825; 541-498-2230
Fax: 541-498-2411
www.thesteamboatinn.com
stmbtinn@rosenet.net

Closest airports: Eugene, OR, and Medford, OR (two hours)
Activities: fishing, hiking, mountain and road biking, rafting, kayaking, cross-country, downhill, and backcountry skiing, snowboarding, snowshoeing, horseback riding, climbing, birding
Season: closed January and February
Guides/Instruction: on-site naturalist
Services: massage, conference facilities
Specialties: fishing and dining
Accommodations: eight cabins, five cottages, two suites, four houses; capacity 60
Rates: $145–$265 per room, double occupancy

Fishing camps occupied this fir-flanked stretch of the North Umpqua River in the early 1900s. In the late 1950s, the inn's original owners earned a following by feeding the construction workers who were building the North Umpqua Highway. To this day, fishing and food define the Steamboat Inn experience. But what keeps guests coming back is the management's genuine belief that once you've stayed here, you're part of the family.

On its way from the Cascades to the Pacific, the river runs through Umpqua National Forest, where the inn is allowed to operate by special permit. That means you're not likely to come across any other buildings on your ramblings through the woods. What you will find are springtime mergansers, summer waterfalls, fall begonias, and occasional winter flurries that vanish on the surface of the river.

AT THE LODGE: The pine-paneled, one-room Streamside Cabins are furnished with handmade quilts, Vermont Castings gas stoves, private baths, and decks overlooking the North Umpqua. A wooded half mile away, the four-person cottages have a master bedroom, sleeping loft, kitchenette, and living room with a fireplace. There's a large, tiled tub in the bathroom. In the River Suites, the tubs are positioned for bath-time river viewing. They have all the amenities of the cottages but are sized for two. The fully furnished, three-bedroom Camp Water houses were built on an old tent campsite across the river, just off the Mott Trail. There are phones in the cabins and suites only, no TVs. Fireside reading in the inn's cozy library is the downtime activity of choice.

THE SPORTS: Set in the midst of 31 miles of catch-and-release fly-fishing waters, the lodge has been a favorite among anglers for as long as it has been around. The steelhead are known to be as finicky as the river bottom is slippery; but with the right fly, some boot traction, and a little luck, you can land a 15-pounder (8 pounds is the average size). Fishing licenses and high-end gear are sold at the inn's well-stocked fly shop—remember, no sales tax in Oregon. Guides and drift boat rentals are also nearby. Hiking and mountain biking terrain in Umpqua National Forest is nearly limitless. Hikers should seek advice from the manager, a knowledgeable birder and naturalist, before hitting the trails. Bike rentals are available on-site. In addition to biking the forest trails, cyclists can ride the narrow, curvy highway that climbs into the Cascades. Nearby outfitters run spring to mid-summer rafting trips on Class III to V rapids. Kayaking is possible year-round, water level permitting. There's adrenaline-free paddling at Diamond Lake, 42 miles east of the inn. Near the lake, you'll find the closest skiing (cross-country, downhill, snowcat), snowshoeing, and horseback riding. The area around the inn isn't really known for its climbing, but obsessive rock jocks can find enough pinnacles and rock faces to keep withdrawal pains at bay. If the activities listed aren't enough to keep you busy throughout a stay, Crater Lake National Park lies within day-trip distance.

MEALTIME: Co-owner Sharon Van Loan and manager Pat Lee have published two cookbooks with many of the dishes you'll find on your dinner plate. Should you require further proof that food is important here, take a peek at one of the inn's regularly held winemaker–guest chef dinner menus—celebrity chefs from award-winning restaurants do their best to create the perfect culinary complement to the lodge's incredible setting. The main dining room is redwood-paneled and has slab tables and a gas fireplace. Meals are also served outside on an enclosed back porch overlooking the gardens and river. Before dinner, there's a half hour of wine and hors d'oeuvres to put you in the mood for a multicourse, gourmet feast. Unlike the ever-changing dinner fare, breakfast and lunch feature a set list of standards like omelets and chili burgers, plus a few creative options like the breakfast sour cream roll-ups filled with strawberry-rhubarb jam. You can also order a sack lunch with a sandwich, fruit, veggie, cookie, and drink. Food allergies and dietary preferences can be accommodated on request.

FINE PRINT:
Pets: leave 'em home
Kids: bring 'em on
Credit cards: MasterCard, Visa
Heads-up: poison oak
Nearest medical: Glide, OR (18 miles)
Weather: Summer temperatures range from 55 to 90°F. Spring and fall low temperatures are in the low 40s, and highs are in the upper 80s. There's an average 40 inches of yearly rainfall. The lodge is at 1,100 feet.

GETTING THERE: Take Interstate 5 to Roseburg, then Highway 138 east 38 miles to the lodge.

See color photo on page 163

TIMBERLINE LODGE

Timberline
Timberline Lodge, OR 97028
Tel: 503-622-7979
www.timberlinelodge.com

Closest airport: Portland, OR (65 miles)
Activities: downhill skiing, snowboarding, snowshoeing, hiking, mountain and road biking, windsurfing, fishing, climbing, horseback riding, rafting, kayaking, canoeing, wildlife watching
Season: year-round
Guides/Instruction: skiing and snowboarding instruction
Services: spa, conference facilities
Accommodations: 71 rooms; capacity approximately 200
Rates: $85–$240 per room, double occupancy

Any visit to Timberline Lodge should start with a toast to the Great Depression. If not for that hefty dose of national misery, this National Historic Landmark would never have been built. It came into existence in the mid-1930s, under the auspices of Franklin Roosevelt's public works program, which allowed out-of-work craftsmen and apprentices to spend more than two years constructing and furnishing what would become one of the most celebrated creations of the era.

With daily history tours given by Forest Service employees, the lodge's past is still very much a part of its present. But most visitors come for what lies outside the lodge's famous walls: Timberline Ski Area and the countless recreation opportunities in Mount Hood National Forest.

AT THE LODGE: A 92-foot-tall volcanic basalt chimney forms the center of the light gray lodge, and the east and west wings extend outward on either side. Every inch of the building was constructed by hand, including the intricate metal- and stonework, textiles, and original art. Since 1975, the nonprofit group Friends of Timberline has taken charge of restoration; their work includes tracking down experts in antiquated crafts techniques that honor the historic integrity of the lodge's design. North-facing rooms have views of Mount Hood. South-facing rooms look onto Mount Jefferson and the Three Sisters. Some rooms have fireplaces; all have Timberline signature feather beds and original artwork. Cold-weather perks include six stone fireplaces at the base of the massive chimney, and a year-round hot tub and sauna. There's also a seasonal swimming pool. Bonus for trivia buffs: Yes, this place does look eerily familiar; shots of the exterior were used in the 1980 movie *The Shining*.

THE SPORTS: That lodge employees go snowboarding on their lunch breaks tells you something of the surroundings. More than 1,000 skiable acres lie just outside the lodge's front door. Six chair lifts, including four high-speed quadruple lifts allow fast access to the 3,590 feet of vertical drop. Rentals and lessons—including Bruno's Learn to Ski/Snowboard for kids—are available (skiing and snowboarding only; there is no gear for other sports). Hiking is the next best thing. The Pacific Crest Trail passes through the grounds, and Mount Hood National Forest's 47,100 acres are thick with trails that lead to waterfalls, creeks, and alpine peaks. Biking is not allowed in the immediate area, but mountain and road bikers will find plenty of terrain nearby. Within an hour's drive, windsurfers can access the world-famous Columbia River Gorge. Guided trout and salmon fishing trips are available through local outfitters, as are guided hikes up Mount Hood, the most frequently climbed mountain in the United States. All of the above activities can be arranged at the lodge's front desk, though you may want to call ahead for information and reservations.

MEALTIME: In most restaurants, "regional cuisine" simply means sharing basic flavor schemes with your neighbors. In the lodge's four-star Cascade Dining Room, it means the chanterelles and morels were plucked from a nearby mountainside, the vine-ripened tomatoes were delivered that morning from a small organic farm in the foothills, and the bay shrimp in your Foglie D'Autuno Seafood Pasta came directly from an Oregon bay. The fresh ingredients and creative dishes are enhanced by fireside seating and views of 11,234-foot Mount Hood and its surrounds. Lighter fare is served in the sofa-laden Rams Head Bar. Burgers, fries, and pizzas are the standards at the Wy'East Cafeteria; its attached outdoor deck is the venue of choice on warm, clear days. Breakfast, lunch, and dinner are available at the lodge. If you plan to spend the day on the slopes or the trails, you can order a sack lunch in advance.

FINE PRINT:
Pets: leave 'em home
Kids: 4 and older
Credit cards: all major cards
Heads-up: roads can be icy in winter
Nearest medical: Mount Hood, OR (45 minutes); medically trained patrol on-site
Weather: Prepare for anything. On a typical summer day, the temperature could be 75°F or it could be snowing. Highs are generally in the mid-80s, and lows can drop to 20 below. Lodge elevation is 6,000 feet. The annual snowfall is 20 feet.

GETTING THERE: From the airport, take Interstate 84 east and exit at Wood Village. Turn left on Burnside Drive and follow Highway 26 east 45 miles to the town of Government Camp. Turn left onto Timberline Access Road. Transportation is available through Luxury Accommodations (503-668-7433; $65 per person).

See color photo on page 164

Washington

FREESTONE INN

31 Early Winters Drive
Mazama, WA 98833
Tel: 800-639-3809; 509-996-3906
Fax: 509-996-3907
www.freestoneinn.com
info@freestoneinn.com

Closest airports: Wenatchee, WA (100 miles), or Twisp, WA (private/charter airstrip, 22 miles)
Activities: hiking, mountain and road biking, rafting, canoeing, climbing, mountaineering, fishing, cross-country, backcountry, and downhill skiing, snowboarding, snowshoeing, horseback riding, llama trekking, hot-air ballooning, sleigh riding, orienteering
Season: year-round
Guides/Instruction: climbing, mountaineering, cross-country skiing, and fly-fishing guides and instruction; on-site naturalist; children's programs
Services: spa, conference facilities
Specialties: kids' programs and cross-country skiing
Accommodations: 21 rooms, 15 cabins, three lakeside lodges; capacity 100
Rates: $100–$245 (rooms), $100–$485 (cabins), $250–$435 (lodges), lodging only, double occupancy

Most lodges fall into one of two categories: down-home friendly or upscale chic. The Freestone Inn manages to fit both. Maybe its cattle-ranch past is what keeps the polished décor and gourmet cuisine from feeling at all pretentious. More likely it's the staff's focus on kid stuff and outdoor fun. It's hard to take yourself too seriously when you've spent the morning rolling in snow.

Situated in the remote Methow Valley on the east side of the raggedy Cascade Range, this 120-acre property is 14 miles from the nearest town. Fortunately, just about everything you'd want is available on-site, from fishing lures to Starbucks coffee (yes, folks, this is Washington).

AT THE LODGE: The architects of the main lodge may have had a classic log cabin motif in mind, but the elegant entry hall, with its high, beamed ceiling of roughhewn logs and its 30-foot-high river rock fireplace, is more suited to sport coats than flannels (it should be noted, however, that dirty jeans are the standard guest attire). Lodge rooms have stone fireplaces, and balconies that overlook the property's 5-acre Freestone Lake and a backdrop of pines climbing up the Cascades. A small fridge, CD player, VCR, and satellite television are standard amenities. Cabins with fireplaces, decks, and kitchenettes are scattered along Early Winters Creek, a gentle stream that cuts through the south side of the property. Six of the cabins were built in the 1940s and refurbished when the main lodge was built in 1996. The separate, three-bedroom Steelhead Lodge and Cutthroat Lodge sit between the lake and stream at the end of their own private drive. Guests have access to two outdoor hot tubs, lakeside and streamside. The massive lake tub can easily accommodate you and your 10 closest friends. Two-bedroom Rainbow Lodge sits alone on the opposite side of the lake.

THE SPORTS: The options are close to limitless. Hiking trails (skiable when there's snow)

crisscross the property, starting with the half-mile path that circles Freestone Lake. You can bring your fishing rod for some catch-and-release angling and then double back to the hot tub. Longer trails run through 2.1 million acres of surrounding national forest and wilderness. Paths run to waterfalls, wildflower-strewn meadows, and outcroppings that overlook snow-tipped peaks. More than 400 miles of trail are open to mountain bikers. Road bikers use a mix of flat valleys and hilly mountain passes. Climbing guides take most peak seekers to nearby Liberty Bell, but the famous Cascades have no shortage of rock and ice to explore. In winter, heli-skiing is available directly from the inn's helipad. Two hundred kilometers of groomed trails keep cross-country skiers busy. Downhill skiing isn't far away. Rounding out the winter menu are sleigh rides. Parents take note: Freestone's KidVenture program takes 8- to 12-year-olds fishing, hiking, horseback riding, climbing, biking, swimming, and orienteering for $45 to $65 per day. All outdoor activities, including gear and guides, can be arranged through Jack's Hut, located just behind the main lodge.

BACKCOUNTRY BONUS: Jack's Hut can arrange backcountry horse or llama pack trips up to a week long, as well as extended alpine mountaineering adventures and hut-to-hut skiing trips that take you deep into the Okanogan National Forest and Pasaytan Wilderness. Packages start at $125 per person.

MEALTIME: Food lovers will feel right at home, with entrées like seared pancetta-wrapped sea scallops carefully crafted by executive chef Todd A. Brown. Local produce is used whenever possible, but the menu isn't limited to

Northwest fare. The wine list is extensive enough for appropriate pairing. Breakfast and dinner are served in the inn's intimate dining room, beneath a towering, two-story fireplace. Sack lunches of whole-grain sandwiches, chips, fruit, an energy bar, and juice can be ordered at Jack's Hut. For an extra $20, the staff will pack it in the inn's signature backpack.

FINE PRINT:
Pets: leave 'em home
Kids: bring 'em on
Credit cards: MasterCard, Visa, American Express, Diner's Club
Heads-up: roads can be icy; the inn is in bear and cougar country; occasional snowmobiles
Nearest medical: Brewster, WA (49 miles)
Weather: Summer highs can hit a dry 90°F; winter lows can dip to 20°. Lodge elevation is only 2,200 feet, but the area gets some snow (82 inches on average).

GETTING THERE: Airport transportation costs $240 round trip from Wenatchee, $75 from Twisp. From Seattle, take Interstate 5 north to exit 208 onto State Road 530 to Darrington. Stay on State Road 530 and exit onto State Road 20 East. Drive over the pass, descend to the valley floor, and look for a blue Department of Transportation sign that says FREESTONE INN NEXT RIGHT. The entrance is a quarter mile up on the right.

See color photos on pages 164 and 165

PARADISE INN

55106 Kernahan Road East
Ashford, WA 98304
Tel: 360-569-2275
Fax: 360-569-2770
www.guestservices.com/rainier

Closest airport: Seattle, WA (80 miles)
Activities: hiking, climbing, mountaineering, cross-country and backcountry skiing, snowshoeing, fishing, road biking, wildlife watching
Season: mid-May through early October
Guides/Instruction: none
Services: none
Accommodations: 118 rooms; capacity 200
Rates: $82–$211 per room, double occupancy

Much has changed since this historic lodge first opened its doors in 1917. Guests no longer bed down in platform tents behind the main building; the dining room manager no longer announces dinner by blowing a whistle from the back porch; and $100,000 no longer buys you a custom-built, Swiss-chalet-inspired, cedar mega-lodge with a living room big enough to contain several homes.

Yet much has stayed the same. Situated within Mount Rainier National Park, Paradise Inn is still surrounded by hardwood forests, glacial peaks, and subalpine meadows as far as you can see. Careful preservation has retained that classic parks lodge feel you can only get from details like the 1919 adz-carved grandfather clock in the lobby. And, most important, the lodge has stayed true to its original purpose: providing a comfortable place to recharge after a day in the Rainier outdoors.

AT THE LODGE: The lodge was built at tree level to allow an unobstructed backdrop of Mount Rainier. Its Alaskan cedar logs were taken from the nearby Silver Forest, so named when a 1915 forest fire turned the charred bark of area trees a grayish silver but left the inner wood unscathed. Peeled-log beams cross the top of the 50-foot-high living-room ceiling. Three massive stone fireplaces decorate the lobby and dining room. The rooms are basic: some have shared bathrooms; none have televisions or phones. All have incredible views of the outdoors. The lodge is a registered National Historic Inn.

THE SPORTS: More than 240 miles of trails fan out in all directions from the lodge. The very short Nisqually Vista Trail starts at Paradise and runs to a glacier lookout. For a longer hike, drive down the hill to the Sunrise parking area and set out on the Burroughs Mountain Trail, a 5-mile loop that starts along the alpine tundra and climbs 1,200 feet through high meadows to mountain ridges. A more challenging five-mile loop is the Skyline Trail, which begins at the Paradise Visitor Center and climbs the west side of Alta Vista Ridge. Trails are generally snow-free from mid-July through September. When there's snow, rent snowshoes and cross-country gear at the Ski Touring Center in Longmire (360-569-2411). Rangers lead guided snowshoe walks throughout the season. The backcountry skiing is on snowfields and glaciers. There are no groomed trails, but you can count on plenty of fresh powder. Climbers have access to endless rock and ice; guide service is available outside the park. Although fishing does not require a permit, there's not much to catch. Check for stream closures before heading out. Bikers have no reason for high hopes either. The trails are closed to mountain bikes, and road riding is discouraged because of limited visibility and the absence of shoulders. If you must ride, try the road from Longmire to Paradise. There's a 2,700-foot elevation gain, and you'll pedal past the point where the Paradise River tumbles 168 feet off a ledge at Narada Falls. If you leave your bike, you can walk the short trail to the base of the falls.

BACKCOUNTRY BONUS: The obvious multiday extension is to summit Mount Rainier (at 14,410 feet, the highest volcanic peak in the Cascades). But you could also work up a longing for a comfortable lodge stay by starting with a two-week backpacking trip on the 93-mile Wonderland Trail, which encircles the mountain. All overnight trips require a wilderness permit. Guide service is available from outfitters outside the park.

MEALTIME: Expect culinary miracles and you'll be sorely disappointed. Breakfasts, lunches, and dinners are served fireside in the dining room, and the regular morning menu features all the expected standards. The Sunday brunch, however, transcends the norm. Sack lunches with a sandwich, trail mix, fruit, carrot sticks, and a drink are available. Daily afternoon tea is served in the mezzanine. The dinner lineup changes every year, but highlights from past menus include a Yakima spinach salad with sliced Washington apples and candied walnuts, seared salmon with blackberry ginger compote and seasoned rice, and bourbon buffalo meatloaf with a Jack Daniels sauce. The emphasis is on regional ingredients. Vegetarian options are always available. From late May through September, the snack bar (soup, chili, sandwiches) is a cheaper, faster alternative to the restaurant.

FINE PRINT:
Pets: leave 'em home
Kids: bring 'em on
Credit cards: all major cards
Heads-up: glacial floods, landslides, debris flows
Nearest medical: Ashford, WA (24 miles)
Weather: Summer temperatures range from the 60s to 70s; winter temperatures drop to the 20s and 30s. The average yearly rainfall is 70 inches, and there's an impressive 680 inches of annual snowfall (the world record for the most snowfall in a single season was set here in 1971–72: 1,122 inches). Lodge elevation is 5,400 feet.

GETTING THERE: Take Interstate 5 south to Highway 512 east to Highway 7 south. At Elbe, turn onto Highway 706 east and continue to the Nisqually Entrance. The inn is 19 miles inside Mount Rainier National Park.

See color photo on page 165

RUN OF THE RIVER

9308 East Leavenworth Road
P.O. Box 285
Leavenworth, WA 98826
Tel: 800-288-6491; 509-548-7171
www.runoftheriver.com
info@runoftheriver.com

Closest airport: Seattle, WA (110 miles)
Activities: birding, hiking, mountain and road biking, rafting, kayaking, canoeing, fishing, climbing, cross-country, downhill, and backcountry skiing, snowboarding, snowshoeing, horseback riding, wildlife watching
Season: year-round
Guides/Instruction: none
Services: spa, conference facilities
Specialties: birding
Accommodations: six suites; capacity 12
Rates: $205–$245 per room, breakfast included

Your first clue is the set of binoculars in your room. Next to them, the birding booklet, which you open to page two: "Top Ten Bird Species You'll See from Your Deck." Booklet in hand, you walk to said deck, take a seat on your private log swing, and before you can lift the binoculars, a goldfinch flutters into view. It doesn't take an ace detective to figure out that this is Birding Central.

If birds aren't your bag, Run of the River's six impossibly romantic suites lend themselves nicely to . . . ahem, indoor pursuits. And nearby outfitters have the outdoors covered year-round. You could choose a different sport each day and stay busy for weeks.

AT THE LODGE: For anyone planning to log a lot of in-room hours (as most guests here do), rest assured that the suites were designed to encourage such intentions. High cathedral ceilings and lots of windows give the rooms an airy feel, perfect for relaxing on the handmade, locally crafted furniture and taking in views of the surrounding mountains, river, and bird refuge. Bathrooms have heated slate floors and walk-in showers with 12-inch showerheads. The hand-hewn, four-poster beds frame high-end mattresses that could challenge your will to get out of bed. If you do leave your bed, it will be to take advantage of fireplaces and in-room Jacuzzi tubs surrounded by stone. The common area is stocked with cushy leather chairs clustered near a river rock fireplace. Around the corner is the open kitchen. Originally built in 1978, the buildings are made of logs and rock that blend with their surroundings. A 2002 renovation took any remaining rough edges and polished them into oblivion. Run of the River is pure luxury.

THE SPORTS: If the in-room amenities, bird book, and peanuts (for feeding the jays) aren't evidence enough of avian presence, consider this: the property is bordered on two sides by a state bird refuge: the Great Washington Birding Trail runs straight through Icicle Valley; and in 2003 the Audubon Society opened an interpretive center a mile away. But recreational opportunities here aren't just for the birds. Hiking and biking trail maps and guides are available in each room; the trail maps cover 399,000-acre Alpine Lakes Wilderness, which is just outside the door. There are hundreds of miles of hiking trails, including some "locals only" paths that

the staff will divulge only to paying guests. Day packs, trekking poles, and trail passes are available for loan. Cyclists can ride wide loops on little-used country roads. Mountain biking terrain ranges from flat fire roads to Devil's Gulch, the best-known singletrack in the state, just 15 minutes away. Class II and III rapids make the Wenatchee River a great first-time rafting spot. Canoeists can paddle Lake Wenatchee or a quiet, portage-free stretch of the Columbia River. The nation's biggest chinook salmon hatchery is a mile upstream from the lodge; May is the best time for angling. Icicle Valley's granite is a rock jock's heaven; you can see Snow Lakes Wall from the decks of the suites. Nearby Eagle Creek Ranch offers two-hour to full-day guided horseback rides through trails tinged with lupine in the spring. Come snowtime, there's downhill skiing and snowboarding at nearby Mission Ride and Stevens Pass, with lots of tree-filled backcountry terrain. Local guides run snowcat trips to Chumstick Mountain. Of the 30 kilometers of the valley's groomed cross-country ski track, 8 are lit for night skiing. Snowshoers need only step out the lodge's front door. Gear that is unavailable at the lodge can be rented in town. You'll find a long list of outfitters in your room.

MEALTIME: Breakfast is the only meal served at the lodge, but it's hearty enough to last most guests until dinner. Locally roasted coffee rouses you to full enjoyment of what follows: pear-huckleberry crumble or a sourdough breakfast bowl filled with chorizo and rice, cinnamon walnut breakfast cake, organic yogurt, fresh local fruit, and creative fruit smoothie concoctions called Boat Drinks that are meals in themselves. Produce and herbs come from an on-site garden or nearby organic farms whenever possible. Vegetarians can have a feast here. Evening meals are a mile away in Leavenworth, where several restaurants do their best to match the high standard set by the lodge's breakfast chef.

FINE PRINT:
Pets: leave 'em home
Kids: adults only, please
Credit cards: MasterCard, Visa, Discover
Heads-up: mosquitoes
Nearest medical: Leavenworth, WA (one mile)
Weather: Summer highs to 85°F, lows in the 50s. Winter temperatures of 20° to 40° with plenty of snow to play in (yearly average is 71 inches). There's not too much rain on this side of the Cascades, but packing waterproof gear is still a good idea. Lodge elevation is 1,100 feet.

GETTING THERE: Drive north on Interstate 405 to Woodinville, then Highway 522 north to Monroe. At Monroe, turn east onto Highway 2 and drive 85 miles through Leavenworth. Take East Leavenworth Road south for exactly 1 mile. Turn right at the lodge sign.

See color photo on page 166

SUN MOUNTAIN LODGE

P.O. Box 1000
Winthrop, WA 98862
Tel: 800-572-0493; 509-996-2211
Fax: 509-996-3133
www.sunmountainlodge.com
sunmtn@methow.com

Closest airport: Wenatchee, WA (98 miles)
Activities: downhill, cross-country, and backcountry skiing, snowboarding, snowshoeing, fishing, hiking, rafting, kayaking, canoeing, mountain biking, birding, climbing, horseback riding, dogsledding, ice skating, hot-air ballooning
Season: year-round
Guides/Instruction: fly-fishing and cross-country skiing guides and instruction; backcountry skiing, mountain biking, and hiking guides; on-site naturalists; children's programs
Services: spa, conference facilities
Specialty: cross-country skiing
Accommodations: 99 lodge rooms, 13 cabins; capacity 250
Rates: $140–$650 per room

This larger-than-life resort dominates a hilltop on the east side of the Cascades Range, and its 3,000 acres of private terrain provide a gigantic playground that accommodates hundreds of guests. The main attraction is its network of cross-country skiing trails, one of the largest in the United States. Hundreds of miles of nearby hiking and biking trails, award-winning cuisine, and a full-service day spa leave ample opportunity for not-so-snowy adventures.

AT THE LODGE: CD players, thick robes, and handmade quilts are standard luxuries in the main lodge rooms. More than half of the rooms also have fireplaces and private decks; all have views of the Cascades or Methow Valley. As you might expect from a lodge of this size, the main building offers more than a place to sleep. There's a library with a fireside

reading nook, a gift shop, two restaurants, and an exercise room (in case you can't find enough ways to sweat outdoors). As you walk across the quartzite floor of the lobby toward the log reception desk and lava rock fireplace, you'll have a clear view of the pool and outdoor terrace. Down the hill a mile and a half is Patterson Lake, where 13 cabins sit amid the cottonwoods. They range in size from one-room studios to loft suites with two bathrooms, full kitchens, living rooms, gas fireplaces, and verandas. The kitchens are stocked with utensils. All of the cabins are quiet: none have phones or televisions. They share a children's playground and barbecue facilities.

THE SPORTS: For aficionados of the skinny ski, nothing compares to a fresh-powder day on Sun Mountain's 200 kilometers of groomed trails. Downhillers and snowboarders will find 1,240 vertical feet at the Loup Loup Ski Bowl, 25 miles away. North Cascade Heli-Skiing (800-494-HELI) can show you the backcountry bowls. Maps of packed, signposted snowshoeing trails are available at the lodge, as is rental gear. In the off-season, the lodge's activities desk doesn't slow down a bit. Horseback riding programs run from mid-April through October. Rides range from 90 minutes to a half day and can be combined with a barbecue dinner or "buckaroo breakfast" on the trail. There's Class III to IV rafting on Methow River from April through July. Guests can sea kayak, canoe, and fish on 130-acre Patterson Lake (on-site; rentals available), and fly-fish on rivers and streams. Trail maps and rental bikes are available for the several hundred miles of trails in Chelan Sawtooth Wilderness, Okanogan National Forest, and North Cascades National Park. Day and evening children's programs treat kids ages 5 to 9 to games, crafts, and field trips for $12 to $25.

BACKCOUNTRY BONUS: The lodge's activity center can arrange overnight horse packing trips in the Chelan Sawtooth or Pasayten Wilderness. A "deluxe trip" with a cook, wrangler, food, packhorses, and two-person tents costs $125 per day. In winter, outfitters offer multiday, hut-to-hut skiing trips on Methow Valley trails. Lodging is rustic, but supplies are delivered to your hut. Prices vary.

MEALTIME: Chef Patrick Miller's creative menu adds Pacific Northwest flare to game, seafood, and vegetarian standards. A big bowl of his much-loved bouillabaisse makes a perfect end to a chilly day, and a 5,000-bottle wine cellar guarantees proper pairing. Breakfast, lunch, and dinner are served in the dining room and Eagle's Nest Café and Lounge. The "Lunches to Go" menu gives new dignity to the paper sack with entrées like the Roasted Vegetable Wrap and the North Cascade Hiker bagel sandwich. Should you get lucky during a day of angling, the kitchen staff will gladly clean and cook your catch. And if dining out requires too much effort, room service is an option.

FINE PRINT:
Pets: leave 'em home
Kids: bring 'em on
Credit cards: MasterCard, Visa, American Express, Discover
Heads-up: bears
Nearest medical: Winthrop and Twisp, WA (9 miles)
Weather: Summer high of 85°F, winter low of 20°. Seven to 9 feet of yearly snow; 15 inches of rain. Lodge elevation is 3,000 feet.

GETTING THERE: Drive north on Highway 97 to Pateros, north on Highway 153 to Highway 20, west on 20 to Winthrop; then follow the lodge signs 9 miles to Sun Mountain.

See color photo on page 166

Canada

CLAYOQUOT WILDERNESS RESORTS

P.O. Box 130
Tofino, B.C.
Canada V0R 2Z0
Tel: 888-333-5405; 250-726-8235
Fax: 250-726-8558
www.wildretreat.com
info@wildretreat.com

Closest airport: Tofino, B.C. (30 minutes)
Activities: hiking, mountain biking, kayaking, canoeing, fishing, mountaineering, snorkeling, diving, surfing, horseback riding, birding, wildlife watching
Season: April through November
Guides/Instruction: hiking, mountain biking, paddling, fishing, mountaineering, diving, bear and whale watching guides; on-site naturalists
Services: spa, conference facilities
Accommodations: 16 rooms; capacity 32
Rates: $480–$844 per person, all-inclusive Eco Adventure Package (transport, meals, gear, activities); three-night minimum; spa packages also available

At some point between the ahi tartare appetizer and the salmonberry lavender sorbet dessert, you're joined at the dinner table by the lodge's sports director, who will take the most important order of the evening. Tomorrow's activities menu is almost too much to digest, but you manage to settle on a morning sea cave expedition and an afternoon mud wrap. Life on Clayoquot's floating Vancouver Island lodge sure is rough, but you'll adapt.

AT THE LODGE: This former fishing lodge, tugged to Quait Bay in 1997 and renovated for a more glamorous existence in 1998, is linked to the shore by a network of docks. On land, there's a longhouse used for special events, a native sweat lodge, and a full-service spa. Most of the buildings have local cedar siding, polished cedar floors, and roughhewn timbers and beams. Slate and river rock are used throughout. Guest rooms have private decks with ocean or mountain views. The private bathrooms are stocked with aromatherapy products and terry robes. Down duvets cover the beds. There are no in-room phones or TVs, but there's a house phone and satellite TV in the library lounge and games area. Downtime is usually spent at the fireside lounge by the open kitchen in the Great Room. There's also a fitness room and an outdoor hot tub.

THE SPORTS: Set inside the Clayoquot Sound UNESCO Biosphere Reserve, the 250-acre property includes two private lakes flanked by old-growth forest and a pristine stretch of coastline. The assumption behind the Eco Adventure Package is that you'll want to participate in all of the activities offered by the lodge. Guided whale and bear watching are included in a stay, as are hiking, mountain biking, sea kayaking, horseback riding on wilderness trails, scuba diving to kelp forests and shipwrecks, and ocean or freshwater fishing for salmon, halibut, steelhead or trout, and more. Expert guides lead all activities (gear is provided), but you can set off on your own instead. Hiking options range from a short interpretive trail to all-day hauls on old logging roads through old-growth forests. You can also take a hike or guided marine trip to Hot Springs Cove. The area offers a good chance to see deer, elk, eagles, whales, seals, and the occasional black bear or cougar. In the spa, you'll have access to hot tubs, a rain forest sauna, and an outdoor shower. Treatments are available à la carte or as a package option.

BACKCOUNTRY BONUS: The resort operates a luxury wilderness outpost at nearby Bedwell River. This 500-acre property borders Strathcona Provincial Park. The outpost's safari-style white canvas prospector tents sit on wooden platforms and are furnished with Adirondack beds, Oriental rugs, antique fur-

niture, and remote-controlled propane woodstoves. There's even enough electricity to power your hair dryer. In addition to the 11 guest tents, there are two dining tents, a games tent, a library tent, two spa tents, and a camp kitchen staffed with trained chefs who prepare slow-roasted stews, game, and seafood dishes and bake fresh breads and pies in huge outdoor stone ovens. All tents are linked by cedar boardwalks. The cost is $720 to $844, all-inclusive (floatplane, meals, activities, gear, spa services); three-night minimum.

MEALTIME: Day trippers from Tofino—which has no shortage of world-class restaurants—often take the 30-minute boat trip just to partake in Clayoquot's gourmet fare. But unlike outsiders, lodge guests won't get a bill at the end of the meal. The staff calls the cuisine "modern natural," meaning health-conscious, flavorful dishes that emphasize local seafood and organic ingredients. After hors d'oeuvres in the lounge, you'll move to the dining room for a four-course feast that may start with watercress and scallion soup with seared scallops and crème fraîche followed by pan-seared stuffed beef tenderloin with a port sediment sauce or a seafood platter with Dungeness crab, oysters, mussels, clams, salmon, halibut, and prawns. The menu changes frequently, depending on the availability of seasonal ingredients. Vegetarians can choose from meatless entrées—real dishes, not just afterthoughts. A take-away lunch might include a grilled veggie sandwich, fruit salad, a homemade granola bar, and apple streudel. Any fish you catch can be cleaned, packed for travel, and shipped home. Sadly, the chef does not come with it.

FINE PRINT:

Pets: leave 'em home
Kids: welcome, if closely supervised
Credit cards: MasterCard, Visa, American Express
Nearest medical: Tofino, B.C. (10 minutes by air)
Weather: Highs in the mid-60s, lows in the low 50s. The

area gets an average 125 inches of yearly rainfall, most of it in the off-season. The lodge is at sea level.

GETTING THERE: Airport transportation (the flight between Vancouver and Tofino, and the water taxi to the lodge) from Vancouver is included in a stay. A $300 credit is given to guests who arrange their own transportation to Tofino. If you're driving, stay on Campbell Street as you enter town, turn right onto 4th Street, left on Main Street, and park in the upper lot between 2nd and 3rd Streets. The pickup point is Method Marine. Parking is free. A floating helicopter pad and floatplane parking are located at the resort.

INCONNU LODGE

Box 29008 OK Mission RPO
Kelowna, B.C.
Canada V1W 4A7
Tel: 250-860-4187
Fax: 250-860-8894
www.inconnulodge.com
info@inconnulodge.com

Closest airport: Whitehorse, Yukon Territory (180 air miles)
Activities: fishing, hiking, canoeing, kayaking, wildlife watching, climbing
Season: mid-June through mid-September
Guides/Instruction: fishing and photography guides and instruction, hiking guides, children's programs
Services: conference facilities
Accommodations: five cabins; capacity 12
Rates: $4,495 per person for five days, $5,495 for seven days, all-inclusive (meals, activities, airport transportation)

When you've got a floatplane, jet boats, and a helicopter at your disposal, scouting for fishing spots takes on a new meaning—especially when the region you're exploring is bigger than the state of Montana and almost entirely devoid of humans. Lines and lures in tow, you soar above peaks and lakes and rivers and valleys before setting down by a ribbon of water that has possibly never been fished. You drop a dry fly on the surface to see if it floats, and just like that, you've nabbed a grayling.

Welcome to the Yukon, Inconnu style. It's all the wilderness you can handle without a hint of roughing it. The lodge's gourmet dining, shorefront cabins, and cedar sauna would appease a finicky debutante. The angling, paddling, hiking and climbing will impress the most seasoned outdoorsperson. And even if you never don your waders or step aboard a chopper, watching the northern lights from a lakeside hot tub would in itself be worth the trip.

AT THE LODGE: Knotty cedar planks line the walls and ceilings of the duplex cabins and 6,500-square-foot lodge. Carpeted floors and in-room heaters help stave off the occasional nighttime chill. There are no phones, but the cabins have electricity and hot and cold running water in the private bathrooms. There's satellite TV in the lodge. Each cabin has a view of McEvoy Lake, and you won't need binoculars to get a good look at the loons. You can shoot pool or toss darts in the lodge's bar before retreating to the formal dining room for dinner. The conference room has slide and video equipment, but if taxidermy makes you queasy, consider holding your meeting in the 10-person outdoor sauna instead.

THE SPORTS: A strict catch-and-release policy in most areas has kept these lakes and rivers as fish-rich as they've ever been. There's a guide for every two lodge guests. All rods, reels, flies, and lures are included, as are the daily fly-ins. You'll fly-fish, troll, and spin-cast for lake trout, Dolly Varden, northern pike, arctic grayling, and inconnu. Two motorboats at each area lake give guests access to waters not reachable by air. Alpine heli-hiking is also included. You and a guide will be dropped off at a trailhead for any trek that suits your mood. Since the tree line is just 700 feet above the lodge, ridgetop hiking is the norm. You'll break for a picnic lunch, then walk a bit more before the guide calls in your location by satellite phone. Ten minutes later, a helicopter is on its way. Paddlers can take a house canoe across 5-by-2-mile McEvoy Lake to a 5-mile, Class II river trip that runs through a chain of lakes. You'll be picked up by a floatplane at the end. Like everything else, the paddling trip is part of the package. The local wildlife roster includes moose, caribou, eagles, loons, ospreys, and the occasional grizzly or wolf.

BACKCOUNTRY BONUS: For a lower-budget option, try Inconnu's do-it-yourself camps. You'll fly from Whitehorse to the lodge before being transferred to the remote camp. There you'll find a simple cabin with a woodstove, deck chairs, a gas cooking stove, a cookware-stocked kitchen, a gas lantern, and a deck of cards. There's also a satellite phone and a 14-foot motorboat with padded swivel seats. Bring your own fishing gear, food, and sleeping bag. Your last night is spent back at the lodge, where you can indulge in a hot shower and a great meal before heading home. The lodging cost for a five-day trip is $2,750 (up to four guests), plus $300 per person for transportation. Lodge guests can opt to include a lake-cabin overnight in their stay. You'll fly in with a guide and two boats, then fish, sleep, fish some more, and fly home the next evening. Another add-on option is for serious climbers only. The lodge's partner airline, Kluane Airways, takes you from Inconnu to the famed, 3,000-foot vertical cliffs of the Cirque of the Unclimbables. At the end of the trip, there's a one-night lodge stay. The cost is about $3,300 for two people.

MEALTIME: Big breakfasts are cooked to order, with fresh baked goods to start. Picnic lunches include deli sandwiches, fruit, homemade cookies and muffins, and drinks. There's also the option of having the guide cook and clean your catch for a shore lunch. The dinner menu changes daily, with starters like asparagus and escargot in phyllo followed by creative salads. Main course dishes range from duck with Grand Marnier sauce to beef tenderloin with foie gras sauce, but the specialty is fresh coho salmon. Restricted diets are always accommodated on request.

FINE PRINT:
Pets: welcome
Kids: bring 'em on
Credit cards: MasterCard, Visa, American Express
Heads-up: mosquitoes
Nearest medical: Watson Lake, Yukon Territory (105 air miles); medivacs to the hospital in Whitehorse, Yukon Territory (180 air miles)
Weather: In-season temperatures range from 50° to 80°F; rain is always a possibility. Lodge elevation is 3,350 feet.

GETTING THERE: The lodge is reachable only by air. Transportation to the lodge from Whitehorse is included in a stay.

See color photo on page 167

ISLAND LAKE LODGE

602a 2nd Avenue
Box 1229
Fernie, B.C.
Canada V0B 1M0
Tel: 888-422-8754; 250-423-3700
Fax: 250-423-4055
www.islandlakelodge.com
info@islandlakelodge.com

Closest airport: Cranbrook, B.C. (one hour)
Activities: backcountry skiing, snowboarding, hiking, canoeing, fishing, mountain biking, horseback riding, climbing, mountaineering
Season: mid-December through early April; mid-June through September
Guides/Instruction: hiking and fishing guides, canoeing instruction, on-site naturalists, children's programs
Services: spa, conference facilities
Specialty: snowcat skiing
Accommodations: 26 rooms; capacity 48
Rates: $240–$340 CAD, double occupancy, including meals (summer); $600–$850 CAD per person, including meals, cat skiing, and gear (winter); three-day minimum in winter

At Island Lake Lodge, three deluxe snowcats scale the slopes each morning, carrying 36 lucky skiers and snowboarders to a private playground roughly the size of Whistler. Some days bring a dozen runs and 15,000 or so vertical feet. Dry, chunky flakes. Deep, empty bowls. No helicopter required.

Partly owned by snowbiz superstars like photographer Mark Gallup and extreme-ski demigod Scot Schmidt, the lodge has drawn such a steady stream of snowcat savants that peak-season rooms fill one year in advance. Last-minute bookings are more easily nabbed in the summer, when the lodge downgrades its status to Just Another Phenomenally Beautiful Canadian Wilderness Hangout.

AT THE LODGE: Rooms are divided among three tamarack lodges, the oldest of which (The Bear) has shared bathrooms and a slight college dorm feel. More grown-up are The Red Eagle and The Cedar, with en suite bathrooms and a private deck off every room. Each lodge has two massage rooms, where you can tackle after-ski kinks with any number of treatments. There are no phones in the rooms, but each lodge has a cellular pay phone. Guests congregate around the common-room fireplaces and in three outdoor hot tubs. The house TV (videos only, no cable) is in the main lodge's game room, where you'll also find the requisite Ping-Pong and darts. Most rooms have great views of the Lizard Range or 25-acre Island Lake. Turbine power and running water come from a natural spring.

THE SPORTS: It's impossible to over-hype the skiing experience at Island Lake Lodge. It starts with a ride to a 7,000-foot mountain summit on a tractor equipped with glove dryers, clothes hooks, and thermoses full of hot cocoa. At the summit, you'll choose from 7,500 acres of alpine bowls, tree runs, cliff jumps, and gentle slopes. You can count on carving fresh tracks on a 20-foot-deep snowpack all the way down the mountain. It's enough to make you swear off ski lifts forever. Skis, snowboards, snowshoes, and poles are available for rent. Bring your own boots. Island Lake Lodge not only owns all of this acreage, they also protect it. Some of the region's oldest cedars grow in the property's woods. In the summer, naturalists lead 90-minute hikes on the Old Growth Trail, where tree hugging requires several sets of arms per massive trunk. Roughly 15 miles of paths constitute the well-maintained trail system, and a separate path connects mountain bikers to fat-tire-friendly, off-site trails. An easy hike is the 1.5-mile walk around the lake. All-day treks to peaks, and plenty in between, are

among the many hiking options. The lodge stocks canoes for guests to take on Island Lake. Horseback rides and fishing guides can also be arranged. Kids ages 6 to 12 can escape their parents every weekday in July and August, when Wilderness Kids Camp counselors teach the finer points of tracking animals, eating berries, and camping out in teepees. At press time, plans were under way to start a climbing and alpine mountaineering program. Call for details.

MEALTIME: Meals are served in the main lodge dining room, where windows frame views of Island Lake and the surrounding peaks. The menu is fixed in winter, featuring a different main dish each night. Summertime choices include international entrées like veal, crab, and chicken pad thai or ostrich-stuffed quail, and creative desserts like banana-walnut spring rolls with caramel-rum sauce. Nonguests can dine for $38.50 CAD (for overnighters, meals are part of the package). Even the lunch menu transcends the ski lodge standard, with dishes like seafood skewers, aged balsamic-soy vegetable chop suey, and a daily soup-and-sandwich combination with fresh baked bread. Trail lunches contain sandwiches, fruit, juice, and cookies or candy bars. Government regulations prevent the lodge from cooking any fish you catch.

FINE PRINT:
Pets: leave 'em home
Kids: bring 'em on (must be 19 or older to ski)
Credit cards: MasterCard, Visa
Heads-up: bears
Nearest medical: Fernie, B.C. (9 miles)
Weather: Summer temperatures range from the low 50s to the mid-90s. Winter temperatures drop below freezing, bottoming out around zero. There's very little rainfall, but the area gets an annual average of 340 inches of snow. Lodge elevation is 4,600 feet.

GETTING THERE: Take Highway 3 east and turn left at the lodge sign, just before Fernie. *In* *summer:* drive through the Mount Fernie Provincial Park campground and take the gravel road approximately 5 miles to the parking area. *In winter:* follow the signs to the parking lot, where overnight guests will be picked up by snowcat at 5:30 P.M. for the 45-minute ride to the lodge. Alternative pickups cost $150 CAD per person (lodge guests only).

See color photos on pages 167 and 168

KILLARNEY LODGE

Box 10005, Algonquin Park
Huntsville, Ontario
Canada P1H 2G9
Tel: 705-633-5551 (summer); 416-482-5254 (winter)
Fax: 705-633-5667 (summer); 416-482-5254 (winter)
www.killarneylodge.com
info@killarneylodge.com

Closest airport: Toronto, Ontario (175 miles)
Activities: canoeing, hiking, wildlife watching, mountain biking, fishing
Season: early May through mid-October
Guides/Instruction: hiking guides, canoeing instruction
Services: none
Specialty: canoeing
Accommodations: 30 cabins; capacity 70
Rates: $139–$259 CAD per person, double occupancy, all-inclusive (meals, canoeing gear)

Researchers in the 1950s made an odd discovery in Algonquin Park: timber wolves respond to human imitations of a howl. The discovery was groundbreaking because it allowed scientists to better track these notoriously elusive carnivores. It also spawned a park tradition, the Public Wolf Howl. Since 1963, thousands of wolf seekers have gathered on August evenings to bellow in unison into the dark woods. When an answer comes—as it does after three howls out of four—it's a distant, eerie song that tingles every spine in the crowd.

Killarney Lodge sits in the quiet, southwest corner of Algonquin Park, on the Lake of Two Rivers. This is prime timber wolf territory, but you're more likely to find a moose on the grounds than to spot a single tail hair from a wolf. If you're nevertheless struck with the impulse to beckon one of these shy animals, you wouldn't be the first guest to paddle out onto the lake and bay at the moon.

AT THE LODGE: The lodge owners can't help smirking when guests ask if there's cell phone reception here. There's no TV, phone, or Internet access either; but the affliction they like to call "e-withdrawal" usually subsides after a day. You can ease the transition by lounging near the woodstove in the main lodge, which was built in 1935 from dark-stained logs accented with red trim, or taking in the views from the comfortable cabins. These are spread around the 12-acre peninsula that dangles off Ontario 60 into the 3-mile-long lake. The pine-paneled or log cabins have one or two bedrooms with decks, sitting rooms, and private bathrooms. In general, those cabins with the best views are priced the highest. The least-expensive units are the duplexes. All have pleasantly nondescript, country décor.

THE SPORTS: Each cabin comes with a 15-foot Kevlar canoe, which you can paddle across the ⅔-mile width of the Lake of Two Rivers and portage 1,000 yards to the seldom-paddled Provoking Lake. Skilled paddlers can attempt a one-day circuit that covers 25 of the park's 930 miles of canoe routes. All guests attend a canoe safety lecture and receive basic instruction (i.e., no standing in the boat, and don't push off without a paddle). Hikers can

walk the 8-mile loop around Provoking Lake or take an easy stroll on the Whisky Rapids Trail, an hour-long riverside ramble that starts 15 minutes from the lodge. If those options aren't enough, 2,850-square-mile Algonquin Park contains numerous other marked trails. Stop in at the visitor center, 6 miles from the lodge, for maps and guidance. There are two mountain bike trails near the lodge, an easy 6-miler and a more technical 16-mile ride. Bikes can be rented nearby. If you come here intent on fishing, you're bound to be disappointed. A day on the lake isn't likely to yield more than a snack-sized lake trout or smallmouth bass. For this reason, the lodge doesn't stock fishing gear.

BACKCOUNTRY BONUS: The Portage Store (www.portagestore.com) offers three- to five-day guided canoeing/camping trips that include all gear, food, permits, and a guide ($395–$575 per person). Group size is limited to eight, and custom trips are available.

MEALTIME: The menu changes daily, but anticipate quality country cooking and a fish dish at every evening meal. Breakfast can include fruit, granola and yogurt, cereal, pancakes, or eggs. Packed lunches are available on request (sandwich, fruit, cheese, granola bar, celery or carrots, home-baked cookies, drinks), or you can eat in and choose from dishes like zucchini lasagna or charbroiled beef tenderloin on a grilled garlic butter bun. Dinner may feature oven-roasted lamb or chicken in addition to pan-fried pickerel, an Ontario staple. If you're lucky enough to catch an edible fish, the staff will cook it if you clean it. The tables seat two to six guests each, by the large stone hearth in the log dining room.

FINE PRINT:
Pets: leave 'em home
Kids: bring 'em on
Credit cards: MasterCard, Visa
Heads-up: mosquitoes in July, some blackflies in June
Nearest medical: Huntsville, Ontario (50 miles)

Weather: Moderate, with highs in the mid-80s, and lows close to 40°F. Lodge elevation is 1,250 feet.

GETTING THERE: From the airport, take Highway 401 east to Highway 400 north to Highway 11 north. At Huntsville, take Highway 60 east. The lodge is inside Algonquin Park at kilometer 33.

See color photo on page 168

KING PACIFIC LODGE

255 West 1st Street, Suite 214 (mailing address)
North Vancouver, B.C.
Canada V7M 3G8
Tel: 888-592-5464; 604-987-5472
Fax: 604-987-5472
www.kingpacificlodge.com
info@kingpacificlodge.com

Closest airport: Prince Rupert, B.C. (75 air miles; floatplane and helicopter only)
Activities: kayaking, canoeing, fishing, hiking, birding, wildlife watching
Season: late May through early October
Guides/Instruction: guided hiking, flight-seeing, bear viewing, and fly-fishing; paddling guides and instruction
Services: spa, conference facilities
Accommodations: 17 suites; capacity 30
Rates: $3,500 CAD and up for three nights, per person, double occupancy, all-inclusive (meals, activities, airport transportation)

King Pacific offers the kind of luxury you'd expect in a Bangkok presidential suite, the service you would hope for at a high-end Bali resort, and the bedroom-window-close wildlife that most people will never see outside a *National Geographic* TV special. It's hard to fathom that this floating hideaway, tucked into a secluded cove on Princess Royal Island, is just a few hours north of Vancouver.

The only access to the lodge is by air. Its floatplane soars above the snow-tipped peaks and chasmed inlets before dropping you into the quiet bay, where you can push a kayak into clear, quiet water in pursuit of humpback whales. The downside, of course, is that such hedonism doesn't come cheap. During a weeklong stay, you can spend what many Alaskans make in a year. Amazingly, you'd be hard-pressed to find a single guest who would say the experience wasn't worth the cost.

AT THE LODGE: Built on a floating barge that's docked at Prince Rupert in the off-season (to protect the lodge from winter weather), King Pacific is 15,000 square feet of impeccably crafted yellow cedar, edge-cut fir, and native stone. Its Great Room has slate floors, wood-paneled walls with windows opening up to the bay, and a two-story stone fireplace surrounded by nap-worthy armchairs and sofas. The enormous guest rooms have down comforters on king-sized beds situated next to windows with expansive views of the ocean or Great Bear Rain Forest. Slate-lined bathrooms have double soaker tubs and detached showers. Many of the suites have separate dining space with room for several guests. All of the furniture was custom designed and crafted from native wood. The over-the-top-decadent Princess Royal Suite encompasses two floors, and has a large master bedroom, an eight-person dining room, and two sunset-view balconies. While other lodge guests have to choose between land and water views, Princess Royal guests get both, plus a waterfall that tumbles over rocks just outside the suite.

THE SPORTS: The basic lodge package includes guided hikes and kayaking trips. You can upgrade to add guided fishing, flight-seeing, heli-hiking/fishing/kayaking, and bear viewing. The guides are a necessity because most of the terrain is without trails. You'll be led through rain forest to waterfalls, ice fields, beaches, and alpine lakes. Kayaking trips cover multiple venues, from protected bays to open ocean, lakes, and island coastlines where orca and humpback sightings are common. Canoeing trips are on gentle lakes and streams. Saltwater fishing yields salmon, halibut, and lingcod; the rivers hold healthy populations of salmon and trout. Bear watching excursions put you on the path of the endemic Kermode, known locally as the Spirit Bear because of its ghostlike white fur. Birders will have a field day at King Pacific. Feeders on the decks draw a steady stream of rufous hummingbirds, and the 20,000 or so miles of surrounding rain forest is home to double-crested cormorants, ravens, loons, and gulls.

MEALTIME: Dinner starts with a teaser like shrimp and avocado salad with golden beet coulis. The main event might be celery-poached salmon with crab risotto, roasted squash, and broccolini in celery broth. Then you'll collapse, face first, into a chocolate-orange mousse or tri-chocolate truffle tart. Meals and local wines are included in the stay; some premium vintages are available for a nominal fee. Vegetarians are accommodated on request, as are successful anglers who wish to have their catch cleaned and dressed for dinner. Packed lunches contain smoked salmon in addition to the usual trailside snacks. All meals are served in the dining room at group or private tables.

FINE PRINT:
Pets: leave 'em home
Kids: 8 and older, please
Credit cards: MasterCard, Visa, American Express
Heads-up: bears, some mosquitoes, poison ivy
Nearest medical: Prince Rupert, B.C. (45 minutes by helicopter)
Weather: In-season temperatures range from 50° to 75°F; wind and rain are always possible. The lodge is at sea level.

GETTING THERE: Access is by floatplane or helicopter only. You'll be picked up at Prince Rupert.

See color photo on page 169

LAKE O'HARA LODGE

P.O. Box 55
Lake Louise, Alberta
Canada T0L 1E0
Tel: 250-343-6418 (in-season);
403-678-4110 (off-season)
www.lakeohara.com

Closest airport: Calgary, Alberta (155 miles)
Activities: backcountry skiing, snowshoeing, hiking, climbing, mountaineering, fishing, canoeing, wildlife watching
Season: late January through early April; June through early October
Guides/Instruction: mountain guides, on-site experts
Services: conference facilities (limited)
Accommodations: eight lodge rooms, 15 cabins; capacity 60
Rates: $420–$625 CAD per room, double occupancy, all-inclusive (meals, winter guides, summer transportation)

This Canadian Rockies classic has been around since 1926, when traipsing through the woods in woolen knickers represented the peak in travel couture. From the beginning, families booked their annual stay a year in advance, while would-be add-ons hovered over the waiting list like vultures. Travel trends have come and gone, but the demand for rooms at Lake O'Hara Lodge hasn't waned—the list is still 500-deep.

The reasons for visiting haven't changed either: jaw-dropping scenery and unparalleled access to the outdoors. Trails that are off-limits to day-trippers take you to obscure parts of Yoho National Park. Mountain guides lead skiing trips into terrain you wouldn't have known existed, let alone explored on your own. At day's end, sip tea in the dining room, gaze onto the lake, and imagine what life was like here before Gore-Tex and fleece.

AT THE LODGE: Built in an era when luxury didn't imply privacy and space, the main lodge rooms are small (sized for two), with shared bathrooms (two for the eight rooms). Guests occupy the upper floor of the Douglas fir-beamed building; the dining area and glacial-stone fireplace are below. The one-room log cabins that line the lakeshores have their own bathrooms. The larger Guide Cabins are cedar duplexes with Murphy beds hidden in the living rooms—four grown-ups can sleep here comfortably. None of the rooms or cabins have televisions or phones. All have comfy beds with thick down comforters and breathtaking views of the lake.

THE SPORTS: Lake Louise is just 15 minutes from the Lake O'Hara parking lot. Banff is less than hour away. But with 45 miles of rarely traveled Yoho National Park trails accessible from the lodge's front door, there's little incentive to leave the grounds. Hikers can cruise the easy, 2-mile path around the lake or tackle a circuit that tops the craggy Wiwaxy Gap and drops down to Lake Oesa before climbing to a Mount Schaffer overlook with panoramic views of distant peaks and alpine lakes. Mountain goats, marmots, and raptors roam the grounds in the summer. Anglers can cast for rainbow and cutthroat trout in Lake O'Hara or any of the immediate area's 12 other lakes. Rock jocks have access to 5.7 to 5.9 multi-pitch climbs near the lodge; countless possibilities, including numerous peaks, await them in the surrounding parkland. The lodge will arrange for guides and instruction through outside outfitters. Another sunny-season diversion is paddling around Lake O'Hara. Canoes and rowboats are available for guests' use. In winter, certified mountain guides are included in the cost of a stay, as is access to the sauna. Skiers must have intermediate skills, but snowshoers can join guided backcountry group tours. Aspiring naturalists can drop in on the twice-weekly talks at a nearby day shelter. Topics range from bears to bugs.

MEALTIME: Old-school as the lodging may be, there's nothing rustic about the cuisine. The set menus change daily, with creative headliners like blackened salmon in a crispy won ton wrap with orange-mango glaze and cinnamon and coconut rice. Meals are served at main lodge tables that face the mountains and the lake. Requests for special dietary needs should be made in advance. Sack lunches include hefty sandwiches and whatever trail snacks, fruits, or veggies you feel like grabbing from the pack-it-yourself O'Hara goodie bar. There's a fish cleaning station set up for guests' use; the staff will prepare your catch for breakfast.

FINE PRINT:

Pets: leave 'em home
Kids: bring 'em on
Credit cards: none
Heads-up: bears (very rare)
Nearest medical: Lake Louise, Alberta (30 minutes)
Weather: Unpredictable year-round. Summer temperatures usually range from the low 40s to the high 70s. Winter temperatures can dip to zero. Lodge elevation is 6,700 feet.

GETTING THERE: From the airport, take Barlow Trail south to 16th Avenue. Head west on 16th Avenue through the Alberta–British Columbia border. Two kilometers past the border, look for the sign marking the Lake O'Hara parking lot turnoff. Park at the lot and wait for the shuttle bus (in the summer) or ski or snowshoe the 11 kilometer access road to the lodge.

See color photos on pages 169 and 170

MOUNT ASSINIBOINE LODGE

P.O. Box 8128
Canmore, Alberta
Canada T1W 2T8
Tel: 403-678-2883
Fax: 403-678-4877
www.canadianrockies.net/assiniboine
assinilo@telusplanet.net

Closest airport: Calgary, Alberta (80 miles to the heliport)
Activities: hiking, cross-country and backcountry skiing, snowboarding, snowshoeing, fishing, climbing, mountaineering, wildlife watching
Season: mid-February through mid-April; mid-June through early October
Guides/Instruction: cross-country and telemark skiing guides and instruction, hiking guides, on-site naturalists
Services: conference facilities
Accommodations: six rooms, six cabins; capacity 30
Rates: $160–$310 CAD per person, including meals and guides

To promote wilderness travel in the 1920s, the Canadian Pacific Railway built a string of backcountry lodges throughout the Rockies. Mount Assiniboine Lodge was one of the first. There are still no roads in the 95,000-acre provincial park that surrounds it, so access is via an eight-minute helicopter flight or a 17-mile hike or ski into a Banff-adjacent valley flanked by deep blue Magog Lake and the lodge's namesake, an 11,870-foot peak sometimes referred to as the Matterhorn of North America.

The lodge has had only two managers since it opened in 1928. Current husband-and-wife team Sepp and Barbara Renner have been at the helm for 20-plus years—on their watch, 75 percent of the guests have been repeat visitors. The reason they return is no mystery. Though it's rustic, the flawlessly run lodge remains an incomparable access point to alpine trails and cross-country terrain ranked among the best on the continent.

AT THE LODGE: This is a back-to-basics backcountry lodge—outhouses, propane lanterns, no running water in the winter. But coal and propane heating will help thaw you after the brisk run to the john, and Sepp will reliably deliver a bucket of hot water to your door every morning for washing. The main building is a rustic, Norwegian-style log lodge with a red roof, hand-painted doors, and unusual elk-hide furniture. Guest rooms are above the heated living room, which keeps the temperature outside your down comforter cozy. The rooms have barely-there, 12-volt lighting and two shared sinks with cold water in the summertime. There's one shared shower and a single flush toilet (plan to use the outhouses behind the main building during peak traffic). The individual cabins sit on a bluff near the lake. Light comes from propane lanterns. Showers and a propane-heated sauna are housed in a separate building, with outhouses nearby. All cabins and the front rooms face the lake and Mount Assiniboine.

THE SPORTS: Skiers can count on backcountry powder for most of the winter season. There's cross-country and alpine skiing, and snowshoeing on ungroomed trails; guides and snowshoes are included in the cost of a stay, and ski gear is available for rent. Sepp, a certified mountain guide, leads many trips himself, breaking trails across open meadows and through Dr. Seuss–like larch forests. Between heavy snowfalls, when the tracks are set, there are more than 30 miles of trails. The conditions are better suited to touring than telemarking, and are best for beginning and intermediate skiers. Snowboarders will be happier elsewhere. In summer, guides take hikers on interpretive walks to the park's lakes and peaks. Two trips leave daily, one for slower-paced walkers and one for peak junkies. The area has 60-plus miles of trails; some scramble up rocky ridges, others meander beside larch-shaded creeks. Keep an eye out for elk, moose, golden eagles, and the occasional cougar or grizzly. There are no fishing guides here, but anglers can take advantage of six nearby lakes stocked with cutthroat and rainbow trout. Fishing licenses are sold at the lodge, where the staff will familiarize unskilled anglers with the art of cleaning their catch.

BACKCOUNTRY BONUS: You can hire a guide in Canmore to take you to the top of Mount Assiniboine. It's a technical ascent for experienced climbers only that's usually done over two days; the first night is spent at the Hind Hut at the base. Contact Yamnuska Mountain School (403-678-4164; www.yamnuska.com) for information.

MEALTIME: Breakfast and dinner are served family style around large birch tables in the historic dining room. You'll start the day with classic mountain fare: fruit, yogurt, muesli, pancakes, eggs, and the occasional frittata. You pack your own sack lunch from a sandwich buffet with homemade whole-grain bread, cold cuts, cheeses, veggies, trail mix, juice, and condiments like fresh sun-dried tomato pesto and hummus. Afternoon tea and lemonade are served with light munchies in the living room. Dinner is a set menu that varies daily. Past dishes have included prime rib with apple horseradish sauce, boneless chicken with lime-cilantro salsa, and tomato halves stuffed with couscous, pine nut pesto, or eggplant parmigiana. Vegetarian options are always available. Save room for desserts like peach cake with custard sauce and chocolate pecan pie.

FINE PRINT:

Pets: leave 'em home

Kids: bring 'em on (10 and older in winter)

Credit cards: MasterCard, Visa

Heads-up: mosquitoes and horseflies (mid-July through mid-August), bears

Nearest medical: Canmore, Alberta (15 minutes by helicopter)

Weather: Summer temperatures range from the low 20s to the low 80s, with occasional snow. In winter, expect highs in the mid-40s and lows to 20 below zero. Average yearly snowfall is about 6 feet. Lodge elevation is 7,200 feet.

GETTING THERE: Drive west to Canmore, then south 25 miles on the Smith Dorian Highway to the Mount Shark Heliport. It's an eight-minute flight or 17-mile hike or ski to the lodge. Helicopter transportation costs $100 CAD per person, each way.

See color photo on page 170

NIMMO BAY RESORT

1978 Broughton Boulevard, Box 696
Port McNeill, B.C.
Canada V0N 2R0
Tel: 800-837-4354; 250-956-4000
Fax: 250-770-7227
www.nimmobay.com
heli@nimmobay.com

Closest airport: Point Hardy, Vancouver Island, B.C. (25-minute flight; floatplane and helicopter only)

Activities: hiking, fishing, rafting, kayaking, whale watching, caving, glacier trekking, birding, wildlife watching

Season: May through October

Guides/Instruction: guides for all activities; fly-fishing, kayaking, river rafting instruction; children's programs, corporate adventure program

Services: spa

Specialty: helicopter access to remote wilderness areas

Accommodations: nine chalets, up to two guests each; capacity 18

Rates: $3,995–$5,995 for four days, per person, all-inclusive (meals, activities, helicopters, airport transportation)

George Bush slept here. So did the CEO of Boeing. In fact, the guest roster reads like a catalog of episodes for *Lifestyles of the Rich and Famous*—which, it just so happens, filmed a segment at Nimmo Bay.

The prohibitive price tag means commoners aren't likely to share the experience. But those who can afford it will be treated to total solitude, impeccable service, and helicopter access to areas that routinely inspire city folk to wax poetic. Take the example of Chicago Bulls head coach Tim Floyd, whose post-trip gushings included, "You'll experience an elevation of the body, of the spirit, and of the soul. . . . " The lodge makes no such promises of enlightenment, but it does guarantee you'll catch a fish. At the end of the day, you may decide that's akin to attaining nirvana.

AT THE LODGE: The cedar, pine, and cypress chalets dot the shoreline at the confluence of the ocean and a river. Each two-bedroom unit has a separate living room and could sleep four quite comfortably, but occupancy is limited to two. Chalets have ocean or river views, full bathrooms with showers and tubs, televisions, phones, and waterfront decks. The main lodge, built in 1980, predates the guest units by 15 years. Many a celebrity guest has pocketed the eight ball at the pool table in the waterfront lounge before retreating to the outdoor wooden hot tub, which has a glacial-rock waterfall as a backdrop. The resort gets 90 percent of its power from this waterfall, which tumbles from 5,000-foot Mount Stephens. The use of alternative energy sources, along with a commendable recycling program, self-composting toilets, and an innovative sewage treatment system has earned Nimmo Bay awards for its environmental practices.

THE SPORTS: When you have a helicopter at your disposal, there's no reason to settle for easily accessible fishing spots. Nimmo Bay's guides will fly you to remote rivers where salmon and trout congregate and help you to perfect the art of catch-and-release. Thirty rivers and five lakes are within the 30,000 square miles of protected land surrounding the lodge. Fishing waders, boots, and spin- and fly-fishing gear are provided, though you're welcome to bring your own. Four- and 8-weight fly-fishing gear is required; you can buy flys at the pro shop. The helicopters are also used for wildlife watching and remote hiking trips. You'll hover over the blue ice before landing for a glacier trek, or set down on a wide, empty beach that's reachable only by air. Hiking boots and all-weather gear are provided by the lodge, as are kayaks and surf bikes for exploring the calm water in a protected cove near the lodge. There's a massage therapist on-site to work out any post-adventure kinks. Special programs include one for kids that offers water sports, hiking, rock climbing, and fishing. Another for corporate groups uses activities like river rafting to facilitate team building. The new First Nations program introduces guests to the region's rich cultural heritage, with visits to native villages and hikes on the historic Grease Trail.

MEALTIME: It's time to redefine your concept of the backcountry picnic. Start by helicoptering to an isolated, snow-dusted plateau. Find a flat spot large enough to hold your folding table. Spread a checkered picnic tablecloth over that table before setting it with silverware and wine glasses. On second thought, do none of the above, because it will be done for you by your hosts. They will also lay out gourmet sandwiches, fruit, cheese, and wine before resuming the activity of the day. The dining experience is no less spectacular at the lodge, where head chef Heather Davis presents five-star creations like Caribbean-style octopus with jalapeño, lime, strawberry, garlic, and onion, with a selection of fresh baked breads. There's an emphasis on fresh seafood and locally grown organic produce and herbs. All dietary restrictions can be accommodated, but if yours would prevent you from partaking in the Glorious Frozen White Chocolate Cheesecake, consider reevaluating your priorities.

FINE PRINT:
Pets: leave 'em home
Kids: bring 'em on
Credit cards: MasterCard, Visa
Heads-up: bears
Nearest medical: Port McNeill, B.C. (15 minutes by helicopter)
Weather: Seasonal temperatures range from 60° to 100°F. The area gets about 20 inches of rain. The lodge is at sea level.

GETTING THERE: Access is by helicopter or floatplane only. You'll fly Pacific Coastal Airlines to Point Hardy, where you'll be picked up for the 25-minute flight to Nimmo Bay. Try to limit luggage to 25 pounds per person; carry-on-sized, soft bags (36 inches maximum) are preferred. Excess baggage can be stored at the Vancouver airport.

PURCELL LODGE

P.O. Box 1829
Golden, B.C.
Canada V0A 1H0
Tel: 250-344-2639
Fax: 250-344-5520
www.purcell.com
places@rockies.net

Closest airport: Calgary, Alberta (three hours)
Activities: hiking, cross-country and backcountry skiing, snowboarding, snowshoeing, wildlife watching, tobogganing
Season: summer and winter
Guides/Instruction: guides and instruction in all activities
Services: massage (by arrangement), conference facilities
Accommodations: 10 rooms, one suite; capacity 30
Rates: $879–$1,350 for three nights, per person, double occupancy, all-inclusive (meals, activities, gear, helicopter transportation); weekly rates, $1,554–$2,415

The guilt-prone may struggle with the accessibility of Purcell Lodge, where the middle of nowhere is as easy as hopping on a helicopter. Settings like this one usually require some suffering, like lugging an overloaded pack through grizzly country and subsisting on stale jerky for weeks. Not only will you be whisked by chopper into this backcountry bliss, but you'll also arrive to find an immaculate, three-story, timber-frame lodge with electric lights, hot showers, a wood-fired sauna, even toilets that flush. What have you done to deserve this?

Get over it. If you're so inclined, you'll have ample opportunity to punish yourself on unforgiving Canadian Rockies trails. Or you could simply resign yourself to an existence in which access to pristine meadows and glacial peaks isn't something you have to earn. Go ahead, prop your feet up on the balcony, take in the views, and relax. No one here will tell a soul.

AT THE LODGE: Every plank, pipe, and bolt on this property was flown in by helicopter. Power is solar and hydroelectric, channeled from a nearby stream. Trash is composted and flown out; sewage is treated at the lodge's macrobiotic plant. The bathrooms are stocked with biodegradable soap and shampoo. It isn't easy to build an amenities-loaded and eco-friendly dwelling in a place this remote, yet Purcell managed to do it with panache. All guest rooms are on the top floor of the lodge, and most have balconies that open to views of surrounding peaks, creeks, and tarns. You can grab a book from the house library and read by the living-room fireplace. Or forgo thinking altogether and retreat to the cedar, wood-fired sauna. There are no phones on-site, but there is a TV (for videos only; no cable out here). Except in the separate honeymoon suite, bathrooms are shared, though each room has its own sink with hot and cold water. Meals are served family style at the dining room's handmade, polished wood tables, by the fire.

THE SPORTS: Purcell stocks day packs, trekking poles, water bottles, and gaiters for guests exploring the 20 miles of developed trails around the lodge. All you have to pack are your boots. Daily guided hikes range from mellow strolls to peak hikes. From the summit of Copperstain Mountain, you can look down onto the lodge—a tiny speck engulfed by wilderness—and appreciate the isolation. In winter, the ridges and bowls of the 160-square-mile property are covered in Purcell powder. Snowshoers can jog across meadows that extend for 10 miles. Telemark skiing is the house specialty, but cross-country and alpine skiers and snowboarders will go home just as happy. Snowboarders and telemarkers generally hike uphill together before floating down pristine powder runs. Gear, guides, and instruction are available for all skill levels.

BACKCOUNTRY BONUS: Purcell is pretty out-there. Getting really, really out-there requires a slightly longer chopper flight. The same folks who built Purcell in 1989 opened **Fortress Lake Wilderness Retreat** in 2001. It's more rustic than the lodge, and set at the edge of a 7-mile-long UNESCO World Heritage Site lake, where you can kayak, canoe, sail, and fish for trout (catch-and-release). Kids are welcome here. A three-night stay costs $1,217–$1,283 per person, double occupancy, including meals, guides, pine-paneled cabins, and helicopter transportation. The weekly rate is $2,105–$2,260. Visit www.fortresslake.com for information.

MEALTIME: With a 24-hour complimentary guest pantry, it's tempting to blow your appetite on something as banal as a candy bar. Resist the temptation. It's worth waiting for a dinner of, say, roast New Zealand lamb leg with balsamic and roasted garlic jus, or maybe grilled herbed tofu with mushroom miso gravy. To take the edge off, you'll get an après-ski (or après-hike) snack like beef satay with peanut sauce or mini chicken burritos. Not that you'll need it after an enormous breakfast of apple and strawberry turnovers, homemade croissants, and made-to-order omelets. Each morning, you'll assemble your sack lunch from a sandwich buffet of homemade breads and cookies. Almost all of the food served is organically grown, freshly baked, and crafted with refined palates in mind. Rest assured, gourmands won't go hungry.

FINE PRINT:

Pets: leave 'em home
Kids: 14 and older
Credit cards: MasterCard, Visa
Heads-up: bears, bugs, bad weather, avalanches (all activities are guided)
Nearest medical: Golden, B.C. (15 minutes by helicopter)
Weather: Summer temperatures average 75°F; winter temperatures hover around zero. There's no rain to speak of, but the area gets an astounding 40 feet of annual snowfall. Elevation is 7,200 feet.

GETTING THERE: Take Highway 1 to Golden, B.C. Helicopter transportation is provided from there. Or you can hike in on a 10.5-mile trail that starts just outside of Golden. Walk-in guests stay at a reduced rate.

ST. JEAN PAVILION

25, boul York est
Gaspé, Québec
Canada G4X 2K9
Tel: 418-368-2324
Fax: 418-368-7353
www.stjeanpavilion.com
info@stjeanpavilion.com

Closest airport: Gaspé, Québec (6 miles)
Activities: fishing, hiking, mountain biking, kayaking, snorkeling, diving
Season: early June through September
Guides/Instruction: fishing guides
Services: none
Specialty: salmon fishing
Accommodations: four cabins; capacity 12
Rates: $690–$900 CAD per person, all-inclusive (meals, guided fishing, airport transportation)

In some spots, the St. Jean River runs so quiet and clear you can't tell where the air stops and the river begins. In its deeper pools, it's a sparkling, costume-jewelry shade of blue-green. But it's not the color scheme that makes anglers grow weepy at first sight; it's the salmon—fat and plentiful and willing to nip at just about any dry fly.

Set at the eastern edge of Québec's sleepy Gaspé Peninsula, at the foot of the Chic-Choc Mountains, St. Jean Pavilion has private access to 20 miles of premier Atlantic salmon fishing. The guides pole their river canoes to the 50 or so holding pools, where anglers can wade amid the swimming shadows. Guests are often as gape-mouthed as the fish.

AT THE LODGE: This is a classic sporting lodge, from the knotty wood paneling to the pool table that's spitting distance from the 14-person dinner table. Reading chairs surround a large stone fireplace, a perfect venue for telling fish tales. The individual log cabins sit at river's edge, each with two bedrooms, a woodburning stove in the living room, a fridge, private bath, and a riverfront porch. You won't find TV or phones, but rooms do come with radios, in case the river isn't music enough. Outdoors, you can contemplate the holding-pool salmon from the vantage point of a peaceful gazebo.

THE SPORTS: The St. Jean River runs 75 miles from the Chic-Choc Mountains to the town of Gaspé. On the Pavilion's 20-mile stretch of water, only eight guests are allowed at a time, two in each sector. The guides have spent decades getting to know every ripple in every pool—this is a one-of-a-kind fishing experience. There's a strict catch-and-release policy on the pristine St. Jean, but anglers with an appetite can catch-and-keep on the nearby York or Dartmouth Rivers. Fly-fishing is the main attraction in these parts, but you can also drive 6 miles to Gaspé and rent a kayak to paddle along the rugged coastline of Gaspé Bay to seal rookeries and seabird nests. Or head for Forillon National Park, where hikers can choose routes that range from the easy, 2-mile loop that runs along Fruing Beach, to a challenging trek on the 11-mile Les Cretes Trail that skirts the Anse-au-Griffon Valley. Mountain biking is not allowed on most of the park's trails, but you can ride the 6-mile La Vallee Trail along the Anse-au-Griffon River to the Le Portage Trail, which takes you into the spruce and poplar forests for 7 more miles. It's a moderately challenging ride on sometimes technical terrain. Bike rentals are available just outside the park. Snorkelers and divers who want to explore the colorful seafloor can rent gear in Gaspé. The park has a cleaning station for washing off your equipment.

MEALTIME: Food is serious business at St. Jean Pavilion. Meals are always a gourmet, multi-course event presented by proud Québecois chefs. Not surprisingly, you'll find many variations on the Atlantic salmon theme—they'll transform your daily catch into a four-star entrée, if you wish. But you're just as likely to find lobster or lamb set before you, along with regional starters like ginger and carrot consommé. All meals are factored into the cost of a stay, including hot shore lunches for anglers. Breakfast and dinner are served around the large dining-room table by the fire.

FINE PRINT:
Pets: leave 'em home
Kids: bring 'em on
Credit cards: MasterCard, Visa
Heads-up: biting insects (some)
Nearest medical: Gaspé, Québec (6 miles)
Weather: Highs to 90°F; lows to 60°F (in-season).

GETTING THERE: Transportation is provided from the airport in Gaspé. If you're driving from Montreal or Québec City, take Highway 132 along the south shore of the St. Lawrence

River. At St. Flavie, you can either travel around the peninsula or cross the Matapedia Valley to the South Gaspesie shore. The lodge is 542 miles from Montreal, 418 miles from Québec.

SENTRY MOUNTAIN LODGE

P.O. Box 97
Golden, B.C.
Canada V0A 1H0
Tel: 250-344-7227
www.sentrymountainlodge.com
info@sentrymountainlodge.com

Closest airport: Calgary, Alberta (168 miles)
Activities: hiking, backcountry skiing, snowshoeing, canoeing
Season: year-round
Guides/Instruction: hiking, backcountry skiing, and snowshoeing guides and instruction; on-site naturalists
Services: spa
Accommodations: four rooms; capacity 14
Rates: $1,495–$1,795 CAD per week, per person, double occupancy, all-inclusive (meals, guided activities, helicopter transportation); three- to five-night packages also available

It isn't easy being the new lodge in town, especially in a part of the world where the snow-obsessed have already selected their favorite backcountry hangouts from a large pool of long-standing contenders. To get noticed, the heli-accessible Sentry Mountain Lodge had to be phenomenal from the day it opened its doors in the fall of 2002.

It was. The lodge drew immediate raves from skiers, hikers, and food lovers alike. With only four guest rooms, it already runs at capacity most of the year. And with rates low enough to lure the masses away from the crowded resorts, there's no reason to believe its popularity will wane.

AT THE LODGE: The red-roofed, wooden chalet sits at tree line in the Selkirk Mountains, with virtually limitless views of Canadian Rockies peaks and pines. The main building's exterior is finished with knotty cedar. Inside, picture windows reach toward the top of the vaulted pine ceiling, and a nap-worthy sofa and armchairs face a woodburning stove. Guest rooms have linen-covered down comforters and fluffy robes to keep you toasty on the short jaunt to the separate bathhouse. There you'll find a shower, changing room, and traditional Finnish cedar sauna (two composting toilets and another shower are located inside the lodge). The separate staff house can be transformed into a Honeymoon Suite on request. Though the lodge is plenty comfy, it's not loaded with resort-style amenities. There's enough electric light to read a book by, but you should expect to scale down your normal plugged-in life-style for the duration of your stay. There's no television or phone—communication with the outside world is by emergency radio and satellite Internet connection (available to guests for a fee). Enjoy the solitude. The bedroom views of the Esplanade Range should help.

THE SPORTS: As powder-mongers go, Sentry ranks as high as any. Professional skiers have said that tree skiing doesn't get much better than this. The 9,400 acres of backcountry terrain contain 500- to 2,500-foot runs on open bowls and ridges. Winter storms consistently dump dry flakes to cover your tracks. Snowshoers can spend all week jogging through meadows and climbing to ridges. Sentry can also arrange off-piste combination packages that marry a lodge stay with snowcat or heli-skiing. This small lodge can tailor activities to any group of guests. Diversity is what sets Sentry apart: the summer hiking is just as good as the

winter schussing. There are no roads to the lodge, so you and the seven other guests have all the trails to yourselves. Routes start at the lodge's front door and run for as many miles as your boots can withstand. Warm up with the Tetras Lake Loop, an easy walk to a nearby lake with steep rock walls shooting up from two sides (there's a canoe anchored to the shore). More challenging treks take you across ridgelines to nearby peaks. There's no technical climbing in the area, but plenty of alpine scrambling. Try climbing the lodge's namesake mountain, a scree-topped, 8,344-foot summit. Guides are provided for all activities. Astronomy tours, photography workshops, and painting trips are offered with sufficient demand.

BACKCOUNTRY BONUS: The lodge will help you plan a hut-to-hut traverse along the Esplanade Haute Route, a weeklong skiing or hiking adventure that traverses the spine of the Esplanade Range and typically ends at Sentry Mountain Lodge.

MEALTIME: Meals are served around a single, butcher-block dining-room table. The French-influenced menu changes daily, in accordance with available fresh ingredients. Breakfast dishes might include baked eggs and mushrooms in a ham crisp; and pancetta, feta, and roasted bell pepper frittatas with potato hash. Trail lunches contain sandwiches with high-end deli meats and fresh baked bread, veggies with homemade dressings and sauces, hot soup or tea, cookies, and a hunk of Swiss chocolate. Your après-skiing or -hiking snack might include sesame beef rice paper rolls with soy-lime dipping sauce, or grilled eggplant and herbed goat cheese roll-ups. And if you managed to save room for dinner, you'll be rewarded with creative entrées like pan-seared pork with an orange bourbon sauce, baked phyllo-wrapped salmon, or pistachio-crusted lamb with a port cream sauce. Vegetarians (but not vegans) can be accommodated with notice. For dessert: crème brûlée, poached pears with Gewürztraminer,

and star anise filled with pastry cream and dashed with mint oil. Not your standard middle-of-nowhere fare.

FINE PRINT:

Pets: leave 'em home

Kids: 14 and older (except by special arrangement)

Credit cards: Visa

Heads-up: mosquitoes and horseflies (in meadows), bears, avalanche danger (skiing is guided)

Nearest medical: Golden, B.C. (20 minutes by helicopter)

Weather: Summer temperatures can swing between the 30s and the 80s with very little warning. In winter, expect dry snow and temperatures that range from the low 20s to below zero. The lodge's first winter season saw more than 16 feet of snowfall. Lodge elevation is 6,920 feet.

GETTING THERE: Take the Trans-Canada Highway (Highway 1) to the staging area at the Heather Mountain Lodge, 34 miles west of Golden, B.C. If you're in a group of two or more, it's cheaper to rent a car than to take a shuttle. You'll be picked up here by helicopter for the 20-minute helicopter flight to the lodge. There's a strict, 40-pound weight restriction for personal luggage.

See color photo on page 171

TUCKAMORE LODGE

P.O. Box 100
Main Brook, Newfoundland
Canada A0K 3N0
Tel: 888-865-6361; 709-865-6361
Fax: 709-865-2112
www.tuckamore-lodge.nf.net
tuckamore.lodge@nf.sympatico.ca

Closest airport: St. Anthony, Newfoundland (17 miles)
Activities: hiking, fishing, kayaking, canoeing, rafting, cross-country skiing, snowshoeing, orienteering, birding, whale watching
Season: year-round
Guides/Instruction: hiking, kayaking, fishing, and naturalist guides; kayaking and fishing instruction; children's activities
Services: conference facilities
Accommodations: nine rooms, three suites; capacity 24
Rates: $110–$160 CAD per room, double occupancy, including breakfast and airport transportation; all-inclusive packages $1,700–$2,500 CAD

Newfies rank just below Texans in the pride they take in their homeland. Ground kissing is not out of the question, nor are spontaneous, public declarations of affection. Tuckamore owner Barb Genge and her locals-only staff are no exceptions. They have no doubt that Newfoundland's Northern Peninsula and its massive Atlantic icebergs represent the very best nature has to offer.

Convincing visitors of this is tantamount to a patriotic duty, though not a difficult one to fulfill. Sometimes all it takes is a kayak trip in a calm, icy bay, or a day hike to a waterfall with a moose near its base. If you're less easily impressed, paddling within splashing distance of breaching whales ought to do the trick. What's certain is that the Tuckamore crew won't give up until you're sold.

AT THE LODGE: Two Scandinavian-style lodges sit at the edge of Southwest Pond. The first, built in 1986, is a pine A-frame with a sauna, hot tub, and exercise equipment. The other is a 1995, white cedar lodge with a fireplace, a billiard table, a library, exercise equipment, and a drying room for soggy clothes. Its three suites, including the large upstairs Honeymoon Suite, have whirlpool tubs. Décor is made-in-Newfoundland, country style. All rooms have electricity and private baths with flush toilets. And as out-of-place as such amenities may seem in a rugged wilderness setting, you'll also find phones, satellite TV, and email access in both lodges.

THE SPORTS: All-inclusive packages cater to specific interests like wildlife watching, kayaking, hiking, and fishing. Anyone curious about Viking culture can spend a week paddling a traditional birchbark canoe through the Bay du Nord Wilderness Area or exploring the thousand-year-old Norse settlement in L'Anse aux Meadows UNESCO World Heritage Site. Outdoor Woman Week focuses on wilderness survival skills. Birders can join the Eider Duck Experience for an up-close look at a local sanctuary project. Nearly every itinerary involves time spent among the mountains, woods, fjords, and moors of 697-square-mile Gros Morne National Park. Guests who don't purchase a package stay can choose from 500-plus miles of nearby trails, many of which trace the coastline. Keep an eye out for moose, caribou, bald eagles, and shorebirds—the lodge stocks books about local birds and butterflies. Canoes are available for use on Southwest Pond. Kayakers can paddle the sea caves and protected area near the lodge in Hare Bay. Guides are available (and required if you're not a resident) for salmon and trout fishing. There are 20 kilometers of groomed, and many more ungroomed, cross-country skiing trails on-site—bring your own gear. Snowshoes are available for rent.

BACKCOUNTRY BONUS: Guests can opt to stay at one of Tuckamore's two remote locations.

One is a four-bedroom, white cedar log lodge on White's Arm Pond that is accessible by eight-wheel machine or fly-in. The other is a basic, boat-in, canvas tent camp on the Grey Islands, 14 miles offshore. Each sleeps 6 guests comfortably; the tent can accommodate up to 10.

MEALTIME: Fresh berries and local fish make daily appearances in the dining rooms, where meals are served family style beneath a cathedral ceiling. For breakfast, the berries top pancakes or cereal, with a side of toast and eggs. The fresh catch served at dinner can be anything from blue mussels to lobster, served with home-style sides like snow peas and carrots, macaroni and cheese casserole, or baked potatoes and creamed corn. Local ingredients feature prominently on the dessert plate, too: fresh strawberries on ice cream, country-style pudding with Newfie rum sauce, and partridgeberry squares, among others. All meals can be customized, including sack lunches, which usually include sandwiches on homemade bread, fruit, cookies, and juice. The lodge will clean and cook whatever seafood you bring home. À la carte meals cost $10 to $30 CAD for guests who don't purchase an all-inclusive package. If you're visiting on a Viking-themed package, expect a culinary homage to the seafaring raiders in the form of a moose and caribou feast.

FINE PRINT:
Pets: sometimes—call ahead
Kids: bring 'em on
Credit cards: MasterCard, Visa, American Express, Diners Club, Interac
Heads-up: bears, mosquitoes, blackflies (in June); the lodge offers hunting and snowmobiling
Nearest medical: St. Anthony, N.F. (17 miles)
Weather: Summer temperatures range from 50° to 80°F,

and winter temperatures can drop well below zero. The average yearly rainfall is 31 inches; annual snowfall is nearly 200 inches. Lodge elevation is 100 feet.

GETTING THERE: Airport transportation from St. Anthony is included in the cost of a stay. If you're driving from the mainland, take the ferry to Port aux Basques (reservations are required), then take the Trans-Canada Highway north to Deer Lake. Follow Route 430 to Route 432 to the lodge. Driving time from the ferry terminal is six to seven hours.

See color photo on page 171

Mexico

COPPER CANYON SIERRA LODGE

Escudero 3109-C, Col. Santo Nino
31320 Chihuahua
Chihuahua, Mexico
Tel: 800-776-3942
www.coppercanyonlodges.com
coppercanyon@earthlink.net

Closest airport: Chihuahua City, Mexico (five hours)
Activities: hiking, mountaineering, burro treks, birding, mountain biking
Season: year-round
Guides/Instruction: hiking guides
Services: none
Accommodations: 17 rooms; capacity 34
Rates: $60 per person, including meals and margaritas

It's time to dispel some gringo-centric myths about travel and the outdoors. First, the quality of a hike is *not* directly proportional to the price of your footwear. Second, electricity is *not* as essential as air or water. Last, and perhaps most shocking, the Grand Canyon is *not* the end-all, be-all of chasmic entities.

These three truths become apparent when you visit Sierra Lodge, where Tarahumara in tire-rubber huaraches cover the rugged canyon trails in a fraction of the time it takes most visitors; lanterns bounce flickers of light around adobe rooms, where there's nary a light bulb to be found; and the Copper Canyon makes the U.S. Grand Canyon look like a glorified sidewalk crack.

AT THE LODGE: The rustic, canyon-top lodge looks like a stretched-out log cabin, with a long, tiled front porch where guests sit to watch the Cusárare River twist through the valley below. Beamed ceilings, kerosene lanterns, and woodburning stoves give the interior an Old World hunting-lodge feel. Each large room has a private bath, with a hot shower, a flush toilet, fluffy towels, and terrycloth robes. There's no distracting television, phone, or even cell phone reception. Rooms have red-tiled floors and stark white walls with original canyon-themed artwork. Colorful homespun bedspreads match the drapes and native rugs. From some rooms, you can see Tarahumara cabins in the distant hills.

THE SPORTS: Roughly four times the size of the Grand Canyon, Copper Canyon extends thousands of square miles outside the lodge. Hiking trails in the immediate area take you as high as 9,000 feet and as low as 5,000 feet, with dramatic ecosystem shifts that range from snow-dusted peaks to subtropical forests on the steamy canyon floor. Guides are highly recommended, since the terrain is tricky (also, solo hikers run the slight risk of stumbling onto marijuana or poppy fields, and—more to the point—the gun-toting guards who protect them). You can hire guides at the lodge for $10 to $30. Burro-supported treks can also be arranged. A great day hike is the three-hour trip to the Cusárare Waterfalls, which tumble 100 feet from a cliff top into a deeper section of the canyon. You can also walk to nearby cave paintings and Tarahumara cave dwellings. Mountain bikers with their own bikes should anticipate tiring, technical rides. Birders, bring your binoculars and keep a lookout for endemic parrots and macaws.

BACKCOUNTRY BONUS: The owners run occasional weeklong canyon crossings that start and end with an overnight at the lodge. Days two through six, you'll walk along little-known trails from sunup to dusk, and camp out under a brighter star cover than you've probably ever seen. Tarahumara guides lead the way, and burros carry much of the load. The cost is $1,200 per person, including guides, cooks, and meals that often feature hand-patted tortillas cooked on an oil drum cover over an open fire. This is a rugged trip without a support vehicle, definitely not for those who require hand-holding. A gentler backcountry

add-on is the one-night campout at Spinach Hot Springs. Call the lodge for details.

MEALTIME: Mornings begin with fruit, yogurt, cereal, and pancakes and eggs made to order—top honors go to the spicy huevos rancheros on homemade tortillas. Your sack lunch will probably contain a burrito, nuts, fruit, and a soda. Dinners are gourmet interpretations of Mexican home-style classics, cooked on a woodstove and served on fine china in the large, lantern-lit dining room. It's good, hearty food that tastes even better after a day on the trail. Start off with a house margarita; afterward, retreat to the leather sofa by the stone fireplace.

FINE PRINT:
Pets: bring 'em on
Kids: 7 and older
Credit cards: none
Heads-up: scorpions, extremely rugged trails
Nearest medical: Creel, Baja (25 minutes)
Weather: Summer days in the upper 80s, nights in the 50s. In winter, expect days in the 60s with some nights below freezing. Average yearly rainfall is just a few inches; snowfall can be as much as a foot. Lodge elevation is 7,500 feet.

GETTING THERE: The train from Chihuahua City to Creel leaves at 6 A.M. and arrives at 11:30 A.M. From there, hire a taxi for the 10-mile drive to the lodge and ask the driver to take you to "Cabañas Cañon del Cobre." It should cost around $30 one-way.

DANZANTE

P.O. Box 1166
Los Gatos, CA 95031
Tel: 408-354-0042
Fax: 408-354-3268
www.danzante.com
info@danzante.com

Closest airport: Loreto, Baja (25 miles)
Activities: hiking, kayaking, fishing, snorkeling, diving, horseback riding, wildlife watching
Season: year-round
Guides/Instruction: whale watching and horseback riding guides
Services: spa, conference facilities (limited)
Accommodations: nine suites; capacity 36
Rates: $135–$175 per person, double occupancy, all-inclusive (meals, activities, gear)

Driving to Danzante is the first adventure. It's like following a pirate map to the X that marks the spot. Once you've made it past the mercado, down the bumpy dirt road, through the stick fence, and around the bay, your treasure awaits: a Sea of Cortez hideaway where you can nibble from a bounty of fresh seafood and tropical fruit in the cool comfort of a palapa-shaded hammock.

After that, the adventures become more conventional (if anything you do in an ocean-front paradise can be called conventional): kayaking among dolphins and manta rays, and horseback riding through cactus-studded arroyos. Better yet, spend each day perfecting the Baja triathlon: play, feast, siesta.

AT THE LODGE: This bay hasn't changed much since the Steinbeck days, when the untouched tide pools and starry skies of the Sea of Cortez inspired the author to philosophize "that all things are one thing, and that one thing is all things." The ecological message wasn't lost on lodge owners Lauren and Michael Farley, who have gone to great lengths to preserve the environment. Aesthetically, that meant using handmade adobe walls and thatch roofs that blend with the surroundings. Power is solar. Produce comes from an organic garden that makes use of gray water and natural composting. All lodge employees are local villagers, and proceeds from Danzante helped build a nearby school. But you needn't sacrifice any comfort for the sake of eco-correctness. All rooms are oceanview suites with two decks and a private skylit bathroom with a Mexican-tile shower that's big enough to sleep in. Ceiling fans and windows ensure cross-breezes, and French doors open to a front-porch hammock. Design details like intricate ironwork, curved glass walls, and wood beams complement furniture crafted by local artisans. There are even built-in shelves with books to borrow for your afternoon downtime on your sitting-room sofa. And you don't have to worry about the distraction of a television or phone. While you're here, you're happily out of touch.

THE SPORTS: The owners have written two Mexico guide books for divers, and used to lead trips for San Diego–based Baja Expeditions. Needless to say, they're familiar with the area's outdoor offerings. Seek their counsel, then take some snorkel gear down the hill to the resort's secluded beach, part of the 120-mile State Marine Sanctuary. Borrow a kayak to paddle in the calm, clear bay, then hop in the water to get a closer look at the parrot fish and soft corals. You can hire a local fisherman to take you trolling in a *panga,* or go deep-sea fishing for dorado and marlin. Certified divers of all levels can rent gear and choose from reefs, walls, sandy bottoms, rocky bottoms, and wreck dives. There's a good chance you'll see sea lions and whales. On land, explore the hundreds of acres of open space on foot (guided or solo) or horseback (guides

and helmets required—this is tough terrain). Trails scale mountains to cliffs overlooking the surf, and follow river beds into rocky canyons fringed with cactus and mesquite. The lodge provides guests with binoculars and birding lists.

BACKCOUNTRY BONUS: Honeymoon Cove is a secluded, white sand beach accessible only by boat. Danzante will take you there, pitch your tent, set up a candlelit dinner on a white linen tablecloth, and leave you with a camp stove and breakfast food. For those who prefer their romantic interludes sans tent, the "beach drop" can also be done as a day trip.

MEALTIME: Buffet meals are served family style in a circular glass dining room and on an outdoor oceanview terrace. Cuisine is health-conscious Mexican-American, with an emphasis on organic produce (grown on-site) and fish caught by local villagers. Vegetarians can be accommodated with advance notice. Continental breakfast includes juices, fruit, sweet rolls, cereals, and a hot entrée—anything from banana pancakes to eggs with nopal cactus in a mild red chile sauce. For lunch, choose from hot dishes like tortilla soup and empanadas, or have a box packed to go (sandwich, chips, fruit, veggies, granola bar, drink). The lodge will clean and prepare any fish you catch. The dinner buffet features regional dishes like chicken enchiladas, sea bass simmered in a mild Veracruz sauce, fish tacos, and chile rellenos. All meals and snacks are included in a stay.

FINE PRINT:
Pets: leave 'em home
Kids: 8 and older
Credit cards: MasterCard, Visa
Heads-up: scorpions, tarantulas, snakes, mosquitoes (rainy season)
Nearest medical: Loreto, Baja (25 miles)
Weather: Summer highs can top 100°F; winter temperatures range from 60° to 70°. There's very little rain, about 5 inches per year. The lodge is at sea level.

GETTING THERE: Zero out your odometer—you'll be watching for landmarks, not street signs. Head south on the main highway for 19.4 miles. Drive past the Tecate Deposito on the left and the Mercado Ligui on the hill. Slow down for the sudden left turn onto a dirt road directly across the highway from a green and white sign that says PARQUE MARINO NATIONAL BAHIA DE LORETO. Look to the left for a school with brightly painted playground tires. Enter through the stick fence and keep to the right when the road splits. At the next Y, turn right again. You'll pass a white church on your left. Keep right to follow the road around the bay. At the next Y, turn right at the sign that says RANCHO to Danzante. The total distance from the dirt road turnoff is 3 miles. If you get lost, ask for Ensenada Blanca and el Rancho de Lorena Y Miquel. A taxi from the airport costs around $50.

See color photo on page 172

HOTEL ECO PARAÍSO XIXIM

Km 10 Antigua Carretera a Sisal
Municipio de Celestún
Yucatán, Mexico
Tel: 800-400-3333; 52-988-916-2100
Fax: 011-52-98-8916-2111
www.ecoparaiso.com
info@ecoparaiso.com

Closest airport: Mérida, Yucatán (68 miles)
Activities: wildlife watching, hiking, road biking, kayaking, fishing
Season: year-round
Guides/Instruction: birding, biking, and fishing guides
Services: massage, conference facilities
Specialty: natural history
Accommodations: 15 bungalows; capacity 45
Rates: $172–$198 per room, double occupancy, including breakfast and dinner

From a distance, it looks like a pink-orange sandbar rising up from the edge of the mangrove. It's not until your boat moves closer that you realize it's a flock of wading flamingos. Thousands of them come to the muddy salt flats of the Ría Celestún Special Biosphere Reserve to feed on the tiny organisms that give the birds their electric color. They're among 300 bird species that nest in the area.

Hotel Eco Paraíso Xixim sits on a white sand beach between the reserve and the Gulf of Mexico. Sea turtles lay their eggs nearby, and endangered crocodiles roam the estuary. White pelicans nearly graze the surf as they zoom past guests watching the sunset from the dunes. Staying here is a reminder to protect what the mainstream resorts have spent decades destroying—the natural beauty that makes the Yucatán unique.

AT THE LODGE: The roomy, thatch-roofed bungalows are spread throughout a quiet, 240-acre coconut grove. Each has two queen beds, a sitting area, a private bathroom, and a private porch with two hammocks and two armchairs. There's no need for air conditioning—ceiling fans keep the well-designed cabañas cool. In step with the lodge's ecological bent, the landscaping consists of indigenous plants watered with recycled shower water. The main building, La Casa Club, houses the restaurant, bar, game room, television, and library, which is stocked with natural-history books and educational videos. The property's only phone is at the front desk. A pergola-shaded, freshwater swimming pool faces the sand dunes and the beach. There's a small, natural-history museum near the reception area.

THE SPORTS: Most activities here are guided, but even tour-phobics should consider this a plus. It takes an expert to navigate a boat through the reserve without disturbing the resident wildlife, and groups rarely contain more than a few guests. The half-day Celestún Inlet trip takes you by boat directly into the flamingo zone, where you'll cruise between mangroves and past a petrified forest; you might even spot a crocodile or ocelot. Binoculars are provided. Offshore fishing trips are led by Celestún fishermen. It takes an hour to boat to the fishing spot, where you'll cast for snapper, grouper, sea trout, and barracuda while your guide prepares fresh seviche for lunch. The half-day bicycle tour gives you access to the salt flats and other parts of the reserve you can't explore from the water. There's also a three-hour moonlight safari, where the eerie silence of your nighttime crocodile hunt is broken only by hoots from great horned owls. Tours start at $15 per person and include all gear and guides. If you prefer solo exploration, you can hike the lodge's half-mile interpretive trail or walk on coastal paths that traverse 60 uninhabited miles. Rental bikes are available for short rides on the sandy dirt roads around the property. Kayaks for open-ocean paddling are available on request.

MEALTIME: The food is surprisingly good for a lodge located far from the resort circuit. Breakfasts start with fresh juice, yogurt, and granola; entrées range from pancakes and French toast to Xixim omelets with shrimp and cheese. The à la carte lunch menu features regional specialties like traditional lime soup and blue crabs stuffed with chipotle-seasoned fish, in addition to international standards like spaghetti pomodoro and Spanish paella. Sack lunches with a sandwich, a hard-boiled egg, crackers, fruit, iced tea, and dessert are available on request. The lodge will clean and cook any fish you bring in from fishing trips. The candlelit, four-course dinners are from a set menu that changes daily. You might start with a shrimp soup and a salad, then enjoy fresh fish or chicken with rice. Dessert could be flan, mango mousse, or lemon sorbet. Vegetarians can be accommodated with notice.

FINE PRINT:
Pets: welcome
Kids: bring 'em on
Credit cards: MasterCard, Visa, American Express
Heads-up: mosquitoes, *tábano* flies, scorpions
Nearest medical: Celestún, Yucatán (6 miles)
Weather: Temperatures range from the low 60s to the upper 90s. The region gets an average of 2.5 feet of annual rain. The lodge is at sea level.

GETTING THERE: Drive to the south of Mérida, toward Uman. Turn right at the second light after the plaza, onto route number 281 to Kinchil-Celestún. At Celestún, head right on the unpaved road that parallels the ocean and drive 6 miles. The resort is at the north end of the village. Airport transportation costs $200 to $330 per carload (up to nine passengers).

See color photos on pages 172 and 173

LAS CAÑADAS CLOUD FOREST ECOVILLAGE

A.P. 24, Huatusco, Veracruz
C.P. 94100
Mexico
Tel/Fax: 011-52-273-734-1577
www.bosquedeniebla.com.mx
bosquedeniebla@infosel.net.mx

Closest airport: Veracruz City, Veracruz (95 miles)
Activities: hiking, birding, mountain biking, mountaineering, rafting
Season: three-day sessions throughout the year; see web site for dates
Guides/Instruction: hiking guides, on-site naturalists
Services: conference facilities
Specialty: natural history
Accommodations: six cabins; capacity 12
Rates: $2,250 MXN for two nights, per person, all-inclusive (meals, guides, and activities)

For cash-strapped villagers in Mexico's highlands, the promise of coffee and cattle income was reason enough to clear away large swaths of cloud forest throughout the 1980s and 1990s. The profits were short-lived, but the environmental damage was not. Now many of those communities are suffering the effects of deforestation: erosion, flooding, and more poverty than ever before.

At Las Cañadas, a private nonprofit reserve on 675 acres of former grazing land, 50,000 native oak, ash, walnut, and beech trees were planted in 1995 in hopes of restoring the cloud forest and developing a sustainable source of income for local residents. Visitors spend three days exploring the moss-dripping trees, bromeliads, orchids, and wildlife that have flourished under a blanket of fog. The proceeds have already helped build a school, develop an organic farm, and educate a community. This is nature travel at its best.

AT THE LODGE: The basic but comfortable cabins are engulfed in ferns and set beside a clear mountain stream, where the sounds of trickling water fill in the gaps between squawks, chirps, and howls. The main building material, a durable mix of steel mesh and mortar called *ferrocemento,* gives the lodge the feel of a papier-mâché, school-project rendition of an ancient village. Paintings are hung outside. Two of the huts are linked by hanging bridges. Two sets of spring-fed showers and composting toilets are shared. There's no electricity—candles light the rooms. Needless to say, there are no phones or TVs. Bedding and purified water are provided.

THE SPORTS: A short interpretive trail takes you over 11 hanging bridges, past two small waterfalls, and into one of Mexico's most diverse biological settings, where giant ferns grow and brilliant orchids peek through moss. Hikes are led by naturalist guides who have a first-name familiarity with each evergreen, bromeliad, and lichen. At least 190 known bird species thrive in the area. On request, the lodge will hire a cloud forest ornithologist from a local conservation group to lead guided tours. Mountain bikes are also available. From the village, you can see Mexico's tallest peak, 18,410-ft. Pico de Orizaba. Guided ascents start from the town of Coscomatepec, about 15 miles from Las Cañadas. Not much farther is Jalcomulco, where rafting outfitters run Class III through V rapids throughout the summer. Other activities include guided tours of the lodge's farm and gardens, yogurt- and cheese-making demonstations, pottery workshops, bonfires, and the Baño de Temazcal, a traditional indigenous sweat lodge.

MEALTIME: Almost everything you'll eat was produced here—from the organic fruits and veggies to the tortillas, breads, and pastas made from homegrown corn, rye, and wheat. Milk comes from the village's herd of Jersey cows. Eggs come from hens kept at the lodge. A few specialty items like macadamia nuts and honey are bartered from neighboring farmers. When each ingredient is fresh, eating is an extraordinary experience. It's made even more so by the setting. Meals (lacto-ovo vegetarian) are served in two dining areas, one an enclosed building with picture windows that frame views of the garden and Pico de Orizaba; the other, a wood and shingle, open-air structure set above a stream in a lush ravine.

FINE PRINT:

Pets: leave 'em home
Kids: 6 and older
Credit cards: none
Heads-up: some mosquitoes (summer)
Nearest medical: Huatusco, Veracruz (20 minutes)
Weather: Daytime temperatures rarely top 80°F, and nights can drop below 40°. The area gets about 70 inches of yearly rain, most of it falling in the afternoon. Lodge elevation is 4,265 feet.

GETTING THERE: Take the Veracruz–Mexico D.F. Highway and exit at "Fortin de las Flores." Take Federal Highway 125 toward Huatusco. 3.7 miles from Huatusco in the direction of Xalapa, turn left under a stone archway—you'll see a sign for Centro de la Universidad Chapingo. Follow the unpaved road 1.2 miles to Las Cañadas. If you're traveling by bus, take the ADO line to Córdoba and transfer to the ADO bus to Huatusco. From there, a taxi should cost about $6.

See color photos on pages 173 and 174

MAJAHUA

Chacala, Nayarit
Mexico
Tel: 011-52-55-5514-2983
Fax: 011-52-55-5211-1612
www.majahua.com
reservations@majahua.com

Closest airport: Puerto Vallarta, Jalisco (56 miles)
Activities: hiking, surfing, horseback riding, fishing, snorkeling, birding, whale watching, kayaking, mountain biking
Season: year-round
Guides/Instruction: whale watching, boating, and horseback riding guides; children's programs
Services: spa, conference facilities
Accommodations: five suites, three tents; capacity 29
Rates: $60–$240 per room, including breakfast

A decade ago, Chacala was a sleepy coastal village whose residents split their time between fishing and surfing. Since then a little bit of tourism has entered the mix, but not much else has changed. There are no high-rise hotels, no high-priced margaritas, no pickup bars pumping tunes only a frat boy in a tequila stupor could enjoy. Just a long, nearly empty beach with some low-key lodging and thatch-roofed *palapas* serving fresh fish tacos to the few travelers lucky enough to have found this place.

Majahua's five villas are tucked away in a private piece of jungle at the south end of the bay. Steps from the water, the breezy suites were designed in 1997 by eco-conscious owner Jose Enrique de Valle, whose sister Laura owns the only other upscale accommodations in the area, Mar de Jade. Both are struggling to protect Chacala from mega-developers, but their efforts may not hold for long. You'd best get here while the getting is still good.

AT THE LODGE: The multilevel, Colonial Mexican suites have a subtle Asian influence. Each has terra-cotta floors and a private bathroom and terrace, some with hammocks. Art from the lodge's outdoor gallery (where the featured artwork actually hangs from the trees) rotates onto guestroom walls. A jungle path lined with delicate, twinkling lights leads to the surprisingly comfortable Jungle Zendo tents, each of which has a mattress on a wooden frame and its own private sitting area with hammocks. The outdoor shower and compost latrine are shared, as is the yoga and meditation area. Be sure to spend time in the oceanview spa, where you can get a massage, a facial, an aromatherapy soak, or a steam bath, set to a soundtrack of jungle birds and crashing waves.

THE SPORTS: Most of the trails are old footpaths to hidden beaches, like the 4-mile hike through guanabana and mango fields to Las Cuevas, where there are coastal caves to explore. Or the two-hour jungle walk to La Caleta, the area's best surfing beach, which is not accessible by car. There's also a three-and-a-half hour hike to the petroglyphs, some of which have been dated to 300 B.C., at Altavista. You can reach the petroglyphs by mountain bike or horseback—well-kept horses can be rented from a guide in nearby El Divisadero. Another short path takes you to the Mastranzo lagoon, where kayaks are available. Paddle around Chacala bay or take a ride on a fishing boat to help net the day's catch of sierra, cazon, or mahimahi. If you brought your own gear, fishing boats are available for rent. Beginning snorkelers can boat to La Penita, a nearby island. In addition to the fast, left-breaking point at La Caleta (mentioned above), several other surf breaks are within an hour's drive. Platanitos, 30 minutes away, is a sandy-bottom, beginner to intermediate break. The white sand beach sits at the edge of a coconut plantation with plenty of nearby hiking for nonsurfers. The summer south swell here can produce anything from gently sloping faces to double-overhead barrels. Winter surfing is more consistent, with fast, steep waves. If you're headed for La Caleta, boat transportation costs 250 pesos (per boatload). Foot protection is a good idea—there are lots of sea urchins and rocks. Bring your own board. Wildlife watching opportunities include the humpback whale migration from January through March, and birding year-round. Look for masked tityras, black-throated magpie jays, Mexican blue-rumped parrots, and endemic hummingbirds in the hills behind the lodge. Birding trips to nearby estuaries and islands can also be arranged.

BACKCOUNTRY BONUS: You can visit Majahua during a weeklong birding trip guided by anthropologist George Otis. After a night in Tepic, you boat through mangroves on Mexcaltitan Island before setting up tents on the beach. Guests spend the next day at Isla Isabel Bird Sanctuary, where they can snorkel around the coral reef and camp on the island. On day four, the group travels to a frigate colony in a lagoon crater before boating to Chacala for a three-night stay. The cost is $520 to $689 per person, including most meals, transportation, and camping and snorkeling gear. You might also consider adding on a stay at a community house in Roseta, a remote mountain community on the Santiago River, two hours from Majahua. Local guides teach Huichol arts and lead day hikes to indigenous communities along the Aguamilpa dam. *Pangas* can be rented for birding trips on the river.

MEALTIME: Breakfasts are basic: fruit, yogurt, granola, fresh bread, and eggs. For lunch, the lodge will pack taquitos or a sandwich to take on the trail. Or you can sit at the restaurant's sculpted terraces overlooking the ocean and order fresh fish, shrimp, lobster, or pasta. At dinnertime, tables are candlelit. If the owner's aunt is in town, specials may include her signature paella or chile rellenos. The kitchen will also clean and serve any fish you caught that day. The food is good, but there's also something to be said for the simple beachfront Chacala *palapas*, where you can sip on a 100-peso Pacifico and pick apart a lobster with your fingers as the sunset silhouettes the sailboats in the bay.

FINE PRINT:
Pets: leave 'em home
Kids: bring 'em on
Credit cards: none
Heads-up: mosquitoes and no-see-ums from July through September
Nearest medical: Las Varas, Nayarit (6 miles)
Weather: November through April, days are warm to hot, with nighttime temperatures dropping as low as 64°F. The rest of the year is just plain hot (add sticky to that in the rainy season, July through September). The lodge is at sea level.

GETTING THERE: From Puerto Vallarta, take the highway north toward Tepic. After 56 miles, turn left at the CHACALA sign. If you get to the town of Las Varas, you went 0.62 mile too far. When you reach the beach, follow the signs to the lodge. It's a five-minute walk down a trail to the reception area. Bring a flashlight if you might arrive at night. Airport transportation can be arranged for 750 pesos.

PICOCANOA ADVENTURE LODGE

Rio y Montaña Expediciones
Guillermo González Camerena #500
Primer Piso
Santa Fe, Mexico D.F.
C.P. 01210
Tel: 866-900-9092
Fax: 011-52-55-5292-5036
www.rioymontana.com

Closest airport: Veracruz City, Veracruz (one hour, 45 minutes)
Activities: rafting, kayaking, hiking, mountain biking, rappelling, climbing, mountaineering, horseback riding, Tyrolean traverse
Season: year-round
Guides/Instruction: rafting, hiking, mountain biking, rappelling guides; kayaking, biking, climbing, mountaineering, raft guiding instruction; on-site naturalists; children's programs
Services: massage, conference facilities
Specialty: river rafting
Accommodations: 24 cabañas; capacity 72
Rates: $816–$1,050 for five days, per person, all-inclusive (meals, activities, airport transportation)

Here's a perk most lodges can't offer: a Class III to IV river running through the backyard. Roll out of bed and into a raft and you're set for the day. A typical stay includes three runs on two of Mexico's wildest rivers, Pescados and Antigua. But Picocanoa's remote location in the mountains of Veracruz makes it just as easy to spend your days swinging from the trees or bushwhacking your way through dense jungle trails.

If you can pardon the hint of Club Medness (buffet meals, paintball wars, campfire shows), the cabaña village is a darn fine place to hang out after a day on the river. After sweating in the subterranean sauna, you can sip cocktails poolside at the open-air bar and practice your Spanish with the other guests, most of whom hail from below the border.

AT THE LODGE: The adobe, thatch-roofed cabañas sleep two downstairs and a third person in the loft. All have electricity and private bathrooms with showers. Everything from the walls to the sinks to the bedspreads was made by hand, giving the rooms an authenticity and charm that transcends their Polynesian cookie-cutter exteriors. To combat the occasional nuisances of mosquitoes and heat, the cabañas are equipped with bed netting and ceiling fans. Porches open up to thick forest vegetation or a manicured lawn, where neatly kept paths lead to the tiled pool, dining patio, sauna, and riverside hammocks. Built in 1996, Picocanoa is the flagship enterprise of adventure outfitter Rio Y Monañas, which has since added villages in two other locations in Mexico. The newest is west of Mexico City, in Valley de Bravo, where the focus is mountain biking.

THE SPORTS: There's a set itinerary for guided activities, but you can break from the group at any time. On the five-day plan, you spend

your first day just getting there. The next morning you can raft the Rio Antigua, riding Class III rapids and paddling through quiet stretches that run past mango and citrus plantations. Then there's an afternoon bike ride through a nearby colonial village. The next day starts with a trek through narrow Cinacatla Canyon to a series of natural pools, then continues with a guided walk through a coffee plantation. The last full day starts with a Class IV stretch of the Rio Pescados, where you'll blast through more than 30 rapids on your way down the deep canyon. To end the trip with another dose of adrenaline, spend the afternoon swinging through the jungle on the Tyrolean traverse. Whenever you're ready to go adventuring on your own, mountain bikes and horses are yours for the asking. There's some singletrack, but old burro paths are the fat-tire terrain of choice. If you're accustomed to amenities like high-end shocks, you'd best bring your own wheels. Hikers can walk the High Plateau Trek, which climbs from the valley floor to a canyon overlook above the Rio Pescados.

BACKCOUNTRY BONUS: A four-day mountaineering add-on costs $1,410 to $1,660 per person (depending on group size). Guides take you up Pico de Orizaba, an 18,410-foot snow-tipped volcano with expansive views of the Veracruz plateau. It's the third highest peak in North America. Camping and climbing gear, transportation, guides, lodging, and meals are all included.

MEALTIME: Meals are served buffet style in the large, open-air *palapa,* which is shaded by mango trees at the edge of the Rio Antigua. Cuisine is regional; the highlight is fresh tropical fruit. Packed lunches with sandwiches, cookies, fruit, and a drink are available on request.

FINE PRINT:

Pets: leave 'em home
Kids: bring 'em on
Credit cards: all major credit cards when booking; only American Express at the lodge
Heads-up: sand flies and occasional mosquitoes
Nearest medical: Jalcomulco, Veracruz (1/8 mile)
Weather: Temperatures rarely stray from the low 70s to mid-80s. Yearly rainfall is 38 inches (most of it falling from July through October). Lodge elevation is 1,800 feet. The river water is fairly warm: getting pitched from a raft is not an entirely unpleasant experience.

GETTING THERE: You'll be picked up at the airport for shuttle transport to the lodge.

See color photo on page 174

The Caribbean

EXOTICA COTTAGES

P.O. Box 109
Morne Anglais, Dominica
West Indies
Tel: 767-448-8839
Fax: 767-448-8829
exotica@cwdom.dm

Closest airport: Melville, Dominica, West Indies (40 miles)
Activities: hiking, mountain biking, kayaking, snorkeling, diving, fishing, horseback riding, birding
Season: closed September 1 through October 15
Guides/Instruction: none
Services: massage
Specialty: organic farming
Accommodations: eight cottages; capacity 32
Rates: $109–$140 per room, double occupancy

Abandon all notions of passively crisping your dermis on a white sand beach. Dominica is about the rugged outdoors, the kind that's muddy and gritty and dripping with ferns. The kind where verdant mountains shoot up 4,000 feet from the jet black coastline before dropping into valleys pocked with boiling lakes. The kind whose answer to its neighbors' listlessly lapping waves is an underwater volcanic *hissss.*

The owners of Exotica's hillside cottages are passionate about preserving Dominica's unique environment—co-owner Atherton Martin is an accomplished organic farmer who has won international awards for his conservation efforts. Ask about the origins of your dinner salad and you'll get an education on the benefits of living green. Should you require any further convincing, just look outside.

AT THE LODGE: The cottages are spread along the terraced western slope of Morne Anglais, one of the island's taller peaks at 3,700 feet, and a good vantage point for watching breaching whales. The Caribbean architecture emphasizes natural materials and wide-open space—cured pine walls, stone accents, high-pitched ceilings, and large living rooms that open to clay-tile verandas with ocean and garden views. Be sure to take a tour of the exotic flowers and fruit trees on the 4-acre farm. Each cottage has a kitchenette with a gas stove, and a private bathroom with solar-heated bath and shower water. Guests are asked to recycle their plastics, bottles, and foil and to add biodegradables to the compost bin. Unlikely as it may seem, the rooms have phones and TVs.

THE SPORTS: Land sports reign supreme on Dominica. Hiking trips are run through Ken's Hinterland Adventure Tours (767-448-4850; www.kenshinterlandtours.com; khatts@cwdom.dm) in nearby Roseau. Guides are highly recommended for this island's difficult terrain and poorly marked trails. Itineraries range from a 15-minute rain forest stroll to Emerald Pool, to a strenuous, all-day trek to Boiling Lake, a 200-foot-wide crater lake fed by two freshwater streams and heated to a steady boil by underground magma. Other island outfitters offer mountain biking, sea kayaking, horseback riding, snorkeling, and diving. Colorful fish, sea horses, sponges, and corals live along the black sand seafloor. Divers can work their way down walls, looking for volcanic bubble streams. Diving gear, instruction, and certification are all available. Anglers can cast for marlin, mahimahi, and wahoo. Birders need not leave the lodge grounds to get their fill of hummingbirds. And even though the island's beaches aren't the wading-in-the-surf sort, there's no shortage of inland rivers and waterfalls to satisfy your splashing needs—the closest is a five-minute walk from the lodge.

MEALTIME: The cuisine is Caribbean Creole, with an emphasis on regional specialties like steamed, fresh mahimahi. Chances are, every bit of produce on your plate was grown on-site. And there's a trained nutritionist in-house to make sure the rest of your dining experience is just as healthful. Breakfast and dinner are served at the cozy Sugar Apple Café, or you can do your own cooking in your cottage (groceries can be found in Roseau, 5 miles away). You can order a trail lunch from the café: your choice of a sandwich, meat or veggie pie, or marinated pasta salad, plus fruit, juice, and a dessert.

FINE PRINT:
Pets: leave 'em home
Kids: bring 'em on
Credit cards: MasterCard, Visa, American Express, Discover, Optima
Heads-up: mosquitoes (some) and sand flies
Nearest medical: Goodwill, Dominica, West Indies (7 miles)
Weather: Temperatures range from the high 60s to about 90°F. The average annual coastal rainfall is 38 inches, with as much as 200 inches in the forest interior. The rainy season is from July through December. Lodge elevation is 1,400 feet.

GETTING THERE: Prepare for a wild ride on the kind of bumpy road that 4×4s were made for. Follow the signs from Melville to Roseau. At the E.C. Loblack Bridge (West Bridge), take Independence Street south to Bath Road and turn right. At the stop sign, turn left onto Victoria Street and drive about a mile to the West Indies Oil/Texaco station. Turn left and then take an immediate right. After another mile or so, turn right at the EXOTICA sign. Continue 1.1 miles to the lodge. Airport transportation costs $55 per person, round trip.

MAHO BAY CAMPS

P.O. Box 310
Cruz Bay, St. John, V.I. 00831
Tel: 800-392-9004; 340-715-0500
Fax: 340-776-6504
www.maho.org
MahoBay@maho.org

Closest airport: St. Thomas, U.S. Virgin Islands (21 miles)
Activities: snorkeling, diving, hiking, windsurfing, kayaking, sailing, horseback riding, birding, road biking, fishing
Season: year-round
Guides/Instruction: snorkeling and diving guides, windsurfing and kayaking instruction, on-site naturalists, marine biologist, solar power expert, children's programs
Services: massage, conference facilities
Specialty: eco-everything
Accommodations: 114 tent-cottages; capacity 450
Rates: $75–$115 per room, double occupancy; one-week minimum during holidays

Long before there was eco-tourism, there was Stanley Selengut. In 1976, the white-bearded eco-pioneer added some resort-style comforts to safari-style camping and gave the resulting hybrid a home on the beach. His simple hillside bungalows-on-stilts helped set the standard for responsible tourism, and are still considered the prototype of the island eco-lodge.

Set on earthy St. John, where expat astrologers, experimental artists, and New Age spiritualists gather in the rain forest to bang drums and howl at every full moon, Maho Bay blends as seamlessly with the local life-style as it does with the natural setting. Don't be surprised if you find yourself gazing onto the turquoise Caribbean in search of a direct link to everything ethereal.

AT THE LODGE: An intricate network of wooden walkways links the tent-cottages that climb the

terraced hillside above a white sand beach. The screened bungalows stand on platforms to minimize erosion. Many of the private decks have Caribbean views—the exact number depends on what the thick vegetation is doing on any given day. There's no running water, but rooms have electric reading lights and table fans, and the shared bathrooms have low-flush toilets and pull-chain showers. There are public phones and email access on the property, but no television ("unless time of war or Super Bowl," says the management). Artists working in the on-site studio specialize in turning empty beer bottles into blown glass creations. There are three sister resorts on the island: **Harmony Studios,** less rustic accommodations built from recycled materials and powered by sun and wind, each with a kitchenette and private bath; **Estate Concordia Studios,** large, remote, open-air properties with full kitchens and baths, freshwater swimming pools, and views of Salt Pond Bay and Ram Head; and Concordia Eco-Tents, similar to the Maho Bay tent-cottages, but with private baths and more modern kitchen facilities.

THE SPORTS: The lodge sits inside the borders of Virgin Islands National Park, which covers two-thirds of the island. Of the park's 20 trails, 12 start nearby. You can walk from thorny coastal scrub to moist tropical forests in minutes. In general, the terrain is rugged and rocky, with strenuous climbs leading to unbeatable views of the Virgin Islands. Top among them is the Bordeaux Mountain Trail to St. John's tallest peak (1,277 feet). Lowland paths lead to pre-Columbian stone carvings and colonial sugar plantation remains. The lodge provides hiking maps, and the park service has guides. Maho Bay also stocks snorkeling and scuba gear for use in the clear, calm bays. The underwater wildlife includes turtles, stingrays, sea fans, spiny lobsters, parrot fish, nurse sharks, octopi, and moray eels, among others. The resident dive masters give open-water PADI courses and lead snorkeling and scuba trips to 14 different locations. Divers can expect reef dives, craggy cliffs, black rock arches, lava tubes, and wrecks at depths of 30 to 60 feet. Single and double sea kayaks can be rented at the lodge, to paddle from the white sand beach to nearby islands. Also available for rent are small sailboats and Cannondale mountain bikes (for road use only—no trail riding allowed in the park). Guided bike trips are available through a local outfitter. Some of the breezier bays are perfect for windsurfing, and Maho Bay offers lessons. Horseback riders can take advantage of the guided beach and trail rides offered by an outside concession. Anglers can fish for barracuda, kingfish, tarpon, shark, bonita, marlin, mahimahi, and king mackerel. Guides, tackle, and bait are available on the island. If you bring your own gear, you can fly-fish near the lodge. Other activities include yoga classes, beach volleyball, and Ultimate Frisbee. You can spend your between-sports recovery time at Maho's pottery workshops and glassblowing demonstrations, or sitting in on a marine biology lecture.

MEALTIME: The eclectic, international menu changes daily, with themed buffet dinners. Caribbean Night features curried chicken, veggie or beef pâté, and jerked steak or duck with island rice. On Mediterranean Night, roast lamb and garlic feta sauce are accompanied by grilled lemon chicken, spanakopita, pilaf, and hummus. A vegetarian option and a salad bar are always offered. Breakfast and dinner are served in the open-air restaurant on a hillside above the beach, and at two dining pavilions positioned for sunset views. Lunch items are sold in the on-site store. Sack lunches with sandwiches, chips, fruit, and cookies are also available. All rooms have propane stoves, ice coolers, and cookware, so you can load up on basic supplies (frozen foods, canned goods, some produce) at the Maho Bay store and cook for yourself.

FINE PRINT:
Pets: leave 'em home
Kids: 4 and older
Credit cards: MasterCard, Visa, American Express
Heads-up: occasional mosquitoes and sand flies, very strong sun
Nearest medical: doctor on call
Weather: From December through April, temperatures range from the low 70s to upper 80s. Temperatures are about 10° warmer during the rest of the year. The rainy season is July through January, but short, light showers are possible any time of year. The annual rainfall is about 43 inches. Lodge elevation is sea level to 400 feet.

GETTING THERE: Take an airport taxi to the Red Hook ferry, then board the ferry to Cruz Bay, St. John. Take Frett's Maho Bay taxi-shuttle from Cruz Bay to Maho Bay Camps.

See color photos on page 175

MOUNT PLAISIR ESTATE

Grande Riviere, Trinidad
West Indies
Tel: 868-670-8381
Fax: 868-670-0057
www.mtplaisir.com
info@mtplaisir.com

Closest airport: Piarco, Trinidad, West Indies (55 miles)
Activities: wildlife watching, hiking, mountain biking, surfing, canoeing, snorkeling
Season: year-round
Guides/Instruction: hiking, birding, turtle watching guides
Services: none
Specialty: leatherback turtles
Accommodations: 13 suites; capacity 46
Rates: $75–$95 per room

You've got to hand it to the leatherbacks—they have excellent taste in beaches. Thousands of these endangered giant turtles nest on Grande Riviere's isolated section of the northeast Trinidad coastline each year, leaving their hatchlings to shimmy seaward at their leisure. It's an event few humans will ever witness, except those staying at Mount Plaisir, where the egg laying and slow exodus to the ocean take place right outside your room.

Of course, cold-blooded critters aren't the only ones who enjoy the warm white sand. You can walk along Grande Riviere beach to the two river mouths that frame the property, then travel upriver by canoe, or hike to rain forest peaks to observe the pristine shoreline from above.

AT THE LODGE: Each of the small suites opens to a large, shared veranda overlooking the Caribbean. Two have private balconies. The backyard view is of Mount Ju rising out of the rain forest. There are no phones or televisions to interfere with the sound of tropical birds rustling surrounding palms. Originally built in the 1970s, the suites were upgraded in the late 1990s. Rooms are bright and airy, furnished with the work of local artisans. If you like what you see, you can probably take it home; much of the furniture, as well as the artwork imported from Asia and Africa, is for sale.

THE SPORTS: The beach is off-limits at night during the March-to-August egg-laying season, but you can watch the turtles by moonlight from your suite. The surrounding 1,200-acre forest reserve offers ample daytime diversion. The lodge's hiking guides, experts on local flora and fauna, can identify rare birds and medicinal herbs at lightning speed. Birders should watch for the yellow-tailed crested oropendola and the nearly extinct piping guan, an endemic species of wild turkey. An easy hike on the Ju Trail leads to a north coast overlook. Other guided hikes take guests to Grande Riviere Waterfall and Sunset Hill, where you can look across the ocean to the island of Tobago. More adventurous hikers can arrange a ride to boat-accessible beaches like Paria Waterfall Beach and Madamas River Bay, where trails run deep into the rain forest. For mountain bikers, the old, rugged roads behind the lodge provide surprisingly challenging terrain. On-the-water activities include canoeing up the Grande Riviere; longboarding on slow, mushy waves; and snorkeling at Langosta, a small cove northeast of the lodge.

BACKCOUNTRY BONUS: Arrangements can be made for guests to spend a night in the rain forest, instead of their room. Or you can explore the island on an organized, weeklong donkey trail hike with Pan Caribe Tours (800-525-6896; www.pancaribetours.com). The route takes you into fishing villages, along beaches, and over rain forest peaks. You'll camp some nights and spend others in rustic guest houses. Afterward, reward yourself with a night or two at Mount Plaisir.

MEALTIME: The cuisine is an eclectic mix of health-conscious Caribbean, Indian, and Italian cuisines, with an emphasis on locally grown organic produce, fresh seafood, and fresh baked breads, cakes, and sweetbreads. There's a wood-fired brick oven for breads and pizzas. Breakfast, lunch, and dinner are served on a veranda overlooking the beach. You can request a sack lunch with a sandwich, fruit, a cooked vegetable, and bread or local "coconut bake." The lodge will clean and prepare any fish you catch. Vegetarian options are always available. Meals range in price from $4 to $20 per person, not including drinks and desserts. For restaurant fare, you can saunter to the village of Grande Riviere for small-town Caribbean food. Back at the estate's beach bar, where there's never a shortage of fresh juice or rum, try the nonalcoholic house special, a tasty blend of soda water and sorrel blossom syrup.

FINE PRINT:
Pets: welcome
Kids: bring 'em on
Credit cards: MasterCard, Visa, American Express
Nearest medical: Port of Spain, West Indies (two hours)
Weather: Temperatures range from the low 70s to the low 90s. The average yearly rainfall is nearly 10 feet. The lodge is at sea level.

GETTING THERE: Take Eastern Main Road to the Valencia–Toco Road. Turn left onto Paria Main Road and follow it 34 miles to the village of Grande Riviere. Mount Plaisir is on the beach on the left side of Hosang Street. The lodge offers airport transportation for $85 one-way, $150 round trip.

See color photo on page 176

PAPILLOTE WILDERNESS RETREAT

P.O. Box 2287
Roseau, Dominica
West Indies
Tel: 767-448-2287
Fax: 767-448-2285
www.papillote.dm
papillote@cwdom.dm

Closest airport: Canefield, Dominica, West Indies (8 miles)
Activities: hiking, diving, snorkeling, kayaking, biking, horseback riding, birding, whale watching
Season: November through August
Guides/Instruction: hiking and birding guides, on-site botanist
Services: spa
Accommodations: four rooms, three suites; capacity 21
Rates: $90–$150 per room, double occupancy

Tucked away in the rain forest near the twin spouts of Trafalgar Falls, Papillote Wilderness Retreat is an Edenic home base for island adventurers. Its botanical gardens exhibit carefully tended begonias, heliconias, and bromeliads under a canopy of breadfruit and banana trees. Fresh fish and prawns get the Creole treatment before landing on your dinner plate. Hot mineral pools, some big enough to soak eight people, are fed by a steady volcanic flow.

AT THE LODGE: It's hard to believe that Hurricane David nearly decimated this side of the island in 1979. Winds blasting at 200 miles per hour wiped out crops and flattened buildings and trees. The power was out for six months, the phone lines for two years. Papillote owners Anne and Cuthbert transformed the disaster into an opportunity to train locals in environmentally responsible building techniques, using international grant money to revive the shattered economy. The tradition of community involvement is evident in each of the rooms, which are furnished with local artwork and locally handmade furniture and quilts. The garden complex has two suites surrounded by endemic plants and flowers. The other building houses two suites and three double rooms that overlook the valley. Stone sculptures and natural mineral baths are scattered throughout the grounds. The rooms have balconies or private verandas and can accommodate two to six guests each. The retreat was designed to be as comfortable as it is tropical. In both respects, it succeeds.

THE SPORTS: On Dominica, land adventures rank higher than ocean sports. Hiking trails cover the island, some starting near Papillote's front door. Most famous is the grueling, six- to eight-hour, out-and-back hike to Boiling Lake, a 200-foot cauldron of water that bubbles at 190°F. Getting there involves a tramp though 17,000-acre Morne Trois Piton National Park, up 2,700-foot Morne Nicols, and into the aptly named Valley of Desolation—a wide, barren bowl with steamy mineral springs, some cool enough to soak in. A slightly less taxing choice is the Syndicate Nature Trail, which climbs a rocky path to the summit of Morne Diabotin, the island's highest peak at 4,747 feet. Some trails can be explored by mountain bike or horseback—outfitters are located 20 miles south of the retreat. Whatever your choice, keep one eye on the treetops; the birding is fantastic. Though the forests get top billing, ocean endeavors are plentiful. Paddlers can explore the calm waters along the rugged coastline in custom kayaks for rent nearby; snorkelers can float above a colorful assortment of Caribbean reef fish; and dive outfitters in Soufrière will lead you to wrecks, reefs, walls, and an underwater sulfur vent that releases a steady stream of noisy bubbles into the sea.

MEALTIME: The distinctly Caribbean aromas emanating from the kitchen are Cuthbert's domain. The menu he developed highlights local produce and island spices. Breakfasts feature eggs from Papillote's chickens, served with an assortment of tropical fruit. Lunch items are flavorful presentations of local fish, meat, and veggies (try the green papaya chicken salad). Packed lunches containing sandwiches, fruit, and chicken are available on request. The set dinner menu changes nightly. Friday's meal might start with pumpkin soup and culminate in a seafood brochette with pasta. Saturday could feature rabbit with mashed potatoes and a dessert of flambéed banana. Vegetarian options are always available. Be sure to sample Cuthbert's rum punch, a secret concoction of rum, lime juice, and spices that's said to have kicked off many a blissful evening.

FINE PRINT:
Pets: leave 'em home
Kids: bring 'em on
Credit cards: MasterCard, Visa, American Express, Discover
Nearest medical: Princess Margaret, Dominica, West Indies (7 miles)
Weather: Idyllic. Temperatures are in the 70s year-round, with an occasional night in the upper 60s. Most of the 200 yearly inches of rain comes at night. Lodge elevation is 1,000 feet.

GETTING THERE: From the airport, drive south to Roseau and turn east on King George V Street toward Valley Road. Take the first major fork left and the second fork right. Continue through Trafalgar Village to Papillote. The lodge provides transportation for $20.

STONEFIELD ESTATE VILLA RESORT

P.O. Box 228
Soufrière, St. Lucia
West Indies
Tel: 758-459-7037; 758-459-5648
Fax: 758-459-5550
www.stonefieldvillas.com
brownc@candw.lc

Closest airport: Vieux-Fort, St. Lucia, West Indies (21 miles)
Activities: hiking, fishing, snorkeling, diving, windsurfing, horseback riding, kayaking, biking, birding
Season: year-round
Guides/Instruction: none
Services: spa
Accommodations: 12 villas; capacity 40
Rates: $120–$535 per villa, double occupancy, including beach and town shuttles; weekly packages available

On this 26-acre former cocoa plantation, hidden at the base of the volcanic Petit Piton on St. Lucia's quiet southwest side, guests meander along lush rain forest trails and sip rum punch on their oceanview verandas before retreating to secluded stucco villas to luxuriate in private, fern-fringed pools. Stonefield Estate is worlds away from the resort-ridden northwest coast, where cruise ships deposit their sunburned patrons at the busy town of Castries to shop for Caribbean trinkets. This is a fantasy land for nature lovers, especially those with a penchant for pampering.

AT THE LODGE: Each of the one- to three-bedroom villas is a self-contained vacation home, with a kitchen or kitchenette, living room, dining room, CD player, and veranda hammocks. Some have outdoor garden showers surrounded by bougainvillea. All have high ceilings, antiques, and four-poster beds draped with colorful, locally woven bedspreads. Louvers are all that cover the open-air windows, which, along with the ceiling fans, make air conditioning unnecessary. The two largest villas, Plantation House and Limemill, have private swimming pools. Many of the buildings have historical significance: Cocoa Villa was the estate's old cocoa processing house, and Limemill Villa was once a lime mill.

THE SPORTS: The property's guests-only nature trail leads to a well-preserved, pre-Columbian petroglyph. Hiking elsewhere on the island is usually guided because the trails are hard to access and are sometimes poorly marked. The Edmund Forest Reserve Trail is the best choice for orchid fans. The climb to the top of the estate's neighboring peak, Petit Piton, is a steep, tricky scramble that can occupy the better part of a day. Or you can take the three-hour, out-and-back Barre de L'Isle Trail along the ridge that bisects the island and tops out at 1,446-foot Morne la Cambe. The same mountainous terrain that makes hiking such a challenge also makes underwater exploration a blast. Divers like the coral slopes of Key Hold Pinnacles off the southwest coast. At Anse Chastanet, just above Soufrière, the sea life prefers shallow waters and is more accessible to snorkelers (be warned, however, that this is where the cruise ship crowd often day trips). All beaches on St. Lucia are open to the public. Your best bet is Malgretoute Beach, a 15-minute walk or five-minute shuttle ride from Stonefield. Windsurfers should head for Vieux Fort or Cas-en-Bas on the island's northeast tip. Horseback riding is available at Morne Coubaril, five minutes from the estate. Nearby hotels also offer deep-sea fishing, sea kayaking, and mountain biking. The resort will help you make arrangements for any of the above.

MEALTIME: The larger villas' fully furnished kitchens may put yours at home to shame. Unfortunately, the same can't be said for the availability of groceries, but guests can order a custom "welcome grocery pack," which includes basics like eggs, bread, tuna fish, beer, and canned soup, for about $25 per person. Anything more exotic requires a trip to Castries. Better yet, let the experts at the Mango Tree Restaurant do the cooking. For breakfast, try the banana pancakes or the more daring West Indian "saltfish" and local cocoa tea. Lunch items range from a ham and cheese baguette to shrimp in Creole ginger sauce. Anything on the menu can be packed to go. Dinner entrées might include pork chops with Lucian beer sauce or fresh fish in a sauce of coconut, capers, and wine. You can also hire a chef to prepare meals at your villa.

FINE PRINT:

Pets: leave 'em home
Kids: bring 'em on
Credit cards: MasterCard, Visa, American Express
Heads-up: mosquitoes (some)
Nearest medical: doctor on call
Weather: Highs in the low 90s, lows in the 70s, with the possibility of hurricanes in the June-to-December rainy season. Lodge elevation is 800 feet.

GETTING THERE: The drive up the west side of the island takes about an hour. Airport transportation costs $55 for up to three people. The trip from George Charles Airport in Castries costs $72. Helicopter transportation is also available through the lodge.

See color photo on page 176

APPENDICES

TOURIST BOARDS

UNITED STATES

ALASKA
Alaska Travel Industry Association
2600 Cordova Street, Suite 201
Anchorage, AK 99503
907-929-2200
www.travelalaska.com

ARIZONA
Arizona Office of Tourism
1110 West Washington, Suite 155
Phoenix, AZ 85007
888-520-3434; 602-364-3700
www.arizonaguide.com

CALIFORNIA
California Division of Tourism
1102 Q Street, Suite 6000
Sacramento, CA 95814
800-862-2543; 916-322-2881
www.visitcalifornia.com

COLORADO
Colorado Tourism Office
1625 Broadway, Suite 1700
Denver, CO 80202
800-265-6723; 303-892-3885
www.colorado.com

FLORIDA
Visit Florida
P.O. Box 1100
Tallahassee, FL 32302
850-488-5607
www.flausa.com

GEORGIA
Georgia Department of Industry, Trade and Tourism
Tourism Division
P.O. Box 1776
Atlanta, GA 30301
800-847-4842; 404-656-3553
www.georgia.org/tourism/tourism.html

HAWAII
Hawaii Visitors and Convention Bureau
2270 Kalakaua Avenue, Suite 801
Honolulu, HI 96815
800-GO-HAWAII; 808-923-1811
www.gohawaii.com

IDAHO
Idaho Department of Commerce
Division of Tourism Development
P.O. Box 83720
700 West State Street
Boise, ID 83720
208-334-2470
www.visitid.org

MAINE
Maine Office of Tourism
#59 State House Station
Augusta, ME 04333
888-624-6345
www.visitmaine.com

MASSACHUSETTS
Massachusetts Office of Travel and Tourism
10 Park Plaza, Suite 4510
Boston, MA 02116

800-227-MASS; 617-973-8500
www.mass-vacation.com

MICHIGAN
Travel Michigan
P.O. Box 26128
Lansing, MI 48909
888-78-GREAT; 517-373-0670
www.michigan.org

MINNESOTA
Minnesota Office of Tourism
100 Metro Square
121 7th Place East
St. Paul, MN 55101
800-657-3700; 651-296-5029
www.exploreminnesota.com

MONTANA
Travel Montana
301 South Park
P.O. Box 200533
Helena, MT 59620
800-847-4868; 406-841-2870
www.visitmt.com

NEW HAMPSHIRE
State of New Hampshire Division of Travel and Tourism Development
172 Pembroke Road
P.O. Box 1856
Concord, NH 03302
800-FUN-IN-NH; 603-271-2665
www.visitnh.gov

NEW MEXICO
New Mexico Department of Tourism
Lamy Building
491 Old Santa Fe Trail
Santa Fe, NM 87503
800-545-2070; 505-827-7400
www.newmexico.org

NEW YORK
New York State Division of Tourism
Empire State Development
Empire State Plaza, Concourse Level, Room 110
Albany, NY 12223
800-CALL-NYS; 518-474-4116
www.iloveny.com

NORTH CAROLINA
North Carolina Department of Commerce
Division of Tourism, Film and Sports Development
301 North Wilmington Street
Raleigh, NC 27601
800-VISIT-NC
www.visitnc.com

OREGON
Oregon Tourism Commission
775 Summer Street, N.E.
Salem, OR 97301
800-547-7842; 503-986-0000
www.traveloregon.com

TENNESSEE
Tennessee Department of Tourist Development
320 Sixth Avenue North, 5th Floor
Rachel Jackson Building
Nashville, TN 37243
800-GO2-TENN; 615-741-2159
www.state.tn.us/tourdev

UTAH
Utah Travel Council
Council Hall
300 North State
Salt Lake City, UT 84114
800-200-1160; 801-538-1030
www.utah.com

VERMONT
Vermont Department of Tourism and Marketing
6 Baldwin Street, Drawer 33
Montpelier, VT 05633
800-VERMONT; 802-828-3676
www.vermontvacation.com

VIRGINIA
Virginia Tourism Corporation
901 East Byrd Street
Richmond, VA 23219
800-847-4882
www.virginia.org

WASHINGTON
Washington State Tourism
128 Tenth Avenue, S.W.
Olympia, WA 98504
800-544-1800; 360-725-4028
www.tourism.wa.gov

WEST VIRGINIA
West Virginia Division of Tourism
90 MacCorkle Avenue, S.W.
South Charleston, WV 25303
800-225-5982; 304-558-2200
www.callwva.com

WYOMING
Wyoming Business Council
Travel and Tourism
I-25 at College Drive
Cheyenne, WY 82002
800-225-5996, 307-777-7777
www.wyomingtourism.org

CANADA

GENERAL
Canadian Tourism Commission
55 Metcalfe Street, Suite 600
Ottawa, Ontario
Canada K1P 6L5
613-946-1000
www.canadatourism.com

BRITISH COLUMBIA
Tourism British Columbia
Vancouver, British Columbia
Canada V6Z 2G3
800-HELLO BC; 604-660-2861; 604-435-5622
www.hellobc.com

NEWFOUNDLAND AND LABRADOR
Newfoundland and Labrador Tourism
P.O. Box 8700
St. John's, NL
Canada A1B 4J6
800-563-6353; 709-729-5919
www.gov.nf.ca/tourism

ONTARIO
Ontario Tourism Marketing Partnership
Corporation
10th Floor, Hearst Block, 900 Bay Street
Toronto, Ontario
Canada M7A 2E1
800-668-2746
www.ontariotravel.net

QUÉBEC
Tourism Québec
P.O. Box 979
Montréal, Québec
Canada H3C 2W3
877-266-5687
www.bonjourquebec.com

YUKON
Tourism Yukon
P.O. Box 2703
Whitehorse, Yukon Territory
Canada Y1A 2C6
867-667-5340
www.touryukon.com

MEXICO

Consejo de Promoción Turística de México
Mariano Escobedo 550, 11580
México DF, Mexico
011-55-52-581-0902

375 Park Avenue
New York, NY 10021
800-446-3942; 212-821-0304
www.visitmexico.com

CARIBBEAN

DOMINICA
Dominica Tourist Office
800 Second Avenue, Suite 1802
New York, NY 10017
212-949-1711

National Development Corporation
Division of Tourism
P.O. Box 293, Valley Road
Roseau, Commonwealth of Dominica
www.ndcdominica.dm

ST. LUCIA
St. Lucia Tourist Board
P.O. Box 221
Top Floor, Sureline Building, Vide Boutielle Highway
Castries, St. Lucia
758-452-4094

800 Second Avenue, Ninth Floor, Suite 910
New York, NY 10017
800-456-3984; 212-867-2950
www.stlucia.org

TRINIDAD AND TOBAGO

Trinidad and Tobago Tourism Office
512 Duplex Avenue
Toronto, Ontario
Canada M4R 2E3
416-485-3490; 416-485-7827

Tourism and Industrial Development Company Ltd.
10-14 Philipps Street
Port of Spain, Trinidad
868-623-1932
www.visittnt.com

U.S. VIRGIN ISLANDS

U.S. Virgin Islands Department of Tourism
P.O. Box 6400
St. Thomas, USVI 00804
800-372-8784

1270 Avenue of the Americas, Suite 2108
New York, NY 10020
800-372-USVI; 212-332-2222

Los Angeles, CA
213-739-0138

Washington, D.C.
202-624-3590
www.usvitourism.vi

OUTDOOR RESOURCES

Adirondack Mountain Club
814 Goggins Road
Lake George, NY 12845
800-395-8080; 518-668-4447
www.adk.org

Adirondack Regional Tourism Council
P.O. Box 2149
Plattsburgh, NY 12901
518-846-8016
www.adirondacks.org

Algonquin Provincial Park
P.O. Box 219
Whitney, Ontario
Canada K0J 2M0
705-633-5572
www.algonquinpark.on.ca

Alpine Lakes Wilderness
Mount Baker–Snoqualmie National Forest
21905 64th Avenue W.
Mountlake Terrace, WA 98043
800-627-0062; 425-775-9702
www.fs.fed.us/r6/mbs

American Mountain Guides Association
P.O. Box 1739
Boulder, CO 80302
303-271-0984
www.amga.com

Andrew Molera State Park
831-667-2315
www.parks.ca.gov/default.asp?page_id=582

Año Nuevo State Reserve
650-879-0227
www.parks.ca.gov/default.asp?page_id=523

Appalachian Mountain Club
AMC Main Office
5 Joy Street
Boston, MA 02108
617-523-0636
www.outdoors.org

Appalachian Trail Conference
P.O. Box 807
Harpers Ferry, WV 25425
304-535-6331
www.appalachiantrail.org

National Audubon Society
700 Broadway
New York, NY 10003
212-979-3000
www.audubon.org

Audubon Canyon Ranch
4900 Highway One
Stinson Beach, CA 94970
415-868-9244
www.nps.gov/ggbr/acr_map.htm

Bay du Nord Wilderness Reserve
800-563-NFLD; 709-635-4520
www.gov.nf.ca/parks&reserves/baydwildres.htm

Beaverhead-Deerlodge National Forest
420 Barrett Street
Dillon, MT 59725
406-683-3900
www.fs.fed.us/r1/b-d

Big Basin State Park
21600 Big Basin Way
Boulder Creek, CA 95006
831-338-8860
www.parks.ca.gov/default.asp?page_id=540

Big Bend Wildlife Management Area
663 Plantation Road
Perry, FL 32347
904-838-1306

Big South Fork National River and Recreation Area
4564 Leatherwood Road
Oneida, TN 37841
423-569-9778
www.nps.gov/biso

Blue Ridge Parkway
199 Hemphill Knob Road
Asheville, NC 28803
828-271-4779
www.nps.gov/blri

Bob Marshall Wilderness
Flathead National Forest
1935 3rd Avenue East
Kalispell, MT 59901
406-758-5200
www.fs.fed.us/r1/flathead

Boundary Waters Canoe Area Wilderness
BWCAW Reservation Center
P.O. Box 462
Ballston Spa, NY 12020
877-550-6777; 518-885-9964
www.bwcaw.org

Bridger-Teton National Forest
P.O. Box 1888
Jackson, WY 83001
307-739-5500
www.fs.fed.us/btnf

Butano Redwoods State Park
650-879-2040
www.parks.ca.gov/default.asp?page_id=536

Canyonlands National Park
2282 South West Resource Boulevard
Moab, UT 84532
435-719-2313
www.nps.gov/cany

Catamount Trail Association
1 Main Street, Room 308A
Burlington, VT 05401
802-864-5794
www.catamounttrail.org

Chattahoochee National Forest
1755 Cleveland Highway
Gainesville, GA 30501
770-297-3000
www.fs.fed.us/conf

Chimney Rock Park
Highway 64/74A
P.O. Box 39
Chimney Rock, NC 28720
800-277-9611
www.chimneyrockpark.com

Clayoquot Biosphere Trust
P.O. Box 67
Tofino, B.C.
Canada V0R 2Z0
250-726-4715
www.clayoquotbiosphere.org

Copper Canyon
Chihuahua State Tourism Office
Edificio Agustín Melgar, Primer Piso
Libertad No. 1300
Chihuahua, Chih. Mexico 31000

888-654-0394; 011-52-1-410-1077 (from the U.S.)
01-800 201-5589; 01-800 849-5200 (from Mexico)
www.coppercanyon-mexico.com

Crater Lake National Park
P.O. Box 7
Crater Lake, OR 97604
541-594-3100
www.nps.gov/crla

Dead Horse Point State Park
P.O. Box 609
Moab, UT 84532
435-259-2614
www.utah.com/stateparks/dead_horse.htm

Eagles Nest Wilderness Area
Arapaho and Roosevelt National Forests
240 West Prospect Road
Fort Collins, CO 80526
970-498-1100
www.fs.fed.us/r2/arnf

Forillon National Park
122 Gaspé Boulevard
Gaspé, Québec
Canada G4X 1A9
418-368-5505
www.canadianparks.com/quebec/forilnp/index.htm

Frank Church/River of No Return Wilderness
Salmon-Challis National Forest
RR2, Box 600
Salmon, ID 83467
208-756-2215
www.fs.fed.us/r4/sc

Gallatin National Forest
3710 Fallon Street, Suite C
Bozeman, MT 59718
406-522-2520
www.wildmontana.org

Gates of the Mountains Wilderness Area
Helena National Forest
2100 Poplar Street
Helena, MT 59626
406-449-5490
www.wildmontana.org

Gila Riparian Preserve
505-988-3867
www.nature.org

Gila Wilderness
HC 68, Box 50
Mimbres, NM 88049
505-536-2250
www.fs.fed.us/r3/gila/rec/wild/wildgila.htm

Golden Gate National Recreation Area
Park Headquarters Building 201
Fort Mason
San Francisco, CA 94123
415-561-4700
www.nps.gov/goga

Grand Canyon National Park
P.O. Box 129
Grand Canyon, AZ 86023
928-638-7888
www.nps.gov/grca

Grand Teton National Park
P.O. Drawer 170
Moose, WY 83012
307-739-3300
www.nps.gov/grte

Great Smoky Mountains National Park
107 Park Headquarters Road
Gatlinburg, TN 37738
865-436-1200
www.nps.gov/grsm

Green Mountain National Forest
231 North Main Street
Rutland, VT 05701
802-747-6700
www.fs.fed.us/r9/gmfl

Gros Morne National Park
P.O. Box 130
Rocky Harbour, Newfoundland
Canada A0K 4N0
709-458-2417
www.canadianparks.com/nfoundland/gmornnp/index.htm

Gulf of the Farallones National Marine Sanctuary
Fort Mason, Building 201
San Francisco, CA 94123
415-561-6622
www.gfnms.nos.noaa.gov

The Gunflint Trail Association
P.O. Box 205
Grand Marais, MN 55604
800-338-6932
www.gunflint-trail.com

Hawaii Volcanoes National Park
P.O. Box 52
Hawai'i National Park, HI 96718
808-985-6000
www.nps.gov/havo

Hiawatha National Forest
2727 North Lincoln Road
Escanaba, MI 49829
906-786-4062
www.fs.fed.us/r9/hiawatha

The International Ecotourism Society
733 15th Street N.W., Suite 1000
Washington, D.C. 20005
202-347-9203
www.ecotourism.org

Julia Pfeiffer Burns State Park
Big Sur Station #1
Big Sur, CA 93920
831-667-2315
www.parks.ca.gov/default.asp?page_id=578

Kachemak Bay State Park
MP 168.5 Sterling Highway
Homer, AK
907-235-7024
www.dnr.state.ak.us/parks/units/kbay/kbay.htm

Kalaupapa National Historic Park
P.O. Box 2222
Kalaupapa, HI 96742
808-567-6802
www.nps.gov/kala

Kalopa State Park
State of Hawaii, Department of Land and Natural Resources
Kalanimoku Building, 1151 Punchbowl Street
Honolulu, HI 96813
808-587-0400
www.state.hi.us/dlnr/dsp/kauai.html

Kenai National Wildlife Refuge
P.O. Box 2139
Ski Hill Road
Soldotna, AK 99669
907-262-7021
kenai.fws.gov

Klamath National Forest
1312 Fairlane Road
Yreka, CA 96097
530-842-6131
www.fs.fed.us/r5/klamath

Koke'e State Park
State of Hawaii, Department of Land and Natural Resources
Kalanimoku Building, 1151 Punchbowl Street
Honolulu, HI 96813
808-587-0400
www.state.hi.us/dlnr/dsp/kauai.html

Lake Clark National Park
Field Headquarters
1 Park Place
Port Alsworth, AK 99653
907-271-3751
www.nps.gov/lacl

Lee Metcalf Wilderness Area
Gallatin National Forest
3710 Fallon Street, Suite C
Bozeman, MT 59718
406-587-2520
www.wildmontana.org

Lewis and Clark National Forest
1101 15th Street North
Great Falls, MT 59403
406-791-7700
www.fs.fed.us/r1/lewisclark

Lily Bay State Park
HC 76, Box 425
Greenville, ME 04441
Park season: 207-695-2700

Off-season: 207-941-4014
www.state.me.us

Marble Mountain Wilderness Area
1312 Fairlane Road
Yreka, CA 96097
530-842-6131
www.fs.fed.us/r5/klamath

Monongahela National Forest
200 Sycamore Street
Elkins, WV 26241
304-636-1800
www.fs.fed.us/r9/mnf

Morne Trois Piton National Park
www.dominica.dm

Mount Hood National Forest
16400 Champion Way
Sandy, OR 97055
503-668-1700
www.fs.fed.us/r6/mthood

Mount Rainier National Park
Tahoma Woods, Star Route
Ashford, WA 98304
360-569-2211
www.nps.gov/mora

Muir Woods National Monument
Mill Valley, CA 94941
415-388-2596
www.nps.gov/muwo

The Nature Conservancy
4245 North Fairfax Drive, Suite 100
Arlington, VA 22203
703-841-5300
www.nature.org

North Cascades National Park
810 State Route 20
Sedro-Woolley, WA 98284
360-856-5700
www.nps.gov/noca

North Country National Scenic Trail
North Country Trail Association
229 East Main Street
Lowell, Michigan 49331
888-454-NCTA; 616-897-5987
www.northcountrytrail.org

Okanogan National Forest
1240 Second Avenue S.
Okanogan, WA 98840
509-826-3275
www.fs.fed.us/r6/oka

Pacific Crest Trail Association
5325 Elkhorn Boulevard, PMB #256
Sacramento, CA 95842
916-349-2109
www.pcta.org

Peacock Springs State Park
Route 2, Box 108
Fort White, FL 32038
386-497-2511
www.peacocksprings.com

Pfeiffer Big Sur State Park
47225 Highway 1
Big Sur, CA 93920
831-667-2315
www.parks.ca.gov/default.asp?page_id=570

Pictured Rocks National Lakeshore
N8391 Sand Point Road
P.O. Box 40
Munising, MI 49862-0040
906-387-3700
www.nps.gov/piro

Pine Butte Swamp Preserve
Highway 89
Choteau, MT 59422
406-466-5526
www.visitmt.com

Pisgah National Forest
1001 Pisgah Highway
Pisgah Forest, NC 28768
828-877-3265
www.cs.unca.edu/nfsnc

Point Reyes National Seashore
Point Reyes, CA 94956
415-464-5100
www.nps.gov/pore

Ría Celestún Special Biosphere Reserve
Calle 18 Av. Pérez Ponce No.110
Col. Itzimná, C.P. 97100
Mérida Yucatán, Mexico

Samuel P. Taylor State Park
P.O. Box 251
Lagunitas, CA 94938
415-488-9897
www.parks.ca.gov/default.asp?page_id=469

San Bernardino National Forest
1824 South Commercenter Circle
San Bernardino, CA 92408
909-382-2600
www.fs.fed.us/r5/sanbernardino

San Isabel National Forest
2840 Kachina Drive
Pueblo, CO 81008
719-553-1400
www.fs.fed.us/r2/psicc

Sawtooth National Forest
HC64, Box 8291
Ketchum, ID 83340
208-727-5000
www.fs.fed.us/r4/sawtooth

Shoshone National Forest
808 Meadow Lane
Cody, WY 82414
307-527-6241
www.fs.fed.us/r2/shoshone

Sierra National Forest
1600 Tollhouse Road
Clovis, CA 93611
559-297-0706
www.fs.fed.us/r5/sierra

Superior Hiking Trail Association
731 7th Avenue
P.O. Box 4
Two Harbors, MN 55616
218-834-2700
www.shta.org

Superior National Forest
8901 Grand Avenue Place
Duluth, MN 55808
218-626-4300
www.superiornationalforest.org

Tomales Bay State Park
Star Route
Inverness, CA 94937
415-669-1140
www.parks.ca.gov/default.asp?page_id=470

Trinity Alps Wilderness Area
Shasta-Trinity National Forest
2400 Washington Avenue
Redding, CA 96001
530-244-2978
www.fs.fed.us/r5/shastatrinity

Umpqua National Forest
2900 Stewart Parkway
Roseburg, OR 97470
541-672-6601
www.fs.fed.us/r6/umpqua

Virgin Islands National Park
1300 Cruz Bay Creek
St. John, VI 00830
340-776-6201
www.nps.gov/viis

Waimea Canyon State Park
Kauai District, Hawai'i State Parks
3060 Elwa Street #306
Lihue, HI 96766
808-274-3444
www.hawaii.gov/dlnr/dsp/kauai.html

White Mountain National Forest
Box 10MG
North Woodstock, NH 03262
800-346-3687; 603-745-8720
www.fs.fed.us/r9/white

Yellowstone National Park
P.O. Box 168
Yellowstone National Park, WY 82190
307-344-7381
www.nps.gov/yell

Yoho National Park
P.O. Box 99

Field, B.C.
Canada V0A 1G0
250-343-6783
www.canadianparks.com/bcolumbia/yohonpk/index.htm

Yosemite National Park
P.O. Box 577
Yosemite National Park, CA 95389
209-372-0200
www.nps.gov/yose

SIZE (BY NUMBER OF ROOMS)

Under 10

UNITED STATES: EAST

UNITED STATES: MIDWEST

UNITED STATES: NORTHERN ROCKIES

UNITED STATES: SOUTH

UNITED STATES: SOUTHWEST

UNITED STATES: WEST

CANADA

MEXICO

CARIBBEAN

Under 50

UNITED STATES: EAST

UNITED STATES: MIDWEST

UNITED STATES: NORTHERN ROCKIES

UNITED STATES: SOUTH

UNITED STATES: SOUTHWEST

UNITED STATES: WEST

CANADA

Clayoquot Wilderness Resorts 224
Island Lake Lodge 228
Killarney Lodge 230
King Pacific Lodge 232
Lake O'Hara Lodge 234
Mount Assiniboine Lodge 235
Purcell Lodge 239
Tuckamore Lodge 245

MEXICO

Copper Canyon Sierra Lodge 250
Hotel Eco Paraíso Xixim 255
Picocanoa Adventure Lodge 260

CARIBBEAN

Mount Plaisir Estate 267
Stonefield Estate Villa Resort 270

Over 50

UNITED STATES: MIDWEST

MINNESOTA
Bluefin Bay on Lake Superior 45

UNITED STATES: NORTHERN ROCKIES

MONTANA
Chico Hot Springs Resort 55
WYOMING
Togwotee Mountain Lodge 76

UNITED STATES: SOUTH

NORTH CAROLINA
Pisgah Inn 91

UNITED STATES: SOUTHWEST

ARIZONA
El Tovar 102

UNITED STATES: WEST

CALIFORNIA
The Ahwahnee Hotel 180
Costanoa Lodge and Camp 182
Tenaya Lodge at Yosemite 198
HAWAII
Sheraton Molokai Lodge and Beach Village 203
OREGON
Timberline Lodge 211
WASHINGTON
Paradise Inn 216
Sun Mountain Lodge 220

CARIBBEAN

Maho Bay Camps 265

RATES

Per night, double occupancy, U.S. dollars
(Canadian rates converted at $1.50 CAD = $1 U.S.)

Under $100

UNITED STATES: EAST

MAINE
The Birches on Moosehead Lake 14
NEW HAMPSHIRE
The Bartlett Inn—rate includes breakfast 20
Nereledge Inn—rate includes breakfast 22
NEW YORK
Adirondak Loj—rate includes breakfast 24
Adirondack Rock and River Lodge—rate includes breakfast 26
Trail's End Inn—rate includes breakfast 31

UNITED STATES: MIDWEST

MICHIGAN
Jolli-Lodge 39
MINNESOTA
Bluefin Bay on Lake Superior—rate includes some activities 45

UNITED STATES: NORTHERN ROCKIES

MONTANA
Chico Hot Springs Resort 55
WYOMING
Togwotee Mountain Lodge—rate includes breakfast, dinner 76

UNITED STATES: SOUTH

GEORGIA
Mountain Top Lodge at Dahlonega—rate includes breakfast 84
NORTH CAROLINA
Pisgah Inn 91
WEST VIRGINIA
Cheat Mountain Club—rate includes activities 100

UNITED STATES: SOUTHWEST

COLORADO
Shrine Mountain Inn 106
Twin Lakes Nordic Inn—rate includes breakfast 109

UNITED STATES: WEST

CALIFORNIA
Costanoa Lodge and Camp 182
Deetjen's Big Sur Inn 185
Rock Creek Lodge—rate includes breakfast, dinner, ski pass (winter) 192
Sorensen's Resort 196
HAWAII
Koke'e Lodge 200
OREGON
Timberline Lodge 211
WASHINGTON
Paradise Inn 216

CANADA

Tuckamore Lodge—rate includes breakfast, transport 245

MEXICO

Majahua—rate includes breakfast 258

CARIBBEAN

Maho Bay Camps 265
Mount Plaisir Estate 267
Papillote Wilderness Retreat 269

Under $200

UNITED STATES: EAST

MAINE
The Birches on Moosehead Lake 14
MASSACHUSETTS
Old Inn on the Green and Gedney Farm 18
NEW HAMPSHIRE
The Bartlett Inn—rate includes breakfast 20
Nereledge Inn—rate includes breakfast 22
NEW YORK
Elk Lake Lodge—rate includes meals 27
Trail's End Inn—rate includes breakfast 31
VERMONT
Blueberry Hill Inn—rate includes breakfast, dinner, winter trail pass 33

UNITED STATES: MIDWEST

MICHIGAN
Big Bay Point Lighthouse—rate includes breakfast 37

UNITED STATES: NORTHERN ROCKIES

UNITED STATES: SOUTH

UNITED STATES: SOUTHWEST

UNITED STATES: WEST

CANADA

MEXICO

CARIBBEAN

Under $500

UNITED STATES: EAST

UNITED STATES: MIDWEST

UNITED STATES: NORTHERN ROCKIES

UNITED STATES: SOUTH

UNITED STATES: SOUTHWEST

UNITED STATES: WEST

CANADA

MEXICO

CARIBBEAN

Over $500

UNITED STATES: EAST

UNITED STATES: NORTHERN ROCKIES

UNITED STATES: SOUTH

UNITED STATES: SOUTHWEST

UNITED STATES: WEST

CANADA

CARIBBEAN

ECOLODGES

Most of the lodges in this book have taken some steps toward protecting and preserving their local wilderness. The following, however, have set themselves apart by making ecological responsibility a top priority. Whenever possible, these lodges use alternative energy, conserve or reuse water, recycle, compost, seek out local goods and labor, and emphasize their region's cultural heritage. Some also donate a portion of their proceeds to community and conservation programs.

INDEX OF LODGES